FREE Test Taking Tips DVD Offer

To help us better serve you, we have developed a Test Taking Tips DVD that we would like to give you for FREE. **This DVD covers world-class test taking tips that you can use to be even more successful when you are taking your test.**

All that we ask is that you email us your feedback about your study guide. Please let us know what you thought about it – whether that is good, bad or indifferent.

To get your **FREE Test Taking Tips DVD**, email freedvd@studyguideteam.com with "FREE DVD" in the subject line and the following information in the body of the email:

 a. The title of your study guide.

 b. Your product rating on a scale of 1-5, with 5 being the highest rating.

 c. Your feedback about the study guide. What did you think of it?

 d. Your full name and shipping address to send your free DVD.

If you have any questions or concerns, please don't hesitate to contact us at freedvd@studyguideteam.com.

Thanks again!

TExES Social Studies 7-12 (232) Study Guide
Test Prep & Practice Test Questions

Test Prep Books

Table of Contents

Quick Overview

As you draw closer to taking your exam, effective preparation becomes more and more important. Thankfully, you have this study guide to help you get ready. Use this guide to help keep your studying on track and refer to it often.

This study guide contains several key sections that will help you be successful on your exam. The guide contains tips for what you should do the night before and the day of the test. Also included are test-taking tips. Knowing the right information is not always enough. Many well-prepared test takers struggle with exams. These tips will help equip you to accurately read, assess, and answer test questions.

A large part of the guide is devoted to showing you what content to expect on the exam and to helping you better understand that content. In this guide are practice test questions so that you can see how well you have grasped the content. Then, answer explanations are provided so that you can understand why you missed certain questions.

Don't try to cram the night before you take your exam. This is not a wise strategy for a few reasons. First, your retention of the information will be low. Your time would be better used by reviewing information you already know rather than trying to learn a lot of new information. Second, you will likely become stressed as you try to gain a large amount of knowledge in a short amount of time. Third, you will be depriving yourself of sleep. So be sure to go to bed at a reasonable time the night before. Being well-rested helps you focus and remain calm.

Be sure to eat a substantial breakfast the morning of the exam. If you are taking the exam in the afternoon, be sure to have a good lunch as well. Being hungry is distracting and can make it difficult to focus. You have hopefully spent lots of time preparing for the exam. Don't let an empty stomach get in the way of success!

When travelling to the testing center, leave earlier than needed. That way, you have a buffer in case you experience any delays. This will help you remain calm and will keep you from missing your appointment time at the testing center.

Be sure to pace yourself during the exam. Don't try to rush through the exam. There is no need to risk performing poorly on the exam just so you can leave the testing center early. Allow yourself to use all of the allotted time if needed.

Remain positive while taking the exam even if you feel like you are performing poorly. Thinking about the content you should have mastered will not help you perform better on the exam.

Once the exam is complete, take some time to relax. Even if you feel that you need to take the exam again, you will be well served by some down time before you begin studying again. It's often easier to convince yourself to study if you know that it will come with a reward!

Test-Taking Strategies

1. Predicting the Answer

When you feel confident in your preparation for a multiple-choice test, try predicting the answer before reading the answer choices. This is especially useful on questions that test objective factual knowledge. By predicting the answer before reading the available choices, you eliminate the possibility that you will be distracted or led astray by an incorrect answer choice. You will feel more confident in your selection if you read the question, predict the answer, and then find your prediction among the answer choices. After using this strategy, be sure to still read all of the answer choices carefully and completely. If you feel unprepared, you should not attempt to predict the answers. This would be a waste of time and an opportunity for your mind to wander in the wrong direction.

2. Reading the Whole Question

Too often, test takers scan a multiple-choice question, recognize a few familiar words, and immediately jump to the answer choices. Test authors are aware of this common impatience, and they will sometimes prey upon it. For instance, a test author might subtly turn the question into a negative, or he or she might redirect the focus of the question right at the end. The only way to avoid falling into these traps is to read the entirety of the question carefully before reading the answer choices.

3. Looking for Wrong Answers

Long and complicated multiple-choice questions can be intimidating. One way to simplify a difficult multiple-choice question is to eliminate all of the answer choices that are clearly wrong. In most sets of answers, there will be at least one selection that can be dismissed right away. If the test is administered on paper, the test taker could draw a line through it to indicate that it may be ignored; otherwise, the test taker will have to perform this operation mentally or on scratch paper. In either case, once the obviously incorrect answers have been eliminated, the remaining choices may be considered. Sometimes identifying the clearly wrong answers will give the test taker some information about the correct answer. For instance, if one of the remaining answer choices is a direct opposite of one of the eliminated answer choices, it may well be the correct answer. The opposite of obviously wrong is obviously right! Of course, this is not always the case. Some answers are obviously incorrect simply because they are irrelevant to the question being asked. Still, identifying and eliminating some incorrect answer choices is a good way to simplify a multiple-choice question.

4. Don't Overanalyze

Anxious test takers often overanalyze questions. When you are nervous, your brain will often run wild, causing you to make associations and discover clues that don't actually exist. If you feel that this may be a problem for you, do whatever you can to slow down during the test. Try taking a deep breath or counting to ten. As you read and consider the question, restrict yourself to the particular words used by the author. Avoid thought tangents about what the author *really* meant, or what he or she was *trying* to say. The only things that matter on a multiple-choice test are the words that are actually in the question. You must avoid reading too much into a multiple-choice question, or supposing that the writer meant something other than what he or she wrote.

5. No Need for Panic

It is wise to learn as many strategies as possible before taking a multiple-choice test, but it is likely that you will come across a few questions for which you simply don't know the answer. In this situation, avoid panicking. Because most multiple-choice tests include dozens of questions, the relative value of a single wrong answer is small. As much as possible, you should compartmentalize each question on a multiple-choice test. In other words, you should not allow your feelings about one question to affect your success on the others. When you find a question that you either don't understand or don't know how to answer, just take a deep breath and do your best. Read the entire question slowly and carefully. Try rephrasing the question a couple of different ways. Then, read all of the answer choices carefully. After eliminating obviously wrong answers, make a selection and move on to the next question.

6. Confusing Answer Choices

When working on a difficult multiple-choice question, there may be a tendency to focus on the answer choices that are the easiest to understand. Many people, whether consciously or not, gravitate to the answer choices that require the least concentration, knowledge, and memory. This is a mistake. When you come across an answer choice that is confusing, you should give it extra attention. A question might be confusing because you do not know the subject matter to which it refers. If this is the case, don't eliminate the answer before you have affirmatively settled on another. When you come across an answer choice of this type, set it aside as you look at the remaining choices. If you can confidently assert that one of the other choices is correct, you can leave the confusing answer aside. Otherwise, you will need to take a moment to try to better understand the confusing answer choice. Rephrasing is one way to tease out the sense of a confusing answer choice.

7. Your First Instinct

Many people struggle with multiple-choice tests because they overthink the questions. If you have studied sufficiently for the test, you should be prepared to trust your first instinct once you have carefully and completely read the question and all of the answer choices. There is a great deal of research suggesting that the mind can come to the correct conclusion very quickly once it has obtained all of the relevant information. At times, it may seem to you as if your intuition is working faster even than your reasoning mind. This may in fact be true. The knowledge you obtain while studying may be retrieved from your subconscious before you have a chance to work out the associations that support it. Verify your instinct by working out the reasons that it should be trusted.

8. Key Words

Many test takers struggle with multiple-choice questions because they have poor reading comprehension skills. Quickly reading and understanding a multiple-choice question requires a mixture of skill and experience. To help with this, try jotting down a few key words and phrases on a piece of scrap paper. Doing this concentrates the process of reading and forces the mind to weigh the relative importance of the question's parts. In selecting words and phrases to write down, the test taker thinks about the question more deeply and carefully. This is especially true for multiple-choice questions that are preceded by a long prompt.

9. Subtle Negatives

One of the oldest tricks in the multiple-choice test writer's book is to subtly reverse the meaning of a question with a word like *not* or *except*. If you are not paying attention to each word in the question, you can easily be led astray by this trick. For instance, a common question format is, "Which of the following is…?" Obviously, if the question instead is, "Which of the following is not…?," then the answer will be quite different. Even worse, the test makers are aware of the potential for this mistake and will include one answer choice that would be correct if the question were not negated or reversed. A test taker who misses the reversal will find what he or she believes to be a correct answer and will be so confident that he or she will fail to reread the question and discover the original error. The only way to avoid this is to practice a wide variety of multiple-choice questions and to pay close attention to each and every word.

10. Reading Every Answer Choice

It may seem obvious, but you should always read every one of the answer choices! Too many test takers fall into the habit of scanning the question and assuming that they understand the question because they recognize a few key words. From there, they pick the first answer choice that answers the question they believe they have read. Test takers who read all of the answer choices might discover that one of the latter answer choices is actually *more* correct. Moreover, reading all of the answer choices can remind you of facts related to the question that can help you arrive at the correct answer. Sometimes, a misstatement or incorrect detail in one of the latter answer choices will trigger your memory of the subject and will enable you to find the right answer. Failing to read all of the answer choices is like not reading all of the items on a restaurant menu: you might miss out on the perfect choice.

11. Spot the Hedges

One of the keys to success on multiple-choice tests is paying close attention to every word. This is never truer than with words like almost, most, some, and sometimes. These words are called "hedges" because they indicate that a statement is not totally true or not true in every place and time. An absolute statement will contain no hedges, but in many subjects, the answers are not always straightforward or absolute. There are always exceptions to the rules in these subjects. For this reason, you should favor those multiple-choice questions that contain hedging language. The presence of qualifying words indicates that the author is taking special care with his or her words, which is certainly important when composing the right answer. After all, there are many ways to be wrong, but there is only one way to be right! For this reason, it is wise to avoid answers that are absolute when taking a multiple-choice test. An absolute answer is one that says things are either all one way or all another. They often include words like *every*, *always*, *best*, and *never*. If you are taking a multiple-choice test in a subject that doesn't lend itself to absolute answers, be on your guard if you see any of these words.

12. Long Answers

In many subject areas, the answers are not simple. As already mentioned, the right answer often requires hedges. Another common feature of the answers to a complex or subjective question are qualifying clauses, which are groups of words that subtly modify the meaning of the sentence. If the question or answer choice describes a rule to which there are exceptions or the subject matter is complicated, ambiguous, or confusing, the correct answer will require many words in order to be expressed clearly and accurately. In essence, you should not be deterred by answer choices that seem excessively long. Oftentimes, the author of the text will not be able to write the correct answer without offering some qualifications and modifications. Your job is to read the answer choices thoroughly and completely and to select the one that most accurately and precisely answers the question.

13. Restating to Understand

Sometimes, a question on a multiple-choice test is difficult not because of what it asks but because of how it is written. If this is the case, restate the question or answer choice in different words. This process serves a couple of important purposes. First, it forces you to concentrate on the core of the question. In order to rephrase the question accurately, you have to understand it well. Rephrasing the question will concentrate your mind on the key words and ideas. Second, it will present the information to your mind in a fresh way. This process may trigger your memory and render some useful scrap of information picked up while studying.

14. True Statements

Sometimes an answer choice will be true in itself, but it does not answer the question. This is one of the main reasons why it is essential to read the question carefully and completely before proceeding to the answer choices. Too often, test takers skip ahead to the answer choices and look for true statements. Having found one of these, they are content to select it without reference to the question above. Obviously, this provides an easy way for test makers to play tricks. The savvy test taker will always read the entire question before turning to the answer choices. Then, having settled on a correct answer choice, he or she will refer to the original question and ensure that the selected answer is relevant. The mistake of choosing a correct-but-irrelevant answer choice is especially common on questions related to specific pieces of objective knowledge. A prepared test taker will have a wealth of factual knowledge at his or her disposal, and should not be careless in its application.

15. No Patterns

One of the more dangerous ideas that circulates about multiple-choice tests is that the correct answers tend to fall into patterns. These erroneous ideas range from a belief that B and C are the most common right answers, to the idea that an unprepared test-taker should answer "A-B-A-C-A-D-A-B-A." It cannot be emphasized enough that pattern-seeking of this type is exactly the WRONG way to approach a multiple-choice test. To begin with, it is highly unlikely that the test maker will plot the correct answers according to some predetermined pattern. The questions are scrambled and delivered in a random order. Furthermore, even if the test maker was following a pattern in the assignation of correct answers, there is no reason why the test taker would know which pattern he or she was using. Any attempt to discern a pattern in the answer choices is a waste of time and a distraction from the real work of taking the test. A test taker would be much better served by extra preparation before the test than by reliance on a pattern in the answers.

FREE DVD OFFER

Don't forget that doing well on your exam includes both understanding the test content and understanding how to use what you know to do well on the test. We offer a completely FREE Test Taking Tips DVD that covers world class test taking tips that you can use to be even more successful when you are taking your test.

All that we ask is that you email us your feedback about your study guide. To get your **FREE Test Taking Tips DVD**, email freedvd@studyguideteam.com with "FREE DVD" in the subject line and the following information in the body of the email:

- The title of your study guide.
- Your product rating on a scale of 1-5, with 5 being the highest rating.
- Your feedback about the study guide. What did you think of it?
- Your full name and shipping address to send your free DVD.

Introduction

Function of the Test

The Texas Examination of Educator Standards (TExES) Social Studies 7-12 (232) test is one of dozens of TExES tests used as part of the certification process for teachers in the state of Texas. Texas law requires every person seeking certification as an educator in Texas to pass comprehensive examinations appropriate to the area in which they wish to teach. The TExES tests have been developed gradually since 2002 as the means by which prospective educators can meet this requirement.

The TExES tests are intended to identify individuals who have the appropriate level of knowledge to teach in Texas public schools. They are governed by the Texas State Board for Educator Certification and the Texas Education Agency. These state agencies have contracted with Educational Testing Service (ETS) to assist in development and deployment of the tests. All TExES tests are based on Texas Essential Knowledge and Skills, the required curriculum for all Texas public school students.

The Social Studies 7-12 (232) test evaluates prospective teachers' skills and preparedness for teaching 7th through 12th grade Social Studies. The test is not used for purposes other than determining whether the test taker qualifies for certification. Understandably, it is almost exclusively taken in Texas, by individuals seeking employment as public educators in Texas. In the 2015-2016 year, the test was taken by 3,000 test takers, of whom 64% passed.

Test Administration

Prospective exam candidates must first get approval to take the test from their Educator Preparation Program (EPP). Once a candidate receives approval from their EPP, he or she can register to take the test through ETS, either online or by phone.

The test is administered by computer at test centers throughout Texas and at selected test centers in states bordering Texas and elsewhere. The test takes five hours, and may be taken in either a morning or afternoon testing session. Candidates taking multiple TExES tests may take different tests in both sessions in one day.

As with all computer-based TExES tests, Texas law requires that a test taker who does not pass the TExES Social Studies 7-12 exam must wait 45 days before retaking the test. A test taker may attempt the test for a maximum of five total administrations (the original plus four retakes).

In accordance with the Americans with Disabilities Act, individuals with documented disabilities can receive testing accommodations. Such individuals must register for their test through ETS and have their desired accommodations approved prior to the testing day.

Test Format

Test takers should arrive at their computer testing center with an admission ticket and appropriate identification. After signing in at the test center, test takers are given the opportunity to secure personal belongings in a locker and then they are assigned a computer. The test consists of 140 scored multiple-choice questions and a variable number of additional multiple-choice questions that are not scored but are used for research purposes for possible inclusion on future tests. Test takers will not be aware of which questions count towards their scores and which are used for evaluation purposes only. The questions cover seven domains of knowledge in the field of Social Studies instruction.

These domains, and the approximate percentage of the test content they comprise, are as follows:

Domain	Approximate Percentage of Test
World History	15%
U.S. History	20%
Texas History	13%
Geography, Culture, and the Behavioral and Social Sciences	13%
Government and Citizenship	13%
Economics and Science, Technology, and Science	13%
Social Studies Foundations, Skills, Research, and Instruction	13%

Scoring

All TExES tests are criterion-referenced, meaning they designed to measure each performance against a reference baseline rather than in relation to other test takers. Raw scores are based on the number of multiple-choice questions answered correctly, with no penalty for guessing incorrectly; therefore, it is prudent for test takers to answer all questions, even if they are unsure of the correct answer. The raw score is then scaled to enable comparison between results on different forms of the test. Scaled scores range from 100 to 300, with a passing score set at 240.

Score reports include both the pass/fail result and the test taker's raw score information broken down by subject matter within the test, for the purpose of aiding preparation for a potential retake attempt. Scores are posted within seven days of the test date to the test taker's account.

Recent/Future Developments

The limit of a maximum five total attempts to pass was instituted effective September 1, 2015. All attempts taken before that date count as one total attempt. No other substantial recent or prospective changes have been announced.

World History

Ancient World Civilizations

The study of history from a global perspective is called *world history, global history,* or *transnational history*. Unlike comparative history, world history examines common patterns across nations and cultures on a global scale. A world historian studies how cultures and nations are drawn together and how they are distinct.

The classical civilizations of the world emerged out of the Iron Age, 1200-1000 BCE, with advanced metal tools, written languages, and specialized farming. The characteristics of a civilization include a written language, a geographic state, metal weapons and tools, and the use of a calendar. The prehistoric world developed near fertile river valleys near the Nile River in Egypt, Mesopotamia near ancient Greece, the Indus River in South Asia, and around the Hwang Ho in China. The classical civilizations that emerged out of the ancient world were Greece, Rome, Persia, India, and China.

Development of Early Classical Civilizations

There were a number of powerful civilizations during the classical period. Mesopotamia was home to one of the earliest civilizations between the Euphrates and the Tigris rivers in the Near East. The rivers provided water and vegetation for early humans, but they were surrounded by desert. This led to the beginning of irrigation efforts to expand water and agriculture across the region, which resulted in the area being known as the Fertile Crescent.

The organization necessary to initiate canals and other projects led to the formation of cities and hierarchies, which would have considerable influence on the structure of later civilizations. For instance, the new hierarchies established different classes within the societies, such as kings, priests, artisans, and workers. Over time, these city-states expanded to encompass outside territories, and the city of Akkad became the world's first empire in 2350 B.C. In addition, Mesopotamian scribes developed systemized drawings called pictograms, which were the first system of writing in the world; furthermore, the creation of wedge-shaped cuneiform tablets preserved written records for multiple generations.

Later, Mesopotamian kingdoms made further advancements. For instance, Babylon established a sophisticated mathematical system based on numbers from one to sixty; this not only influenced modern concepts, such as the number of minutes in each hour, but also created the framework for math equations and theories. In addition, the Babylonian king Hammurabi established a complex set of laws, known as the Code of Hammurabi, which would set a precedent for future legal systems.

Meanwhile, another major civilization began to form around the Nile River in Africa. The Nile's relatively predictable nature allowed farmers to use the river's water and the silt from floods to grow many crops along its banks, which led to further advancements in irrigation. Egyptian rulers mobilized the kingdom's population for incredible construction projects, including the famous pyramids. Egyptians also improved pictographic writing with their more complex system of hieroglyphs, which allowed for more diverse styles of writing. The advancements in writing can be seen through the Egyptians' complex system of religion, with documents such as the *Book of the Dead* outlining not only systems of worship and pantheons of deities but also a deeper, more philosophical concept of the afterlife.

While civilizations in Egypt and Mesopotamia helped to establish class systems and empires, other forms of government emerged in Greece. Despite common ties between different cities, such as the Olympic Games, each settlement, known as a polis, had its own unique culture. Many of the cities were oligarchies, in which a council of distinguished leaders monopolized the government; others were dictatorships ruled by tyrants. Athens was a notable exception by practicing an early form of democracy in which free, landholding men could participate, but it offered more freedom of thought than other systems.

Taking advantage of their proximity to the Mediterranean Sea, Greek cities sent expeditions to establish colonies abroad that developed their own local traditions. In the process, Greek merchants interacted with Phoenician traders, who had developed an alphabetic writing system built on sounds instead of pictures. This diverse network of exchanges made Greece a vibrant center of art, science, and philosophy. For example, the Greek doctor Hippocrates established a system of ethics for doctors called the Hippocratic Oath, which continues to guide the modern medical profession. Complex forms of literature were created, including the epic poem "The Iliad," and theatrical productions were also developed. Athens in particular sought to spread its vision of democratic freedom throughout the world, which led to the devastating Peloponnesian War between allies of Athens and those of oligarchic Sparta from 431 to 404 B.C.

Alexander the Great helped disseminate Greek culture to new regions, also known as *diffusion*. Alexander was in fact an heir to the throne of Macedon, which was a warrior kingdom to the north of Greece. After finishing his father's work of unifying Greece under Macedonian control, Alexander successfully conquered Mesopotamia, which had been part of the Persian Empire. The spread of Greek institutions throughout the Mediterranean and Near East led to a period of Hellenization, during which various civilizations assimilated Greek culture; this allowed Greek traditions, such as architecture and philosophy, to endure into the present day.

Greek ideas were later assimilated, along with many other concepts, into the Roman Empire. Located west of Greece on the Italian peninsula, the city of Rome gradually conquered its neighbors and expanded its territories abroad; by 44 B.C., Rome had conquered much of Western Europe, northern Africa, and the Near East. Romans were very creative, and they adapted new ideas and innovated new technologies to strengthen their power. For instance, Romans built on the engineering knowledge of Greeks to create arched pathways, known as aqueducts, to transport water for long distances and devise advanced plumbing systems.

One of Rome's greatest legacies was its system of government. Early Rome was a republic, a democratic system in which leaders are elected by the people. Although the process still heavily favored wealthy elites, the republican system was a key inspiration for later institutions such as the United States. Octavian "Augustus" Caesar later made Rome into an empire, and the senate had only a symbolic role in the government. The new imperial system built on the examples of earlier empires to establish a vibrant dynasty that used a sophisticated legal code and a well-trained military to enforce order across vast regions. Even after Rome itself fell to barbarian invaders in fifth century A.D., the eastern half of the empire survived as the Byzantine Empire until 1453 A.D. Furthermore, the Roman Empire's institutions continued to influence and inspire later medieval kingdoms, including the Holy Roman Empire; even rulers in the twentieth century called themselves Kaiser and Tsar, titles which stem from the word "Caesar."

In addition, the Roman Empire was host to the spread of new religious ideas. In the region of Israel, the religion of Judaism presented a new approach to worship via monotheism, which is the belief in the existence of a single deity. An offshoot of Judaism called Christianity spread across the Roman Empire and gained popularity. While Rome initially suppressed the religion, it later backed Christianity and allowed the religious system to endure as a powerful force in medieval times.

Individuals, Events, and Issues that Shaped the Development of Early and Classical Civilizations

The earliest "hearths of domestication" established and dispersed farming practices and breeding techniques that helped small villages in Egypt, Iraq, Pakistan, China, Mexico, Central America, and Peru blossom into complex cultural civilizations. Agriculture likely did not originate in just one of these hearths first, but rather formed independently around the same time. Prior to the First Agricultural Revolution, animals such as horses, pigs, cows, dogs, cats, camels, sheep, and goats roamed wildly in their natural environments. During the Old Stone Age, nomadic hunters would stalk, stampede, and hunt wild creatures for their hides, marrows, and meats. Archaeological evidence, such as Paleolithic paintings and site-based soil samples, illustrate that Stone Age hunters slaughtered meals by stampeding herds of animals off prehistoric cliffs. These epic, cliff-side bloodbaths allowed nomadic bands of hunters and gatherers to carry out quick, massive kills that clothed and fed packs of thirty or more people for extended periods of time. With the advent of domestication, or the taming of animals, however, humans created even more sustainable food sources, driving herds into human-made grazing enclosures instead of rocky ravines. Within these enclosures, residents tamed, bred, milked, skinned, and butchered animals for a more consistent and sustaining source of food. Gradually, through the processes of animal husbandry and selective breeding, many wild species evolved into domesticated livestock that assisted with the Neolithic Age's higher demand for farm labor.

As feral beasts became extra farmhands via the practices of animal husbandry and selective breeding, several "culture hearths" around the globe began employing new agricultural techniques that tapped into the potential of animal labor. By around 5500–3500 BCE, Neolithic farmers began using domesticated livestock as a source of farm labor. Livestock became crucial contributors to the new plowing and towing processes that allowed settlements to make the full transition from hunter-gatherer communities to sedentary agricultural societies. Domesticated animals also provided Neolithic farmers with the fertilizer, wool, hides, and leather that assisted with systematic crop production.

Most of the world's earliest hearths of domestication had similar features:

- They were typically located near major sources of water (usually rivers) or on hillsides that attracted natural flow of rainwaters.

- They were typically located in lands with a mild climate that proved favorable for crop growth.

- They all developed similar irrigation systems (canals and ditches) that helped grow surplus crops.

- They all employed animal labor in some capacity to assist with crop production.

Many Neolithic farms also employed new systematic practices such as slash-and-burn farming or terraced farming. The practices helped develop new extensive crops such as wheat and barley. One of the earliest centers of wheat and barley production emerged in an unlikely place: the rolling foothills of the Zagros Mountains, located in the so-called Fertile Crescent of Mesopotamia (modern northeastern Iraq). Today, the Zagros Mountains remain arid and eroded by the unstoppable forces of history; nevertheless, many scholars, including Robert Braidwood, an archaeologist who conducted his world-renowned research in Iraq in the 1950s, believe the Zagros region of Mesopotamia once hosted the world's first hotbed for primitive agriculture. In fact, some scholars believe the village of Jarmo, the target of Braidwood's archaeological dig, laid the foundation for modern life by hosting the world's first domesticated barley and wheat fields some nine thousand years ago.

These early hearths of domestication produced sustainable forms of living that laid the foundations for later classical civilizations such as the Egyptian Empire, the Babylonian Empire, the Incan and Mayan empires in the Americas, and the Macedonian, Greek, and Roman empires of the Mediterranean. These early classical civilizations all suffered similar demises: They became dysfunctional from within and succumbed to outside enemies and attacks. Often these empires were led by charismatic leaders such as Alexander the Great, Julius Cesar, and Montezuma II. These great empires, however, also crumbled in the hands of charismatic leaders.

Major Political, Economic, and Cultural Developments in the Civilizations of Africa, the Mediterranean Basin, Mesoamerica, Middle and Near East, and Asia

Ancient Greece
Alexander's father, King Phillip II of Macedon, conquered the Greek city-states, ultimately achieved at the Battle of Chaeronea in 338 BCE, and established the first centralized Greek state in ancient history. Phillip II then set his sights on the Persian Empire and began preparing for an invasion; however, he was assassinated by sources disputed by contemporary historians. Some speculate they were Persian assassins; others claimed that unhappy leaders of the recently conquered city-states executed the assassination. In any event, Alexander the Great succeeded his father and seized control over their new empire at twenty years old.

In the thirteen years between Alexander's accession to the throne and his own death, he conquered the Persian Empire, which stretched from the Mediterranean to India, fulfilling his father's plans. During this period, education and literacy spread, and new genres of writing were created. The rich cultural interactions between the great ancient civilizations ushered in the Hellenistic period. Architecture was more lavish, and the scientific advancements that began with Aristotle continued throughout the empire. The spread of Greek culture, as well as its interaction with foreign civilizations, had a lasting effect on religion, language, and innovation that endured until Rome conquered Greece and adopted much of the Hellenic culture.

Roman Empire
The formation of Rome is steeped in legend and lore befitting its status as the greatest successor to all previous empires. According to legend, twin brothers Romulus and Remus set out to found a new city but disagreed as to its location. Tensions led to Romulus killing his twin brother and founding a city on the Palatine Hill called Rome. Conquering land from Britain to northern Africa and the Middle East, Rome solidified itself as the greatest empire of the ancient world. At its height, Rome's military conquered and held an unprecedented amount of territory.

Throughout its history, Rome transitioned from a monarchy to a republic and then to an autocratic empire. Historians dispute when Rome was founded, but most agree that it was established somewhere between the tenth and eighth centuries BCE by the Latin tribe of Italy. The Etruscans established control over the region by the late seventh century BCE and were ruled by an aristocratic elite and monarch. Sometime during the latter half of the sixth century BCE, the Latin tribe regained power and established the Roman Republic. Around 509 BCE, a constitution and system of government based on checks and balances and separation of powers was established. The senate functioned as the elected legislative branch, and nobility known as *patricians* controlled it. Consuls functioned as the executive branch, and the senate appointed the consuls for limited terms. The Roman Republic would rise to greatness after first defeating Carthage in the Punic Wars and then the Macedonian and Seleucid empires in the second century BCE. Although still a republic, Rome constituted the premier empire in the Mediterranean, well positioned for expansion.

Persian Empire

Cyrus the Great established the First Persian Empire in 550 BC after stifling the great rebellion of the Medes and subsequently defeating the kingdom of Lydia and the Neo-Babylonian Empire. Initially nomadic shepherds, the Persians steadily consolidated power and created a strong infrastructure and military. At its height, the Persian Empire was the largest in the ancient world and stretched from Eastern Europe to Central and South Asia. His successors, including Darius I, continued to expand the empire until Alexander the Great conquered much of Persia, creating the largest empire until the founding of Rome.

Maurya Empire

The Maurya Empire was the most powerful and influential kingdom in the history of ancient India, ruling from 322 BCE to 185 BCE, and it was one of the largest empires in the word for its time period. The first emperor of Maurya was Chandragupta Maurya, who overthrew the Nanda Dynasty, unified India, and expanded the empire. His success occurred after Alexander the Great's armies withdrew from India, and Chandragupta's armies defeated the satraps and Greek armies that were left behind.

Africa

Between the 1500s and 1800s, over 12 million African slaves were shipped across the globe as free labor for agricultural markets. Slavery had a cultural impact not only on Africa, but also the entire globe, especially the developing colonies and nations of North and South America. The spread of African languages and cultures to the New World (called the African Diaspora) created an entirely new culture in the Americas.

Africa is also responsible for exporting important agricultural and animal domestication techniques, textile creation skills, and other technological advances to the rest of the world in antiquity. North Africans shared shipbuilding techniques with Greek and Roman civilizations, and they became leaders in mathematics and engineering. Ethiopians were the first to cultivate coffee and recognize its energizing properties. The Nile River Valley region is also believed to be one of the first to develop cotton as a textile and agricultural export.

Americas

During the Age of Exploration, indigenous Americans taught European explorers how to cultivate such plants as maize (corn), beans, pumpkins, squash, cacao, beans, vanilla, sweet potatoes, peppers, peanuts, pineapples, sunflowers, gourds, plums, and tobacco. Native American agricultural techniques and harvesting technologies transformed the diets of people around the world. Native Americans also exported domestication techniques for turkeys and certain dog breeds, transforming the trade market for household and farm animals. Additionally, the Native American civilizations advanced studies in mathematics, engineering, and astronomy. In the United States, indigenous culture and mythology still pervades the national psyche even though many Native Americans were slaughtered by the colonial and revolutionary governments of the New World.

Revolution, in and of itself, is also one of the greatest exports of the Americas. The American Revolution, the first of its kind in the New World, became a focal point of later revolutions. Today, many revolutionary forces still look to the American Revolution for inspiration.

Europe

Much of the West's political and philosophical heritage is owed to the Greek and Roman civilizations of European antiquity. The Greeks established democracy, and the Romans established the framework of republicanism. During the Enlightenment, these classical values helped shape the revolutionary sentiments of the Founding Fathers of the United States. Christianity is another essential European export. Europe adopted the religion during Late Antiquity and the Middle Ages. Eventually, Christianity was dispersed throughout the world during the Age of Exploration. During the Enlightenment and Age of Exploration, Europe also became a leader in science, mathematics, and technology, thanks in part to the influences of North Africa, the Middle East, and the Arab world. Europeans became expert shipbuilders and explorers, refining such exploratory tools as the astrolabe and compass.

Middle East

The Middle East has always been a hub of early civilization. Middle Easterners helped develop early mathematical principles (number systems, algebra, geometry) as well as advanced mathematics (trigonometry and calculus). Likewise, Middle Easterners were leaders in engineering and architecture during Late Antiquity and the Middle Ages. Their architectural styles influenced European and American buildings. The Middle East is also the epicenter of monotheistic religion, as the original home of Judaism, Christianity, and Islam.

Asia

Asia was responsible for dispersing gunpowder, silk, fireworks, tea, and spices throughout the world during the Age of Exploration. Following the success of overland travels across the Silk Road in the 1200s and 1300s, Europeans began to develop a fascination with the Far East. This Orientalism drove explorers to find faster sea routes to China and Japan. In many ways, the Far East's grip on the European consciousness is, perhaps, the driving force of the Age of Exploration.

Political Organization, Cultural Characteristics, and Contributions of Ancient Civilizations

Ancient Greece

Ancient Greece formed from scattered farming communities between 800 BCE and 500 BCE. In this early era of Greece, the polis, or city-state, held all of the political power locally. City-states were self-ruling and self-sufficient. The idea of a self-governing state had an enduring effect on the government of Greece and would result in the demokratia (rule by the people), which would spread and influence the world. As farming villages grew and marketplaces were built, a government with laws, an organized army, and tax collection took shape.

Each city-state was different from one another, but some unifying traits included a common language, a shared belief system, an agriculturally based economy, and rule by several wealthy citizens instead of rule by a king or queen. However, these few aristocratic rulers, known as *oligarchs,* often owned the best and most land, which created tension as the population grew. As a result, many citizens moved to less populated or newly conquered areas. By 800 BCE, there were over 1500 city-states, each with its own rulers and rules. Greek city-states were concentrated on the coast, resulting in greater contact with other civilizations through trade. City-states' governments and culture continued to diverge as time progressed. For example, in the fifth century BCE, Athens became the first direct democracy in the world, and Athenian citizens would vote directly on legislation. Only adult, male, landowning citizens could vote, but it was a remarkable departure from all contemporary forms of government to provide for direct democracy, especially relative to other city-states' oligarchies. Another world-renowned example is Sparta, which based its entire social system and constitution on military training and ability.

The Greek religion was polytheistic. Every city-state had a temple dedicated to a particular god or goddess; however, the whole of ancient Greece believed that Zeus, residing in Mount Olympus, was the most powerful of the gods. The physical presence of the temple, the rituals and festivals that dotted the Greek year, and the widespread belief in the gods controlling every aspect of human life heavily influenced their agricultural economy, government, and interactions with other ancient civilizations.

The ancient Greeks were known for their citizen-soldiers, known as *hoplites*. No ancient civilization could field a professional military due to economic restraints, such as a lack of a banking system and the need for agricultural laborers, but the hoplites were famous in ancient times for their tactics and skill. Hoplites were armed with spears and large shields, and they would fight in a phalanx formation. The Romans would later adopt many of the Greek military principles. Greek city-states fought numerous wars among each other, the largest being the Peloponnesian War, as well as wars against Persia. Fought between 499 BCE and 449 BCE, the Greco-Persian Wars pitted the Greek city-states against the mighty Persian Empire after the latter invaded. Although ancient sources are difficult to authenticate, it is certain that the Persian forces vastly outnumbered the Greeks who historically struggled to unite, even against a common enemy. This conflict included the legendary Battle of Thermopylae where three hundred Spartans, led by the Spartan king Leonidas, held off the elite contingent of the Persian army, the Immortals, for two days. After several setbacks and disastrous turns, the Greeks eventually defeated the Persian fleet at the naval Battle of Mycale and forced the Persians out of Europe. Greek unification did not last beyond this victory, and by 404 BCE, Sparta crushed Athens in the Peloponnesian War. Athens would never again attain its status as the leading city-state.

Roman Empire
Although already one of the world's most powerful civilizations, Rome began to strain under political pressure and domestic unrest in the mid-first century BCE. In 48 BCE, Gaius Julius Caesar seized power over the republic, but his assassination in 44 BCE on the Ides of March threw the republic back into turmoil. Caesar's great-nephew turned son adopted by will, Octavian, eventually emerged as the sole leader of Rome, and historians define this point as the beginning of the Roman Empire. Octavian would serve as the first emperor under the name Augustus. His rule would be one of the most peaceful and prosperous in Roman history, often referred to as the *Pax Romana* or *Pax Augusta*. Although the Roman Empire did not adhere to the republic's democratic principles and separations of powers, the Roman Empire would be the vehicle that enabled Rome to conquer and administer enormous territory.

As Rome became an empire, its influence both in the ancient world and in the modern world began to take shape. Rome's ability to absorb and adapt the cultural achievements of Greece and push them on conquered cultures was a key to their success. Rome was highly influenced by Greek culture, religions, ideas, literature, and politics but kept at its roots the Roman ideals of simplicity, honesty, and loyalty. Rome was able to hold together a government that included multiple races, languages, and cultures in peace through the successful use of these ideas. In addition, Rome applied concepts developed by the Persians in the administration and political organization of its territories. By the time Rome became an empire, the government was highly structured with a complex civil service that addressed and administrated localized affairs.

Rome's decline began well before its eventual fall. There are many aspects to Rome's demise, including social, political, moral, religious, and economic. Each took their toll on the strength of the empire, and by 400 A.D., Rome collapsed under public unrest and religious discord, along with the invasion of the Huns of Mongolia and Germanic tribes. Although ultimately defeated, Rome's legacy extends all the way through to the present day. The Roman Republic's democratic elements and robust civil service would be the model for much of the West, especially the United States. That is to say nothing of the advancements in literature, technology, architecture, urban planning, and hygiene across the empire that influenced every future Western civilization.

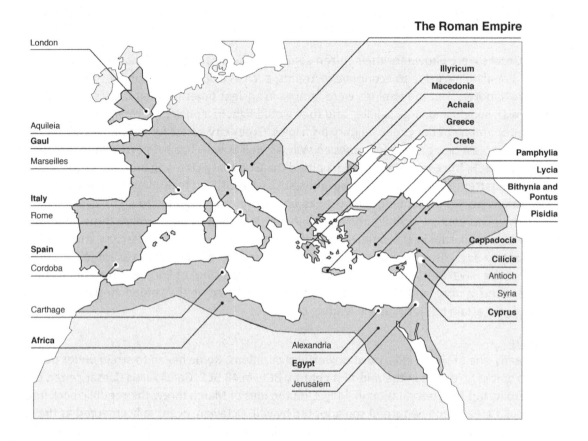

Persian Empire

The Persian Empire consisted of multiple countries, religions, languages, and races governed by a central government. Cyrus the Great was known for his social and political acumen. He was able to navigate the empire's diversity with his "carrot or stick" approach. Cyrus the Great would offer foreign civilizations some degree of home rule, as long as they paid tribute to Persia and adopted some of its norms, or else the might of the legendary Persian military would crush them. As long as the citizens of Persia paid taxes and were peaceful, they were allowed to keep their own religious customs, local culture, and local economies. It was not until his successors that this political policy began to wan with the onset of multiple rebellions that weakened the centralized government.

The government of Persia delegated power among four governing capitals. Each state had a satrap, or governor. The satrapy government allowed for regional self-governance with a military leader and an official record-keeper that reported to the central government. The empire was also innovative in its road construction and postal systems. By allowing some degree of regional autonomy, Persia was able to rule over an unprecedented territory in ancient history. For example, Babylon even requested to be part of Persia because of its unique policies. The empire's enormity and vast scope influenced world history for centuries. Persian scholars and political philosophers would later influence rulers in the Renaissance and Enlightenment eras.

Maurya Empire

The Maurya Empire established a centralized government to govern its vast territories, and it specialized in tax collection, administration, and the military. It was modeled after the Greek and Persian governments, who, through trade and invasion, had influenced Chandragupta's government layout. Previously, regional chieftains and small armies governed India, which led to continuous skirmishes and wars. Chandragupta cleared out the chieftains and imposed regulated laws and tax reforms. The centralized form of government allowed for a period of peace, scientific advancement, and religious growth.

The centralized government was made up of four provinces organized under one capital. Each emperor had a cabinet of ministers known as a *Mantriparishad,* or Council of Ministers, to help guide him—an idea that is still used in governments across the world. Princes, or Kumaras, likewise oversaw each province, with a council of ministers called the *Mahamatyas*. A civil service was developed to govern many aspects of life and infrastructure, including waterworks, roads, and international trade. The army was expanded into one of the largest in the world at the time. Trade became a major source of revenue as other empires sought spices, food, and cloth from India.

India's three main religions flourished in this period. Hinduism, a blend of multiple beliefs, appeared in the Epic Age and became a central religion. Buddhism appeared as a consequence of the harsh social structure that had left a wide gap in the social and economic freedoms of the people. Chandragupta later accepted Jainism, a religion of total peace and unity with the world. Overall, the Maurya Empire featured a balance of religions that promoted peace as foundational and sought social harmony. The centralized government discouraged the infamous Indian caste system, which organized society by social status and led to discrimination against the lower castes.

Chinese Empire

Between 1000 BCE and 500 A.D., ancient China was unified under three successive dynasties: the Zhou Dynasty, the Qin Dynasty, and the Han Dynasty, in respective chronological order. The Zhou Dynasty was the longest dynasty in Chinese history and began after the fall of the Shang Dynasty. Originally, the Zhou Dynasty had moved away from the Shang Empire, created their own government, and formed alliances with enemies of the Shang. When war eventually broke, the people of Shang, so angered by their own government's foolishness, put up little resistance against the rebellion.

Under the Zhou Dynasty, the kingdom's ruler legitimized their power through the Mandate of Heaven, meaning they believed the rulers of the land were put in place by a higher being that could not be disposed. The Zhou claimed that the Shang Dynasty had forfeited their claim due to their mismanagement of the kingdom. This would be a common theme for dynasty takeovers. A centralized government was established, but the Zhou Dynasty never achieved complete centralized control across the kingdom. The economy was heavily agricultural and organized based on feudalism, an economical system in which a wealthy, landowning class rules the peasant class. These aristocratic rulers retained considerable power and regularly rebelled against the central government.

The Qin Dynasty was the first imperial dynasty, originally organized under Emperor Qin Shi Huangdi. The imperial state had a more centralized government, which limited the aristocratic landowners' power, stabilized the economy, and boosted the army. The Qin Dynasty formed a political structure that allowed China to start major building projects like the Great Wall of China. Its form of government would be adopted by many dynasties in China's history. The Qin Dynasty was short-lived and ended when Emperor Qin Shi Huangdi died prematurely, and rebel leaders fought for control of the kingdom.

Liu Bang of Han defeated Xiang Yu of Chu at the Battle of Gaixia in 202 BCE, establishing the Han Dynasty.

Like the previous imperial dynasty, power was consolidated under a single emperor who dominated the Han Dynasty's centralized government. Under the emperor, a cabinet of ministers and chosen nobility acted as advisors who retained limited power. The Han dynasty was a golden era of Chinese innovation and technology, all driven by the tremendous growth in commerce and trade. To facilitate commerce, the Han Dynasty issued one of the world's earliest currencies under a money economy. Han coinage would remain the dominant currency from its introduction in 119 BCE until the Tang Dynasty in 618 A.D.. A uniform currency was an essential part of the legendary Silk Road, which began under the Han Dynasty.

World History from 600 A.D. to 1450 A.D.

World Civilizations from 600 A.D. to 1450 A.D.

Early Middle Ages
The Middle Ages refers to the period from the fifth century to the fifteenth century, beginning with the fall of the Roman Empire and ending with the Renaissance and Age of Exploration. Sharp population decline, intensely localized governance, frequent invasions, famine, and disease defined the early Middle Ages and explain why it is sometimes referred to as the *Dark Ages*. Manorialism and feudalism were the dominant economic systems of the period. Peasants would rent patches of land to farm on enormous manors of aristocrats, while knights and lower nobles would exchange military service with the aristocracy in exchange for control over a manor. In addition, much of the knowledge gained during the Age of Antiquity was lost during this period.

High Middle Ages
During the High Middle Ages, signs of revival began to emerge. Christians began to see the need to live out the fundamental convictions of Christianity and also saw the need for the clergy to exemplify Christ. After several reforms, religious orders developed, such as the Franciscans and Dominicans. The orders protected the knowledge and texts of the church, becoming a strong intellectual body. As a consequence, there was a revival in learning in the monasteries that trickled out to the cathedrals and then to schools.

Around 570 A.D., the Islamic prophet Muhammad was born in Mecca. Muhammad was a trade merchant who, coming into contact with Christian and Jewish traders, blended their religions with his own religious experience in which he believed that Allah was the one true god. He believed that Allah had called him to preach the Islamic religion. At first, he met with little success, as most Arabs believed in many and differing gods. However, in a few years, he was able to unite the nomadic tribes under Islam.

After Muhammad's death, his successors, known as *caliphs,* developed the religion of Islam into a system of government and spread the faith and government control into the Middle East, North Africa, Spain, and southern France. At one point, the Islamic Empire was larger than the Roman Empire. With invasion, Islam spread the Arabic language and embraced Greek science and Indian mathematics. From 900 A.D. to 1100 A.D., Islam experienced a golden age.

In 1095, European Christians launched military strikes against Muslims in the Holy Land, and the entire series of armed religious conflicts is known as the *Crusades*. During the Crusades, Italy's trade flourished because the movement of people facilitated commerce and communication with the Middle East and Africa. In the High Middle Ages, Italy expanded trade into Europe, and merchants across Europe began to settle in areas with good trade routes. Others who had a trade to sell settled in these areas, forming towns and local governments. The development of commerce would be the impetus for the Renaissance.

Major Developments in Mesoamerica, Andean, and Asia

India

The classical age of India came to a sudden end in 535 A.D. when the Huns invaded. Under Hun rule, India held on to its religious and cultural traditions. By the 600s, a Hindu confederation pushed back the Huns, and Harsha, the Hindu king, united the empire once again. At first, his rule was peaceful and humane, but in his later years, oppressive acts caused another overthrow of the empire. This time, it was from the Rajput Indians, descendants of central Asians who had intermarried with Hindus after invading some centuries before.

The Rajput kingdoms were small, regionally ruled areas weakened by disunity. After the spread of Islam in the Middle East, Muslim Turks began to invade India. Beginning in the north, Muslims streamed in and began to convert Hindus to Islam. It took from 712 A.D. to 1236 A.D. for Muslims to control the northern part of India and another hundred years to gain the southern part.

After setting up a new capital in Delhi, the Muslim invaders used sultans, or Muslim authorities, to rule over India. Their government was called the *Delhi Sultanate,* and it was cruel toward those who had not converted to Islam. The sultans remained in power until 1526 A.D.. The laws established higher taxes for non-Muslims, which caused many to convert. The strict caste system of Hindu also caused many to convert to the socially equal Muslims. As a result of the invasion and religious conversion, India was divided into Hindus and Muslims, and it remains a dividing point today.

China

The harsh terrain between China and the rest of the world kept it in relative peace and stability for most of Europe's Middle Ages. However, after the Han Dynasty fell, China was in turmoil for nearly four hundred years until a Chinese general, Yang Chien, founded the Sui Dynasty in 581 A.D.. It was the Sui Dynasty that rebuilt the foundations of the government and allowed the next two dynasties to flourish with two more golden ages.

Following the collapse of the Sui Dynasty in 618 A.D., the Li family took control of the empire and established the T'ang Dynasty, which lasted for almost two hundred years. Under T'ang, the government moved to a highly centralized, highly regulated form of government run by the empire's scholars. The economy grew with building projects that opened new avenues of trade. Canals and ports allowed thousands of foreign merchants to trade in China. The dissemination of ideas and culture, combined with long peaceful stability, allowed the Chinese time to create world-changing inventions, such as gunpowder and block printing. The decline of the T'ang Dynasty began after a series of weak emperors, overtaxation, and persecution led to the deposition of the last T'ang emperor by Chao K'uang-yin.

In 960 A.D., Chao K'uang-yin established the Song Dynasty. Though it would last until 1279 A.D., the Song Dynasty was often fighting off Mongol invaders. The early Khitan invaders were paid off with silver and silk, but the Tungusic people, known as the *Jurchen,* from Manchuria, divided the empire into two— Jurchen's Jin Empire to the north and the Song Empire to the south. Under Song rule, the southern empire flourished, despite the split. Trade increased with the opening of new commercial colonies and ports. As the Chinese began to travel to trade their wares, they introduced new ideas and technology to the world. They also improved sea travel and invented important navigational equipment.

With the empire split, the Jin Dynasty came under attack by Mongols, and after many years of tribute or fighting off, the dynasty gave way under the attacks of Genghis Khan, a brutal but highly effective military commander. In 1215 A.D., Genghis Khan conquered the Jin Dynasty and moved to the West, occupying parts of Russia, Persia, Iraq, and northern India. Genghis Khan's grandson, Kublai Khan, united the empires once again by overthrowing the Song Dynasty in 1279 A.D. and adding the Asian states of Burma, Annam, and Cambodia. He then established the Yuan Dynasty, making Kublai the first foreign ruler in Chinese history.

After the Collapse of the Western Roman Empire

Feudalism

In medieval Europe, feudalism was a legal system that included participation among lords (people who owned the land), vassals (people who were given possession of the land), and fiefs (the land itself). When the lord granted land to the vassal, the vassal would pledge fealty (sworn loyalty) to the lord in return. From 9th century to 15th century A.D., feudalism was a way of managing land in exchange for nobility.

Manorialism

Manorialism was another economic, social, and political system in medieval Europe that lasted well into the 18th century, and gradually died out after that. Manorialism involves lords of a manor receiving payment from their subjects through labor. Serfdom was a characteristic of manorialism, where tenant farmers were given a plot of land to cultivate by the lord of the estate. Manorialism was different from feudalism in that there was no ceremony involved in manorialism to establish a relationship between a lord and a vassal. Instead, manorialism was an economic arrangement that effectively managed the lands of the aristocracy and clergy.

Roman Catholic Church and Eastern Orthodox Church in Medieval Europe

Following the collapse of the Roman Empire into fragmented territories in 476 A.D., the former eastern territory retained its power and regained control over some of Rome's other territories, establishing the Byzantine Empire. Although originally part of the Roman Empire, the Byzantine Empire adopted significantly different policies and cultural practices during and after Rome fell. Under Theodosius I, the Byzantine Empire adopted Christianity as the official religion during the third century. During the sixth century, under the reign of Heraclius, the empire adopted Greek as the official language in its administration and military. The Byzantine Empire protected and advanced the rich culture of art, literature, and philosophy developed by the Romans. The emperor Justinian is by far the most heralded and influential Byzantine ruler. He successfully invaded to reorganize governments and spread law. The Code of Justinian, also known as the *Corpus Juris Civilis*, issued from 529 A.D. to 534 A.D., is a fundamental collection of jurisprudence, and it was intended to be the complete collection of laws governing the Byzantine Empire. The Code of Justinian is one of the most influential pieces of legislation in world history, serving as the basis for future civil law jurisdictions and canon law of the Roman Catholic Church.

Christianity played a special role in the Byzantine Empire, as it was able to take over much of the authority lost by civil and military rulers. Christianity was also able to keep literacy, culture, and philosophy of the ancient world alive. In addition, the Byzantine Empire's Christian faith would pit it against Muslims in numerous bloody conflicts. By Justinian's time, the church of the east and the west had grown apart. Concerned with growing differences between the two, Justinian sent out missionaries and suppressed heresy and paganism. His attempts failed in the long term and, as a result, the east and west churches split irrevocably into Roman Catholicism and Eastern Orthodox Christianity with the Schism of 1054 A.D.

In 768 A.D., Charlemagne, or Charles the Great, took power and worked to unify an empire under the Roman Catholic Church. By 800 A.D., he was crowned emperor of the Holy Roman Empire. The Holy Roman Empire controlled a complex set of territories in central Europe from the early Middle Ages until it dissolved in 1806. The predominance of Christian thought in Charlemagne's government covered all aspects of government and allowed for a revival in literature and the arts. It also included copying Latin text to preserve knowledge for future generations. This contrasted sharply with the rest of the West, where much of the former Roman territories lived in localized and unorganized communities. The Holy Roman emperors claimed to be the heir to the Roman Empire and clung to the prestige of that claim. Even in the Holy Roman Empire, the West failed to develop the technology and advance the knowledge gained under the Roman Empire. Although the Holy Roman Empire retained the name and wielded substantial power, the actual government was extremely decentralized, like that of other feudal territories with lesser names.

Comparison of Social, Political, Economic, and Religious Aspects of Medieval Europe with Previous Civilizations

As central feudal governments weakened in the High Middle Ages, the church emerged as the most powerful institution in both Western Europe and Byzantium. With the infamous crowning of Charlemagne as the emperor of the Holy Roman Empire in the West, the Catholic Church sought to expand its political role in Europe. The church, once a weakened spiritual institution, became a political machine in Europe. Feudalism still reigned as the dominant social and economic structure, but the church swiftly began to take control of these socioeconomic affairs. While feudalism and the manor/serfdom system created division, the church strove for unification through faith. The Catholic Church provided both physical and spiritual security during these dark times. The church became the center of every community, controlling the daily lives of its participants. Even the legal system was based on Catholic canon, which unified church and state. During this time, popes wielded as much power as kings. They had the ability to rule the people, deny salvation, and excommunicate members from the community. The church also had the power to execute members who threatened the sanctity of canon law. The local clergy of the Catholic Church demanded as much respect as the feudal knights. The emergence of the church as a social, economic, and political leader set the stage for the wave of Crusades in later centuries. Additionally, it set the stage for the battle between church and state that would carry throughout the Early Modern period. With church and state so closely unified during this period, corruption ran rampant as the Catholic Church asked its followers to pay for their salvation. Diplomatic ties with the Middle East remained tenuous during this time as the Catholic Church declared holy wars on the Muslim Turks.

Political, Religious, and Social Impact of the Crusades and Other Religious Interactions

In 1093, Pope Urban II teamed with the Byzantine emperor Alexius Comnenus to declare a series of "holy wars," or "Crusades," on the Muslim Turks who were knocking at the door of the Byzantine capital, Constantinople. For two centuries, several waves of Crusades were carried out in the Holy Land, specifically in Jerusalem. The Crusades were not only religious in character, but also economic. On the ground, the Crusades maintained a religious zeal—knights traveled throughout the Mediterranean to fight for their Lord. Behind the scenes, rulers and merchants profited off loans and leases. The Crusades helped make Genoese and Venetian merchants some of the wealthiest in Europe, if not the world. Politically, the Crusades helped unite quarrelsome knights who had been previously warring across Europe. The knights united in a common enemy: Muslims. In terms of a social impact, the Crusades helped further diversify the Holy Land as Jerusalem shifted hands between Western Europe, Byzantium, and the Muslim Turks. By the 1200s, the Crusades had become so common that the sporadic campaigns had too often led to failure. As a result, the power of the pope and the Byzantine Empire began to weaken. The power of feudal nobles also began to weaken. This helped usher in the end of feudalism in Europe, paving the way to the rise of stronger monarchies and nation-states. As the power of feudal nobles declined, the power of Italian merchants began to increase. This accumulation of wealth eventually paved the way to the trade-driven Age of Exploration in the Early Modern period. Specifically, trade grew between Europe and Asia, spawning an increase in European "Orientalism." This Orientalism encouraged Europeans to find new trade routes to Asia by sea. Additionally, European technology advanced to allow for easier trade and travel. The cultural exchanges between the Muslims and Christians opened the doors to technological advancement in Western Europe. Nevertheless, the bitterness of the Crusades left Christians and Muslims at "war" for centuries to come. The Crusades are still viewed as a historical example of the dangerous roots of Christian hegemony in the Middle East.

World History from 1450 A.D. to 1750 A.D.

While Europe was experiencing a low point in the Middle Ages, with little progress in the arts, technology, or culture, India and China were experiencing multiple golden ages. However, by the 1300s, the tide had shifted. Europe was coming out of its dark age and moving toward a period that would surpass the cultural achievements, wealth, and power that India and China had gained during the Middle Ages. In this emerging Western dominance, the East declined, but it did not remain isolated due to European exploration and colonization.

For Europe, the Middle Ages were a time of feudalism and religious orthodoxy. As the period ended, people began to shift toward the idea of individualism, as they began to seek out political and economic freedom, independence of thought in religious matters, and a desire for greater knowledge. The idea of a "Renaissance man" developed, with Leonardo da Vinci representing the ideal: a person who achieved mastery in many forms or subjects.

World Civilizations from 1450 A.D. to 1750 A.D.

Fall of Constantinople
The fall of Constantinople happened in May 1453 and marked the end of the Roman Empire, a 1500-year imperial state. The Ottoman Empire invaded the capital of the Byzantine Empire following a fifty-three day siege, led by the young Mehmed the Conqueror, sultan of the Ottoman Empire. For some historians, the fall of Constantinople marks the end of the Middle Ages.

Western Religion
The major division between Christianity occurred in the 1500s as a result of the Protestant Reformation. Catholics and Protestants fought several wars to decide what religion would dominate in a particular region. The wars were often for political and economic gain but fought on the basis of religion. In particular, the Thirty Years' War was the bloodiest conflict in world history until the First World War. The Thirty Years' War directly led to the concept of the nation-state, one of the most important developments in modern history. The need for an identifiable nation-state grew out of the need for regions to determine their own religion to prevent future conflict.

During periods of strife and persecution, different denominations of Christianity migrated to the United States, especially during the colonial period. Such groups who sought religious freedom and tolerance included the Quakers, who settled in Pennsylvania; the Dutch Anabaptists and Calvinists, who settled in New York; and the Catholics, who settled in Maryland, among others. The Great Awakening, a religious revival in colonial America during the 1730s and 1740s, contributed to the American Revolution by encouraging people to challenge authority in their pursuit of salvation. Many colonists believed that the war was just in the eyes of God, and so it gave them a moral reason to fight. Ministers, like Jonathan Mayhew, who coined the phrase "No taxation without representation," preached that the revolution was a religious crusade and that it was the Christian's duty to do battle against tyrants and oppressors.

Martin Luther

Martin Luther, a priest, monk, professor, and composer, was an influential part of the Protestant Reformation. Martin Luther disagreed with the Catholic Church in its then-belief that salvation could be bought instead of bestowed by grace, and nailed his *Ninety-Five Theses* to the wall of a chapel in Wittenberg, Germany in 1517. In addition, Luther also translated the Bible into the German vernacular instead of its usual Latin, allowing the masses to interpret the text on their own. Luther was later excommunicated by the Catholic Church for not renouncing his writings.

The Black Death

Peaking in Europe from 1346 to 1353, the Black Death was a pandemic that is believed to have destroyed nearly half of Europe's total population, an estimated number of 75 to 200 million people. The Black Death was thought to have been carried to Europe by rats on the Silk Road from Central Asia. The symptoms of the plague consisted of buboes (swollen lymph notes in the armpit or groin) followed by vomiting and fever. The plague made reappearances in Europe until the 19th century, and the world population of 450 million, pre-plague numbers, did not return until the 17th century.

Leonardo da Vinci

Leonardo da Vinci set the ideal for the "Renaissance Man," a person whose genius and talent is depicted in many different areas. He was best known for being a painter, having created the famous works of *Mona Lisa* and *The Last Supper*, but was also know for being an engineer, mathematician, inventor, sculptor, architecture, and scientist, among other things. Leonardo was born to a peasant woman and educated in the studio of Andrea del Verrocchio, a famous Florentine painter. Leonardo is credited with conceptualizing flying machines, the double hull, an adding machine, and concentrated solar power.

Advancements in Technology

Advancements in technology can have positive and negative consequences, but all change the world in some way. Examples of major innovations include the printing press, cotton gin, electricity, gunpowder, and Internet. These discoveries have laid the groundwork for numerous adaptations and new inventions.

Invented by Johannes Gutenberg around 1440, the printing press spread ideas that fueled the Reformation, the American and French revolutions, and the Enlightenment. As a cheaper and quicker way to spread information, the printing press led to an explosion in literacy. Prior to the invention of the printing press, books were handwritten; thus, few copies were available, and the copies that were available were very expensive, so only the elite could read and write. In particular, the explosion of books dramatically altered people's relationship with religion. Before Gutenberg's invention, religious scholars were the only people who could read the Bible, and religious services were the only place where people heard Christianity. After its invention, millions of people could read the Bible for themselves, directly leading to the Reformation, as people arrived at their own interpretations.

Similarly, the political order was challenged, as people could more easily communicate and gather news across long distances.

Electrical energy was observed in ancient civilization, but it wasn't until after the spread of information through the printing press that electricity became studied and used. In the 1800s, electrical knowledge was furthered by numerous inventions, such as Alexander Graham Bell's telephone and Thomas Edison's light bulb and phonograph. George Westinghouse's electricity distribution system improved on Edison's direct current with alternating current, which is a much more reliable method of conducting electricity safely across long distances. Electricity completely changed the face of manufacturing and further spurred the Industrial Revolution.

The Chinese invented gunpowder in the ninth century, and the written formula appears in records of the Song dynasty in the eleventh century. Gunpowder spread along the Silk Road, from central Asia to the Middle East to Europe. Gunpowder totally changed the way war was waged, decimating nations and cultures without the technology and making empires for those who had it. Although Europeans did not start using gunpowder until the thirteenth century, gunpowder would provide the means for Europeans to quickly conquer the Americas, including toppling the powerful Incan and Aztec empires. Gunpowder naturally led to the invention of more deadly explosives. War on land, air, and sea became bloodier and more devastating.

Originally created by the United States in the 1960s to connect military networks, the Internet became available for commercial usage in the early 1990s and exponentially increased ever since. The Internet empowers people and nations in various ways. Knowledge is now available at the fingertips of anybody with a working Internet connection. The Internet is the modern-day printing press. Politicians and economists can easily share incredible amounts of technical data and information in an instant. Furthermore, the capital necessary for large-scale investment is more readily available, thanks to improvements in communication technology. Within society, the Internet increases civic engagement by expanding citizens' knowledge of public affairs and broadening political participation. People can now directly communicate with their elected representatives, and those representatives are able to modify their positions based on the will of the people. In addition, watchdog groups are capable of closely monitoring the actions of public officials. More recently, social media networks have further connected people.

Along with these inventions and adaptions, discoveries and improvements in transportation and medicine have dramatically impacted world history. The invention of the steamboat, train, automobile, and airplane allowed people to efficiently travel across long distances. Improvements to transportation would continually increase commerce and communication; however, transportation also served devastating military purposes. During World War II, tanks steamrolled through enemy lines, planes dropped millions of tons of explosives on cities, and submarines sunk unsuspecting ships. Medical improvements, such as penicillin, x-rays, and vaccinations, have saved innumerable lives. People are living longer, healthier lives with a higher standard of living. In 1900, the average life expectancy was thirty-one, and by 2010, the world average was sixty-seven. However, life expectancy is higher in the developed world relative to the developing world where medical advances have not yet fully reached.

Developments in Africa, the Americas, Western and Eastern Europe, Middle East, and Asia

<u>Age of Exploration</u>
The traveling merchants, the Crusades, the conquests of foreign lands, and the writings of ancient Greece expanded the known world of Europeans to include Europe, northern Africa, the Middle East,

and Asia. Early explorers such as Marco Polo brought back amazing stories and exotic goods from Asia, while ports in the Middle East and around the Mediterranean spread cultures through trade. However, the very existence of America and Australia was unknown to the ancient and medieval world. Likewise, there was very little knowledge of sub-Saharan Africa until the late Renaissance era.

In an effort to find better trade routes to China, explorers discovered unknown lands that would change the world in dramatic fashion. Over a two hundred year period from 1450 to 1650, the great explorers of the age would discover new lands, unknown people, and better trade routes to the silks, spices, precious metals, and other sought-after goods Europe was eager to own.

Portugal and Spain funded the first explorations and, along with Italy, dominated the discovery of new lands and trade routes for the first one hundred years of exploration. In 1488, Portuguese explorer Bartolomeu Dias became the first European to sail around the Cape of Good Hope in South Africa and the first European to sail from the Atlantic Ocean to the Indian Ocean. On a voyage lasting from 1497 to 1499, Vasco da Gama, another Portuguese explorer, followed the route of Dias and became the first European to reach India by sea.

Portuguese explorers' success led to Portugal's dominance over trade with Africa and Asia. In West Africa, the Portuguese traded for slaves, and in east Africa, they captured city-states and opened trading posts. The coastal trading posts were utilized to launch further exploration and trade farther east with China and Japan. During a voyage launched in 1500, Dias went on to reach Brazil after his ship was blown off course to Africa. Brazil would later become Portugal's most lucrative colony due to the sugar plantations farmed by African slaves and indigenous people.

By the 1530s, France, England, the Netherlands, and Scotland were beginning to send explorers on their own expeditions. In 1534, the king of France sent Jacques Cartier to discover a western passage to the Asian markets, and during his voyage in 1534, Cartier became the first European to travel down the Saint Lawrence River and explore Canada, which Cartier named after Iroquois settlements that he encountered. Englishman Francis Drake was the first European to successfully circumnavigate the world, completing the three-year voyage in 1580. Another Englishman, Henry Hudson, was hired by the Dutch East India Company to find a northwest passage to India, and he explored the modern New York metropolitan area in the early seventeenth century. The Dutch would use this knowledge to colonize the area around the Hudson River, including New Amsterdam.

Even more devastating than the loss of their land, contact by Europeans exposed the indigenous people of America to devastating new diseases. Without any type of immunization, mild European diseases decimated the populations of the natives. Often the illness and death of natives made conquering the areas swift, and with it the loss of the culture, traditions, and languages of the native people. However, diseases such as syphilis and cholera were brought back from expeditions, ravaging European countries. The high death toll from disease, coupled with the deaths from native-born slave labor, caused a labor shortage that the Spanish replenished with slaves from their trade deals in West Africa. These slaves were mainly brought to the Caribbean Islands, though they were shipped to other Spanish colonies. The British colonies would later import millions of slaves to the modern-day American South to harvest cotton.

Colonialism

Although the European explorers never did discover an effective northwest passage to Asia, Europe quickly realized the economic value of their discovery. Mercantilist economic policies viewed the exploitation of colonies and slaves as a positive because it increased the wealth of the home country.

Often European nations sought wealth, first through the possibility of finding areas rich in gold, then through agricultural endeavors. The colonies were a way for a country to import goods from their own colonies, becoming more self-sufficient and reducing their reliance on trade with rival powers. As the trade routes became more efficient and the colonies more stable, the transfer of slaves for plantation work in sugar cane and tobacco fields became an ever-increasing source of revenue. To incentivize the creation of permanent colonies, colonists were often given more freedoms than in their home country. Colonial populations also increased as a result of religious persecution throughout Europe.

Spain set up the first colonies in the Caribbean Islands, Florida, California, Mexico, and South America. New Spain, as they called their colonies, was established in the mid-1500s. In 1565, the fort, St. Augustine, was established in modern-day Florida, making it the oldest European settlement in the modern-day United States. Colonies founded by the French, Dutch, and English in the Americas began in the 1600s, including settlements along the eastern coast of North America, eastern Canada, Newfoundland, Great Lakes area, and later along the Mississippi River. In 1624, the Dutch, seeking arable ground, established the New Amsterdam settlement near modern-day Manhattan, which would become an important trading center. The English would capture the New Amsterdam settlement in 1664 and rename it New York City, after the Duke of York.

Sir Walter Raleigh sent an expedition to settle land in the Americas in 1585. The initial attempt to settle Roanoke Island, North Carolina, failed, and the colonists sailed back to England with Sir Francis Drake, who arrived after successfully raiding and pillaging the Spanish colonies in the Caribbean. A second attempt in 1587 also failed. The fate of the "Lost Colony" remains disputed as a relief ship, returning to the area in 1591, found no trace of the settlement. England's first permanent settlement was founded in Jamestown, Virginia, in 1607, and subsequently the Virginia Colony was established.

In 1620, the Pilgrims, an English religious group of Anglicans and Separatists, settled in the Cape Cod Bay area of Massachusetts and drew up their own plans for governing their colony. After enduring religious persecution in England, the Mayflower Compact detailed the plan for a colony founded in fair and just laws, offering citizenship to all adult males. Unlike most other colonies, the Plymouth colony did not have a royal charter, so the Mayflower Compact is unique in that it provided one of the first forms of self-government in the colonies. By their eighth year, the Pilgrims had successfully established the Massachusetts Bay Colony, the second of the eventual thirteen British colonies in North America.

The rest of the thirteen colonies formed when royal charters were granted, either to individuals or corporations. The thirteen colonies were allowed limited self-rule. A governor for the colonies was appointed by England, but each colony could rule by its own laws enacted by colonial assemblies. The method in which these men were appointed, and the laws of each colony, differed based on the type of charter each had, if any. In royal colonies, those of Virginia, Massachusetts, New Hampshire, New York, New Jersey, North Carolina, South Carolina, and Georgia, the king of England was the direct authority of the colony and chose the governor, among other things. Proprietary colonies, which included Pennsylvania, Delaware, and Maryland, were under the authority of the owner of the colony, while Rhode Island and Connecticut were self-governing and had no direct authority.

The colonies were divided into sections: New England, Middle Colonies, and Southern Colonies. New England's economy was based on fishing and forest harvesting. The Middle Colonies had arable ground and developed a farming economy with heavy yields in wheat for export. The Southern Colonies, having a warm climate like southern Europe, with rich soil, grew crops such as tobacco, rice, and cotton. By the 1700s, the thirteen colonies were invaluable, making England much wealthier. In early years of colonization, indentured servitude provided much-needed labor. These servants pledged a certain amount of years, usually between five and seven, to pay for their passage and some land and tools to become prosperous citizens once their indentured time was completed. Initially, Africans came as indentured servants. This occurred first in Jamestown in 1619; however, by the late 1600s, slavery within all of the colonies was introduced. The bulk of African slaves were used in the Southern Colonies to work on plantations.

From the 1500s to the 1700s, Spain and Portugal colonized the areas of Mexico, the West Indies, and places in South America. Later, the French and English would gain control of places in the Caribbean Islands and the West Indies. Unlike the thirteen colonies, Spanish rule was authoritarian and centralized, with the government having more power and fewer restrictions. The economies in Mexico, the West Indies, and Latin America were based on mining, plantations, and livestock. Slave labor was in heavy use. In no other place was the Roman Catholic Church more influential abroad than the colonies of the southern Americas. They were second only to the Spanish government, having influence politically and socially. The church owned nearly half of the land, with church officials being part of the wealthy landowning aristocracy.

Founded in 1788, the British colony in Australia was originally a penal colony populated by convicts deported from Britain. Between 1788 and 1868, more than 160,000 British convicts were transported to the Australian penal colony. Criminals were used to settle the area and work the land. If they finished their sentence, they could begin to work for themselves. Many had families that were freed from forced labor. The fertile areas of Australia were used for crop raising and grazing sheep. More and more land was seized from the Aboriginal Australians for agriculture and grazing, pushing the Aboriginals into the less desirable desert region. By the mid-nineteenth century, Australia would be a desirable place for non-convicts due to numerous gold rushes and a booming agricultural industry. Established in 1841, the nearby New Zealand colonists similarly drove out the native Maori tribes and used their land to graze sheep and raise crops. Unlike Australia, New Zealand was never used as a penal colony, though some of its occupants were escaped convicts. Most settlers were former sailors, whalers, or sealers. The exportation of exotic woods, and later the capture and trade of natives into slavery in Australia, were sources of revenue for the colony.

The introduction of new diseases to the Aborigines and the Maoris decimated their numbers. The Maoris' numbers decreased significantly again when, after adopting the English musket as a method of warfare, intertribal wars led to more deadly conflicts. Like Australia, the New Zealand settlers also pushed out the native people, leading to a series of armed conflicts between 1845 and 1872, collectively known as the *New Zealand Wars*. In the end, the settlers prevailed, and the number of Maoris greatly diminished.

Attempts were made to colonize Africa, but disease, resistance, and the difficult terrain caused Europe to limit settlements to trade ports and coastal forts. However, through colonization, indigenous African civilizations were decimated by the slave trade.

European Renaissance and Reformation

The Italian Renaissance
The Renaissance, meaning *rebirth*, began in the fourteenth century in Italy and spread throughout Europe during the fifteenth century. Its philosophy was humanism, or the study of man and his relationship with the world. It was a time when reason and knowledge were highly valued. The Roman Catholic Church kept pace with Europe's focus on mankind and nature, instead of heaven and heavenly beings. Popes sponsored educational enhancements and were, in some instances, as is the case with

Pope Pius II, trained as classical scholars. In the early 1500s, Julius II had masters such as Michelangelo create artistic masterpieces that celebrated humans. Indeed, the arts moved toward a more realistic and proportional style with Italian painters such as Leonardo da Vinci, Raphael, and Titian leading the way.

The literary greats of the age were writing in their own vernacular, or language, instead of Latin. This was one of the greatest leaps forward; it not only built their native language, but it also allowed the Italian people to learn and grow in literacy. This and the advances in printing made the written word more accessible and widely dispersed than ever before. The dissemination of knowledge to larger groups of people would change the world, especially as the Renaissance spread to other European nations.

Renaissance in Northern Europe

The ideas in Italy began to spread northward, allowing the arts to flourish in Germany, such as Albrecht Dürer, and in the Netherlands, like Johannes Vermeer and Rembrandt. England began a long history of great literature with Geoffrey Chaucer's *The Canterbury Tales* and Edmund Spenser's *The Faerie Queene*. The highest literary achievements of the Renaissance came from two English playwrights, Christopher Marlowe and his better-known contemporary, William Shakespeare. But the Renaissance did not stray far from religious themes; instead, they humanized them, as is the case of Italian works of art. It was also an early changing point in Christianity, as theologians like Meister Eckhart, Thomas à Kempis, and Sir Thomas More began to use humanism to question the need for priestly intervention, favoring instead direct worship of God.

The invention of movable type by Johannes Gutenberg in 1439 started a revolution in printing that saw the expansion of books go from approximately 100,000 laboriously hand-copied books in Europe to over 9 million by 1500. The literacy rate in Europe improved vastly, as did the printing of religious writings. News could now travel to distant places, allowing for unprecedented communication both locally and globally. Movable type would be one of the major inventions of the Renaissance, heavily influencing the Reformation and Enlightenment.

The Reformation

In 1517, Martin Luther, a German monk and professor of theology, nailed his famous *Ninety-Five Theses*, or *Disputation on the Power of Indulgences*, to the door of the cathedral in Wittenberg, Germany. Pope Leo X demanded Luther to rescind, but Luther stood his ground, which launched the Protestant Reformation. There were serious problems in the Catholic Church, including clergy accepting simony, or the sale of church offices; pluralism, or having multiple offices; and the violation of vows. In addition, the worldly behavior of the church leaders and the biblical ignorance of the lower clergy prompted Luther to ignite a fire that could not be swept away or cleared up. The Roman Catholic Church could not weather this call for reform like it had done before. This was instead a call to cast off the Catholic faith for Protestantism. Many church denominations were formed under Protestantism, the first being Lutheranism, which gained strength in Germany and Switzerland.

Shortly after, the Roman Catholic Church issued a Counter Reformation in an attempt to quell the spread of Protestantism by addressing some of the complaints. In its initial stages, the Counter Reformation had little effect, and many Germans adopted Lutheranism as its officially recognized religion. By 1555, the Catholic Church recognized Lutheranism under the Peace of Augsburg, which allowed rulers to decide on which religion their kingdom would follow. In Germany there was peace, but civil wars broke out in France and the Netherlands. The Spanish-ruled Netherlands' struggle was as political as it was social, with other countries joining the fight against Catholic Spain.

In the 1600s, the peace in Germany faded as the country allied itself with either the Protestant Union or the Catholic League. The Thirty Years' War broke out in 1618 and became one of the most destructive wars in European history. It was a war of political and religious hostility that would involve Germany, Denmark, France, Austria, Spain, and Sweden, to some degree. Though it ended in 1648 with the Peace of Westphalia, France and Spain would wage war until 1659. The Treaty of Westphalia emphasized national self-determination, which directly led to the development of the nation-state. For the first time in human history, local people controlled the right to build a nation-state with the accompanying legitimacy to control their region. The new states, most of which were carved out of the Holy Roman Empire, were allowed to determine their religion, including Catholicism, Lutheranism, and Calvinism.

The Enlightenment
In the Enlightenment, also known as the *Age of Reason,* that followed the Renaissance, Europe began to move toward a view that men were capable of improving the world, including themselves, through rational thinking. The Enlightenment placed a heavy emphasis on individualism and rationalism. During the Renaissance, scholars looked at the Middle Ages as a lost period and considered their own time as modern and new. The Enlightenment, building on the foundations of humanism, began a prolific era of literature, philosophy, and invention.

By the 1700s, Europe had entered the High Enlightenment Age, where events started to take place as a result of the rational thought promoted by the first half of the age. The idea that everything in the universe could be reasoned and cataloged became a theme that set Diderot to work at the first encyclopedia and inspired Thomas Paine and Thomas Jefferson during the initial political unrest in the American colonies.

In the later years of the Enlightenment, the ideal vision that society could be reborn through reason was tested in the French Revolution of 1789. Instead of becoming a leader in rational thinking and orderly government, the revolution turned into the Reign of Terror that saw the mass execution of French citizens and opened the way for the rise of Napoleon.

European Expansion

Columbian Exchange
European exploration in North America dates back to around 1000 AD when Scandinavian Vikings, led by Leif Eriksson, first made their way to Greenland and then journeyed on to modern-day Newfoundland. They settled briefly in an area now known as L'Anse Meadows. However, clashes with the Native American people living nearby caused them to return to Greenland a few years later. The first permanent settlements in North America began after Italian sailor Christopher Columbus landed in the Caribbean in 1492. This was a significant breakthrough since most Europeans did not know that this huge landmass even existed. It initiated a period of discovery, conquest, and colonization of the Americas by the Europeans. Often referred to as the *Columbian Exchange*, this period allowed people who had been cut off from each other for 15,000 years to share knowledge, ideas, culture, food, plants and animals, technology, and religion; this led to significant changes and enhancements for both regions.

Atlantic Slave Trade
Slavery is believed to be as old as civilization itself, likely beginning during the First Agricultural Revolution nearly ten thousand years ago. The enslavement of human beings was integral to such early civilizations as Egypt, China, the Mayan Empire, Greece, and Rome. Nevertheless, race did not become the primary driving force behind human captivity and forced labor until the so-called Age of Exploration.

Previously, slaves were held captive as prisoners of war. In the case of Egypt, the Jews were enslaved because of their ethnic origins and religious beliefs, but not their "race." Race is a construct that did not develop fully until the Early Modern period of world history. Once the Europeans made contact with the New World, they developed a new system of slavery in the Atlantic World that categorized black and indigenous persons as naturally inferior. The so-called Atlantic Slave Trade was built upon the foundations of racial constructs and racism. Slavery in the Americas became a hereditary phenomenon during the peak centuries of the Atlantic Slave Trade. This slave trade was also economic in origin: The sugar and tobacco plantations of the Americas demanded an excess of cheap or free labor. Initially, Europeans looked to Native Americans as their enslaved labor supply. Quickly, however, millions of Native Americans died because of the spread of unfamiliar diseases. As a result, the Atlantic Slave Trade reared its ugly head in history, and millions of Africans were uprooted to work the fields in the Thirteen Colonies, the Caribbean, and Brazil in place of their Native American brethren. This slave trade lasted from the 1400s well into the late nineteenth century.

Impact of Political, Economic, and Cultural Imperialism on Both Colonizers and the Colonized

Expansion of the Ottoman Empire
The Ottoman Empire came into existence in the early 1300s as the Byzantine Empire's grasp on the Middle East and Balkans slowly dwindled. Anatolian Turks—a group of militaristic nomads—began to settle in the region formerly known as Christian Byzantium. These Turks believed they were ghazis, or "warriors for Islam." They began raiding Christian territories in hopes of forcing these so-called infidels into submitting to their strict Islamic codes. The most successful ghazi at this time was named Osman I. Osman I became known as Othman by westerners, and he eventually adopted the name, calling his followers Ottomans. At first, the Ottomans acted kindly to the people they conquered, protecting them with Turkish armies. The dramatic expansion of the Ottoman Empire, however, did not occur until nearly 150 years after its founding. Under the leadership of such powerful conquerors as Mehmet II, the Ottoman Empire expanded rapidly in the late 1400s and 1500s. Mehmet II is famous for conquering the Christian capital of Constantinople and renaming it "Istanbul" in 1453. In the century that followed, the Ottoman Empire was led by three more powerful sultans who expanded the empire into North Africa, Mesopotamia, the Middle East, the Balkans, Egypt, and eastern Europe. From the late 1500s until the end of World War I, the Ottoman Empire entered a period of slow decline. Internal corruption and external conflicts brought the empire to its knees. At the end of World War I, the Ottoman Empire was finally dissolved with the creation of Turkey.

Conquest of the Aztec
Hernàn Cortés was the first great Spanish explorer and conquistador, and he conquered present-day Mexico, defeating the mighty Aztec Empire. Within two years of his landing in 1519, most of the vast Aztec Empire fell under Spanish rule. Gold and silver were the prizes for the Spanish in Mexico, as they robbed the Aztecs of much of their precious metals. Francisco Pizarro explored modern-day Peru and conquered the Incan Empire in 1533, making it the second of the two most powerful ancient civilizations in the history of the Americas to fall under Spanish rule. Spain sent thousands of new settlers to America to mine precious metals and start plantations and ranches.

World History from 1750 A.D. to the Present

World Civilizations from 1750 A.D. to the Present

Prohibition and The Great Depression

Prohibition (the 18th Amendment to the U.S. Constitution) was passed in 1919 and prohibited the production and sale of alcoholic beverages. This amendment fueled corruption since people made, sold, and transported liquor illegally. The 21st Amendment repealed it in 1933. Women had been campaigning for the right to vote since the 1840s, and these suffragettes used the outbreak of World War I to leverage their fight, stating they would help support the war if they were granted the right to vote. The 19th Amendment, which guaranteed women the right to vote in federal elections, was finally passed by Congress in 1919 and ratified the following year. On October 29, 1929 (referred to as Black Tuesday) the stock market crashed, marking the beginning of the Great Depression that lasted through the 1930s. President Franklin Delano Roosevelt's solution was the *New Deal*—a variety of new programs and laws to provide government funding to help rebuild America's economy.

Holocaust

Aside from the incredible casualties resulting from intense fighting and bombings of cities, World War II is marked by the worst war crimes in human history. Germany conducted a systematic genocide of six million Jewish people during the Holocaust, sending two-thirds of Europe's Jewish population to be executed in death camps. Millions of non-Jews were also exterminated during the Holocaust, including Slavs, Poles, Romani, people of color, Communists, homosexuals, and disabled people, among others. It is estimated that anywhere between six and eleven million people were executed in the Holocaust.

Decolonization

The start of decolonization in India occurred after World War I, with the Government of India Act of 1919. While the war was raging, Britain promised India more self-rule if they supported the war effort. However, the act did not grant freedom in taxation, foreign policy, or justice and only went as far as allowing local matters to be addressed by native-born citizens. For the Indian National Congress, India's largest political party, this fell short of what they had expected. In the 1920s, Mahatma Gandhi, leader of the Indian National Congress, protested using civil disobedience. In August 1947, England granted independence to India and split the British Indian Empire into India and Pakistan.

Political Revolutions and Movements of the Eighteenth Through the Twentieth Centuries

American Revolution

The American Revolution occurred as a result of changing values in the Thirteen Colonies that broke from their traditional relationship with England. Early on in the colonization of North America, the colonial social structure tried to mirror the stratified order of Great Britain. In England, the landed elites were seen as intellectually and morally superior to the common man, which led to a paternalistic relationship. This style of governance was similarly applied to the colonial system; government was left to the property-owning upper class, and the colonies as a whole could be seen as a child dutifully serving "Mother England."

However, the colonies' distance from England meant that actual, hereditary aristocrats from Britain only formed a small percentage of the overall population and did not even fill all the positions of power. By the mid-eighteenth century, much of the American upper class consisted of local families who acquired status through business rather than lineage. Despite this, representatives from Britain were appointed to govern the colonies. As a result, a rift began to form between the colonists and British officials.

Uncertain about whether they should remain loyal to Britain, representatives from twelve colonies formed the First Continental Congress in 1774 to discuss what they should do next. When Patriot militiamen at Lexington and Concord fought British soldiers in April 1775, the Revolutionary War began. While the rebel forces worked to present the struggle as a united, patriotic effort, the colonies remained divided throughout the war. Thousands of colonists, known as Loyalists or Tories, supported Britain. Even the revolutionaries proved to be significantly fragmented, and many militias only served in their home states. The Continental Congress was also divided over whether to reconcile with Britain or push for full separation. These issues hindered the ability of the revolutionary armies to resist the British, who had superior training and resources at their disposal.

Even so, the Continental Army, under General George Washington, gradually built up a force that utilized Prussian military training and backwoods guerrilla tactics to make up for their limited resources. Although the British forces continued to win significant battles, the Continental Army gradually reduced Britain's will to fight as the years passed. Furthermore, Americans appealed to the rivalry that other European nations had with the British Empire. The support was initially limited to indirect assistance, but aid gradually increased. After the American victory at the Battle of Saratoga in 1777, France and other nations began to actively support the American cause by providing much-needed troops and equipment.

In 1781, the primary British army under General Cornwallis was defeated by an American and French coalition at Virginia, which paved the way for negotiations. The Treaty of Paris in 1783 ended the war, recognized the former colonies' independence from Great Britain, and gave America control over territory between the Appalachian Mountains and Mississippi River. However, the state of the new nation was still uncertain. The new nation's government initially stemmed from the state-based structure of the Continental Congress and was incorporated into the Articles of Confederation in 1777.

French Revolution

Unlike the United States' revolution against a ruler across the ocean, the French Revolution was an internal fight. In 1789, tension between the lower class (peasants) and middle class (bourgeois) and the extravagant wealthy upper class of France came to a head. The Old Regime, headed by the monarchy, was overthrown, and the Third Estate, made up of the bourgeois class, seized power. The American Revolution, overtaxation, years of bad harvests, drastic income inequality, and the Enlightenment influenced the French Revolution. In August 1789, the National Constituent Assembly, a democratic assembly formed during the French Revolution, passed the Declaration of the Rights of Man and of the Citizen, which defined the natural right of men to be free and equal under the law.

Napoleon

France radically changed the government from a monarchy to a democracy with provisions for civil rights, religious freedoms, and decriminalization of various morality crimes, like same-sex relationships. Two political powers emerged: liberal republicans called *Girondists* and radical revolutionaries, known as *Jacobins*. Conflict between the parties resulted in the Reign of Terror—a period of mass executions— and eventually the rise of Napoleon who set up a nationalist military dictatorship. During the revolution, Napoleon Bonaparte consolidated power after becoming famous for his heroism during the revolutionary wars against Britain, Austria, and other monarchies that sought to retain their right of royal rule. However, by 1804, Napoleon declared himself emperor and remilitarized France, and he conquered most of Europe in a series of global conflicts collectively known as the *Napoleonic Wars,* starting in 1803 and continuing until Napoleon's defeat at the Battle of Waterloo in 1815.

After the chaos sparked by the French Revolution that fanned across Europe during the revolutionary wars, European powers met at the Congress of Vienna in November 1814 to June 1815 to rebalance power and restore old boundaries. The Congress of Vienna carved out new territories, changing the map of Europe. France lost all of its conquered territories, while Prussia, Austria, and Russia expanded their own. With the restoration of a balance of power, Europe enjoyed nearly fifty years of peace.

Latin American Wars of Independence

Fueled by the successful American Revolution, Napoleon's rise to power, and the writings of the Enlightenment, a spirit of revolution swept across the Americas. The French colony in Haiti was the first major revolution occurring in 1791. The Haitian Revolution was the largest slave uprising since the Roman Empire, and it holds a unique place in history because it is the only slave uprising to establish a slave-free nation ruled by nonwhites and former slaves. In 1804, the Haitians achieved independence and became the first independent nation in Latin America. When Napoleon conquered Spain in 1808, Latin American colonies refused to recognize his elder brother, Joseph Bonaparte, as the new Spanish monarch and advocated for their own independence. Known as the *Latin American Wars of Independence,* Venezuela, Colombia, Ecuador, Argentina, Uruguay, Paraguay, Chile, Peru, and Bolivia all achieved independence between 1810 and 1830. In 1824, Mexico declared itself a republic when, after several attempts by the lower classes of Mexico to revolt, the wealthier classes joined and launched a final and successful revolt. When Napoleon overtook Portugal, King John VI fled to Brazil and set up court. Later he left his son Pedro behind to rule. Pedro launched a revolution that saw him crowned emperor.

By the mid-1800s, the revolutions of Latin America ceased, and only a few areas remained under European rule. The U.S. president James Monroe issued the Monroe Doctrine, which stated that the Americas could no longer be colonized. It was an attempt to stop European nations, especially Spain, from colonizing areas or attempting to recapture areas. England's navy contributed to the success of the doctrine, as they were eager to increase trade with the Americas and establish an alliance with the United States.

Simon Bolivar

Simon Bolivar was a wealthy Venezuelan creole who helped inaugurate a chain of revolutions in South America in the early nineteenth century. Declaring independence from Spain in 1811, Simon Bolivar and his fellow revolutionaries entered a brutal war with its former Mother Country. At first, Bolivar and his army suffered a series of devastating defeats at the hands of the Spanish army in Venezuela. In August 1819, after years of a back-and-forth struggle for independence, Bolivar, who had previously been forced into exile, marched across the Andes Mountains with two thousand men to face the Spanish army in modern-day Colombia. This daring tactic proved to be fruitful—Bolivar surprised the Spanish army in Bogota, inaugurating a decisive victory. In 1821, in just two years after this infamous sneak attack, Simon Bolivar and his revolutionaries officially won their independence. However, the independence of Venezuela was not enough for the famous creole rebel—Bolivar continued marching south into Ecuador, meeting up with fellow revolutionary Jose de San Martin. The meeting of these two revolutionaries catalyzed yet another string of hard-fought independences in South America.

Russian Revolution

The first shots of the Russian Revolution occurred on January 22, 1905, as a result of a growing discontent among workers and their families. The Russian masses rose up against the government in response to the rapid industrialization of the nation, which paved the way to the unchecked economic exploitation of Russian citizens. Anger over socioeconomic inequalities encouraged workers to push back against the oppressive rule of Russian czars such as Nicholas II. These agitated workers not only protested against the government, but also against the traditions of the Russian Orthodox Church. On January 22, 1905, hundreds of thousands of workers and peasants stormed the czar's Winter Palace in St. Petersburg, demanding better working conditions and an elected national legislature. At this time, czar Nicolas II of Russia was not in his palace. However, his generals ordered soldiers to fire on the angry mob of 200,000-plus people. Nearly one thousand unarmed citizens were killed as a result. This day, known as Bloody Sunday, provoked a wave of strikes and violence that eventually encouraged Nicholas II to establish some political reform, including the creation of the Duma, Russia's first parliament. Nonetheless, the Duma remained essentially powerless, as the czar dissolved it in less than ten weeks. This angered the people even more, setting the stage for the March Revolution of 1917, which witnessed the creation of a provisional Soviet government. The March Revolution succeeded in forcing Nicholas II to abdicate his throne, but it failed to create a strong central government. The weakened provisional Soviet government eventually toppled as a result of the Bolshevik Revolution in the fall of 1917. The Bolshevik Revolution was led by Vladimir Lenin, who eventually quelled a civil war and carried out Marxist political reforms that were integral in establishing the USSR.

Political, Economic, and Cultural Expansion

British Empire
The British Empire stretched across the world, and at one point had over 450 million people under its rule. With the loss of its American colonies, England began to focus on other areas of the world. In the mid-1700s, India was the first target of British imperialism. Opposition to the ruling Mughal Empire allowed the British army an inroad at the Battle of Plassey in 1757, where General Robert Clive and his army overtook Bengal in northeast India. Next, the British forced the Mughal emperor to give all tax-collecting rights to England. In 1784, Parliament passed the East India Company Act, also known as *Pitt's India Act,* which brought the East India Company's rule in India under control of the British government. Railway systems to expedite the shipment of goods to Great Britain were built, and a new government called the *British Raj* was established. Indians were educated to work in the government and, at first, used their education to promote reform in India. Many of these civil service workers would take on the mantle of nationalism and advocate for India's independence. Great Britain further expanded its empire into areas of Africa and solidified its rule in Australia, capitalizing on exports from Australia and Canada. It also had what is seen as an informal empire in China and other nations due to its ability to dominate trade and influence economic policy.

Japanese Imperialism
Imperialism was also seen in Japan, a country that moved from a primitive and feudal system to a strong empire quickly and overtook Taiwan, Korea, many islands in the Pacific Ocean, and parts of China. It was not until the end of World War II that Japan was forced to surrender control of its accumulated empire. Germany, Russia, and the Ottoman Empire also gained land through imperialism during the years before World War I, most of which was lost by the end of the Great War. The United States was initially against imperialism after having been a colony itself and even solidified these ideas in the Monroe Doctrine; however, by the late nineteenth and early twentieth centuries, the United States defeated Spain in the Spanish-American War and annexed Hawaii, Guam, and the Philippines.

Industrial Revolution

Economic Revolution
During the Renaissance, commercial trade was revived and caused a revolution in the European marketplace and economy. The division of labor, urbanization, and population growth led to a more advanced market economy. Europeans were buying what they had historically made for themselves and

were working in a particular trade, which transformed the economy and increased commercial productivity. By 1760, the Industrial Revolution began in England and revolutionized commerce when mechanized textile manufacturing, steam power, and iron making became the norm.

Europe mainly traded among itself, as India and China were not interested in Europe's exports, seeing them as primitive. Europe, however, desired the spices, silk, and tea only available from the East. China especially demanded coin money for exchanges, which at first made it difficult and expensive to purchase such items. The need for a monetary system was evident. During the sixteenth century, European countries would adopt mercantilism as their economic policy, which promoted governmental regulation of the country's economy for the purposes of increasing national wealth. Mercantilist policies developed national currencies, monetary reserves, and positive trade balances to ensure that imports exceeded exports. The Commercial Revolution transformed Europe from a humble trading system into a sophisticated market economy with banking, stocks, and government protection to promote trade. The revolution of trade coincided with exploration and colonization, which brought slave labor into the market, further increasing productivity.

Industrial Revolution

While Europe was in the midst of colonization and revolutions, they experienced an industrial revolution that would impact the social and economic fabric of life. Starting in the 1760s, with humble origins in England's textile economy, it lasted until the 1820s and changed the way people worked and lived. The revolution brought new scientific developments and improvements to agriculture and textile manufacturing. It was also a time of great invention in steam- and water-powered engines, machines, tools, chemicals, transportation, factories, lighting, glass, cement, medicines, and many more. Additional information concerning the Industrial Revolution and the Second Industrial Revolution are included in the section called "The Major Economic Transformations that Have Affected World Societies."

In some ways, it improved people's standard of living, but in many ways, it made life harder. Falling prices on goods made nutrition levels improve and allowed people more buying power. Medicines and better transportation also improved the quality of life for many. However, crowded living quarters in the booming urban centers were often appalling, as were the diseases brought on by working in factory conditions. The use of child labor eventually brought about reform, and labor unions had an effect on working conditions, but it took many years for either of these problems to be properly addressed.

Totalitarianism in the Twentieth Century

Totalitarianism is a political ideology where the state controls all aspects of public and private life. It is an extreme version of authoritarianism, which is only concerned with the state consolidating political power and retaining dominance over the political system. In contrast, totalitarianism utilizes extensive propaganda, surveillance, and state-controlled mass media to dictate all aspects of life within the country. Totalitarianism often involves a single political party led by a dictator, oppression of political opponents, state monopoly over weapons and communication, centralized political direction and economic control, and the use of terror, such as a secret police. Fascism is a form of totalitarianism that became popular in Europe after World War I. Fascists advocated for an all-powerful government led by a strong dictator that would be prepared for total war and the mass mobilization of resources for the benefit of the state. Fascism is often tied with nationalism.

Adolf Hitler's Nazi Party is the most infamous example of a fascist totalitarian government. Italy was also considered a fascist regime in the years between 1922 and 1943, with Benito Mussolini as the head of government. Italy allied with Nazi Germany in World War II. The Union of Soviet Socialist Republics had emerged through the Bolshevik Revolution in 1917 in Russia and militantly supported Communism—a socialist system of government that called for the overthrow of capitalism. Although the Soviet Union formed an alliance with the United States during World War II, relations chilled, and the Cold War began in 1947. Although no true war was declared between the two nations, both the Union of Soviet Socialist Republics and the United States engaged in indirect conflict by supporting and overthrowing foreign governments.

World War I and World War II

First World War

The onset of World War I began with the precarious balance of power and the geographic divisions written by the Napoleonic Wars' Vienna Congress.

Austria-Hungary's large empire was diverse in culture and included various peoples of several races, languages, and beliefs. However, minorities in their lands in the Balkans grew tired of foreign control. This was especially true in Bosnia, which was all but under control by the nationalistic secret military society, the Black Hand. This nationalistic sentiment grew until, in 1914, Gavrilo Princip, a Serb patriot and member of the Black Hand, assassinated Archduke Franz Ferdinand, heir presumptive to the throne of Austria-Hungary. In response, Emperor Franz Joseph I of Austria-Hungary declared war on the kingdom of Serbia, officially launching the First World War.

Europe had tied itself into a tangled web of alliances and mutual protection pacts. Germany and Austria-Hungary were allies. Russia promised protection to France and Serbia, and England maintained a tacit support to its past allies throughout the mainland. Each of the Allies soon mobilized to support each other. Germany had already planned for declarations of war, however, and was nervous about fighting a two-border war against both France and Russia, so it developed the Schlieffen Plan—a strategy to quickly demolish French resistance before turning around to fight Russia on the Eastern Front. However, this plan relied on the neutrality of England; after Germany invaded Belgium to attack France, England's declaration of war ensured that a long war would be inevitable.

The Great War lasted from 1914 to 1918 and was the deadliest war in European history until World War II, with approximately 16 million combatants and civilians dying in the conflict. The carnage was largely a result of technological innovation outpacing military tactics. World War I was the first military conflict to deploy millions of soldiers and the first war to involve telephones, tanks, aircrafts, chemical weapons, and heavy artillery. These twentieth-century technological innovations were deployed alongside outdated military tactics, particularly trench warfare. As a result, hundreds of thousands of troops would die during battles without achieving any meaningful strategic gains. Countries were devastated by the loss of the male population and struggled to cope with a depleted workforce, and widows and orphans struggled to regain any degree of normalcy.

Due to the high death tolls, the Allies' need of the financial support, and the anger associated with the war, the Treaty of Versailles harshly punished Germany, who the Allies blamed for the war. The Allies coerced Germany into signing the treaty that was a death sentence to their country's economy. It contained a "guilt clause," which, unlike the Congress of Vienna's terms for the similarly belligerent France, made oppressive demands on Germany. The treaty took German lands, enforced a heavy reparations debt that was impossible to pay, and stripped Germany of its colonies. After suffering enormous losses during the war itself, the Treaty of Versailles ensured that no national recovery would be possible.

In the aftermath, Russia, Italy, and Germany turned to totalitarian governments, and colonies of Europe started to have nationalistic, anticolonial movements. The Russian Revolution of 1917 led to a civil war in which the Bolsheviks, or Communists, took control under the guidance of Communist revolutionary Vladimir Lenin and established the Soviet Union. The Communist government turned into a dictatorship when Stalin emerged as leader in 1924. Stalin ruled with an iron fist and executed all of his political opponents, including the Bolsheviks. Dissatisfaction with the treaty in Italy led to the rise of fascist leader Benito Mussolini. Germany suffered through several small revolutions, splintering political parties, and class division; this, combined with wartime debt and hyperinflation—a result of the Treaty of Versailles—caused many to become desperate, especially during the throes of the Great Depression. Adolf Hitler, a popular leader in the National Socialist German Workers' Party (Nazi Party), organized street violence against Communists. In the 1932 parliamentary elections, the Nazis emerged as the largest party in the *Reichstag* (German Parliament), but the Nazis did not have enough votes to name Hitler as chancellor. The street violence against Communists and Jews continued unabated, and on January 30, 1933, political pressure led to President von Hindenburg naming Adolf Hitler the chancellor of Germany. Hitler immediately expelled Communists, the second most popular political party, from the *Reichstag*, and coerced the *Reichstag* to pass the Enabling Act of 1933, effectively creating a dictatorship.

Second World War

Nazi Germany had risen to power through the 1920s and 1930s, with Hitler's belief that Germany would only recover its honor if it had a resounding military victory over Europe. Nazi ideology adhered to an extreme nationalism advocating for the superiority of the German people and the necessity of expanding their lands into an empire. Jews, Communists, and other nonconformists were banned from political and social participation.

In 1936, German troops violated the Treaty of Versailles by moving outside Germany's borders, with a remilitarization of the Rhineland. The Rome-Berlin Axis, an alliance between Germany and Italy, was forged in the same year. Germany was the only European power to support Italy's invasion and annexation of Ethiopia, and in exchange, Italy supported Germany's annexation of Austria. In 1936, a civil war broke out in Spain between Spanish nationalist rebels and the government of the Spanish Republic. Mussolini and Hitler supported the Spanish nationalist general Francisco Franco and used the Spanish Civil War as a testing ground for their new alliance. The Allies did not respond to these actions, and when Germany demanded the return of the Sudetenland, a territory in Czechoslovakia, France and Great Britain agreed in hopes of an appeasement despite the protests of the Czech government. Hitler then moved into more areas farther afield, which prompted the Soviet Union to sign a nonaggression pact with Germany. On September 1, 1939, Germany invaded Poland, and on September 3, 1939, France and Great Britain declared war on Germany, jumpstarting the deadliest conflict in world history.

Although less discussed than the Holocaust, the Japanese military committed similar war crimes across Asia, executing between three and ten million Chinese and Koreans, among others, between 1937 and 1945. In one event, the Rape of Nanking, Japanese soldiers captured Nanking and brutally murdered 300,000 civilians. An additional twenty thousand women, children, and elderly were raped during the massacre. Japanese newspapers closely covered a contest between two Japanese officers to see who could kill more people with a sword during the Rape of Nanking. Stalin also committed heinous war crimes during World War II, with estimates ranging from four to ten million deaths as a result of executions and sentences to the Gulag. The United States has also faced criticism for its decision to drop two nuclear bombs on the Japanese cities of Hiroshima and Nagasaki, killing more than 129,000 civilians, leveling both cities, and ending the war. The American government justified the use of nuclear weapons as the only way to avoid a ground invasion of Japan that would have cost more Japanese and American lives than the bombs.

Towns and cities had been leveled, civilian and soldier death tolls were crippling to economies, and countries struggled well into the 1950s to recover economically. It became a breeding ground for Communism, and in China, the end of the war meant a reprisal of the civil war between Mao Zedong's Communists and nationalists that had been interrupted by world war. Another result of the war was a changed map of the world, as countries were divided or newly formed, and the end of most of Britain's colonialism occurred as a result of the empire's economic and military losses. Following the war, Great Britain, France, Portugal, Belgium, Italy, the Netherlands, and Japan had either granted freedom to colonies or lost areas during the war. Many African and Middle Eastern countries would be granted their independence; however, the newly formed countries' borders were drawn according to those of the former colonies, creating ethnic and religious tensions that still exist today.

In an effort to stop a world war from occurring again, the Allies created the United Nations to be a safeguard and upholder of peace. This proved especially important, yet difficult, as the world was divided between a capitalist Western bloc and a Communist Eastern bloc. Germany was divided between the United States and Soviet Union to maintain peace and to better control the reconstruction of Germany; occupation zones were established, with East Germany occupied by the Soviet Union and West Germany occupied by Great Britain, France, and the United States.

Spread and Fall of Communism and the Post-Cold War World

Cold War
Within two years of World War II, the world was involved in a different kind of war—a Cold War—that pitted capitalism and Communism against each other. World War II left Europe on the brink of collapse, leaving the United States and Soviet Union as the world's undisputed remaining superpowers. The United States and its Allies embarked on a campaign of containment in an attempt to keep Communism from spreading to other countries.

In the 1940s, U.S. president Harry S. Truman, in an effort to contain Communism, offered U.S. military and economic protection to any nation threatened by Communist takeover. By 1949, the United States, Canada, and ten European nations agreed to the same idea in an alliance known as the *North Atlantic Treaty Organization (NATO)*. When West Germany was invited into NATO in 1955, the Soviet Union responded with a similar alliance known as the *Warsaw Pact*. The Warsaw Pact and NATO were vehicles for the United States and Soviet Union to flex their military might. In addition to conventional arms, the two superpowers competed in a nuclear arms race throughout the Cold War. The nuclear arms race created a situation where each country could destroy the world many times over at the push of a button. There were several close calls during the conflict due to mixed signals, misunderstandings, or provocation—the most notorious being the Cuban Missile Crisis when the Soviet Union placed nuclear missiles in Cuba, ninety miles away from Florida.

The United States fought a series of proxy wars against the Soviet Union to prevent the spread of Communism. The Korean War, 1950-1953, was an attempt to keep Communism from spreading into Korea. China and the Soviet Union joined together to fight the United States and Allies until an armistice was signed that divided Korea into a Communist North and a democratic South along the thirty-eighth parallel. The thirty-eighth parallel was an important demarcation during the war itself, as America was cautious to pursue the North Koreans back across the parallel or else risk escalating the proxy war into a conventional one against the Soviets.

The Vietnam Conflict, 1955-1975, was another proxy war pitting the United States against Communism. China and the Soviet Union provided extensive aid to the Communist Viet Cong guerilla fighters and the more conventional North Vietnamese army. Although the United States was the superior conventional military force, the American military struggled mightily against the guerillas using the dense jungle as cover. As intense opposition to the war mounted in the United States, the United States withdrew after the North Vietnamese captured Saigon in April 1975. The Soviet Union similarly struggled against guerilla forces backed by the United States during the Soviet-Afghan War, which lasted between 1979 and 1989. The United States provided military and financial support to the Afghans during the conflict, many of who would later found al-Qaeda or join the Taliban to fight the United States, including Osama bin Laden.

Protests and new leaders gave some economic freedom and recovery to these European nations after WWII, but East Germany was excluded. In 1961, a wall was built to separate East and West Germany in an attempt to keep people from fleeing the Soviet-controlled East. However, in 1985, Mikhail Gorbachev became the Soviet leader and began to change politics in the Soviet Union, with *glasnost*—a policy of government transparency and openness—and *perestroika,* a government reform. He allowed the Eastern European satellite countries more economic freedom and limited self-government. The Soviet economy could not keep up with the United States, especially when President Reagan increased American military spending. Pushed to the brink of economic collapse, the Soviet Union could no longer maintain control over their satellites and Allies, who were increasingly agitated for complete autonomy. On November 9, 1989, the Soviet Union ordered the Berlin Wall to be knocked down, an important step toward thawing the Cold War. On December 26, 1991, the Soviet Union officially collapsed and broke up into fifteen distinct countries.

Post-Cold War World
The collapse of the Soviet Union left the United States as the sole world superpower. In addition, Communism no longer represented a viable political ideology, cementing the market economy as the leading economic system, which is later discussed in greater detail in the section "The Major Economic Transformations that Have Affected World Societies." In the mid-1990s, the Internet emerged as a driving force in globalization, connecting people across the world and providing instantaneous access to vast stores of information. Globalization further presented itself in the form of supranational governance. In 1992, the European Union was established for the purpose of creating a common market for goods and capital. Other supranational political entities would lead the way toward the creation of a globalized economy.

Founded in 1995, the World Trade Organization is a supranational organization composed of 164 member states, and it establishes regulations, norms, and dispute resolution to govern trade agreements between countries. Trade agreements between two entities are referred to as *bilateral agreements,* and any larger type of agreement is classified as *multilateral.* The entity entering into the trade agreement can be either a single nation-state or a trade bloc—an informal group of countries who negotiate as a single entity. The most common type of trade agreement is free trade, which offers preferential treatment through the elimination of trade restrictions, like tariffs and quotas. Trade agreements force countries to rely on the economic health of their trade partners, which naturally leads to interdependence. Examples of trade agreements include the North America Free Trade Agreement and Association of Southeast Asian Nations.

Trade agreements form the basis of a globalized economy as countries seek to maximize the economic principle of economies of scale, which defines how countries can function most efficiently within markets and vis-à-vis competitors. It encourages countries to specialize in what they do best and devote the bulk of their resources to maximizing that specialty. In theory, increasing production will make the output more efficient and cost effective. Incentivizing countries to boost their production and pursue their competitive advantage inherently leads to greater economic interdependence and globalization; trading countries are necessarily dependent on their partners to meet some need. For example, in the North America Free Trade Agreement, the United States provides technology and white-collar skills, while Mexico primarily focuses on manufacturing.

Despite the trend toward supranational political and economic entities, nationalism has reemerged as a powerful force in the post-Cold War Era. Nationalism is best understood as people seeking independence for some collective reason, like geographical proximity or cultural similarities. In addition, nationalism is primarily expressed via its opposition to external influences. Just as nationalism served as a rallying cry for colonial people fighting to gain their independence, nationalism has come back into vogue as the means for people to advocate for greater local control.

The Yugoslav Wars of 1991 to 2001 and eventual collapse of Yugoslavia illustrate how ethnic nationalism exists as a powerful countervailing force to globalization trends. The former Socialist Federal Republic of Yugoslavia contained several republics that consisted of distinct ethnic groups, including Bosnia and Herzegovina, Croatia, Macedonia, Serbia, and Slovenia. Additionally, Serbia was further divided between Kosovo and Vojvodina. After the death of Yugoslavia's founding authoritarian ruler, Josip Broz Tito, the country eventually collapsed under separatist nationalist movements. Following a series of bloody wars and war crimes, collectively known as the Yugoslav Wars, seven newly independent states emerged out of Yugoslavia—Bosnia and Herzegovina, Croatia, Kosovo, Macedonia, Montenegro, Serbia, and Slovenia.

Nationalism is also on the rise in Western democracies as people grapple with the consequences of a globalized economy and greater involvement of supranational political entities beyond their control. In June 2016, the United Kingdom held a referendum on the country's membership in the European Union, and British citizens voted to withdraw, which is commonly referred to as the "Brexit" (British exit). Nationalism greatly influenced British citizens' reluctance to cede any degree of sovereignty, pay taxes, or follow regulations from the European Union.

Significant Individuals of the Nineteenth and Twentieth Centuries

Charles Darwin

Charles Darwin is known as the Father of Evolution, and was a naturalist and geologist. Darwin collected samples and made extensive observations in his Voyage of the Beagle from 1831 to 1836. His most famous spot was the Galápagos Islands, where he discovered varying species of finches from island to island. His theory of natural selection proposed that organisms best suited to their surrounding environment were most likely to survive.

Mao Zedong

In China, Mao Zedong, the chairman of the Communist Party and leader of the People's Republic of China, attempted to quickly transform China into a Communist state through an ineffective and devastating economic program known as the *Great Leap Forward,* which abolished private ownership of property and featured collective communes. The Great Leap Forward caused a humanitarian disaster, resulting in tens of millions of deaths, due to inefficient economic planning under a poorly devised Communist system.

Mohandas Gandhi

Mohandas Gandhi became the leader of the Indian independence movement following the passage of the Rowlatt Act, which allowed the British colonial government to jail Indian protesters without a trial by jury. Returning World War I veterans and human rights advocates in India violently rejected the Rowlatt Act as a stumbling block to Indian self-government and a threat to Indian rights. In an act of defiance against the colonial British government in the spring of 1919, ten thousand Hindu and Muslim protesters flocked to Amristar, the capital city of the Punjab province in India. During this protest, British troops killed over four hundred Indians and injured over one thousand protesters. This controversial moment in history paved the way for Gandhi to emerge as the respected leader of Indian resistance. Unlike other revolutionaries at that time in history, Gandhi urged his followers to employ nonviolent noncooperation tactics against the British government. The former lawyer called upon the nonviolent principles of world religions to instill in his followers the principle of satyagraha ("truth force"). In the Western world, Gandhi's principle of satyagraha has become colloquially known as passive resistance or civil disobedience.

In the 1920s and 1930s, Gandhi launched a passive resistance campaign that combined peaceful marches with economic boycotts. These nonviolent means of resistance eventually led to the passage of the Government of India Act by the British Parliament in 1935, which offered Indians limited democratic elections and local self-government. This act, however, was not respected by the British government during World War II when it deployed Indian troops without the consent of local government officials. During this time, Gandhi pressed the Indian people to find peace during these controversial times. Nevertheless, in the postwar years, by 1947, Indians were becoming increasingly violent, not only with British officials, but also with each other. Muslims and Hindus grew increasingly at odds with one another in the postwar years. Despite all his passive efforts, Gandhi's hope for a united, independent India was only half realized: On July 16, 1947, the British government partitioned the Indian subcontinent into two countries, Pakistan and India. In 1948, Mohandas Gandhi's life was taken by a Hindu extremist who disliked his attempts to achieve equal treatment for both Muslims and Hindus. Gandhi's nonviolent ethos has, nevertheless, continued to reverberate through history, namely in the work of such civil rights advocates as Martin Luther King Jr. and Nelson Mandela.

Adolf Hitler

Adolf Hitler was an Austrian-born soldier who was awarded the Iron Cross on two occasions for his service in the German army during World War I. Following the end of the war, Hitler joined a small, right-wing political group that threatened to overturn the Treaty of Versailles, which placed sanctions on the postwar German military, government, and economy. Hitler also joined the group in vowing to destroy global Communism. As the group expanded, it became known as the National Socialist German Workers' Party, often abbreviated as "Nazis." Nazism became the German brand of fascism, promising to protect the middle and lower-middle classes from postwar sanctions and the global overreach of Communism. Like Benito Mussolini, the Fascist leader of Italy, Adolf Hitler had the ability to command and manipulate a crowd with his fiery speeches. His public-speaking skills eventually led to his assumption of the position as chosen *der Führer*—or "leader" —of the Nazis. A failed attempt to seize power in Munich in 1923 landed Hitler and many of his fellow Nazis in prison. While in prison, Hitler wrote his famous book *Mein Kampf* (*My Struggle*). This book served as the blueprint for Nazism, labeling Jews, Slavs, gypsies, and other groups as "subhuman" and calling for the eugenic creation of the Aryan race. By 1933, Hitler and his book *Mein Kampf* had gained so much popular support that he became chancellor of Germany, paving the way to World War II, the Holocaust, and the eventual fall of Nazism in Germany.

Nelson Mandela

Born to a royal family of the Xhosa-speaking South African Thembu tribe in 1918, Nelson Mandela became one of the premier civil rights activists in world history. In the 1940s, Mandela joined the African National Congress party, joining fellow black leaders in South Africa in their fight against the white

41

minority's oppressive regime. This regime had its roots in colonial practices that legitimized the oppression and marginalization of black and interracial South Africans. The white minority leadership created an apartheid system of social segregation. Mandela joined other revolutionaries in protests and armed conflicts, leading to his eventual imprisonment. Following his release from prison in 1990, Nelson Mandela continued his civil rights battle in the racially divided South Africa. He eventually helped end apartheid in South Africa, becoming the first black president in 1994. As president, he formed a multiethnic government, using his position of power to fight racial prejudice throughout the globe. He died in 2013 at the age of ninety-five.

Mother Teresa

Born Agnes Gonxha Bojaxhiu, Mother Teresa (1910–1997) became one of the most beloved religious figures and missionaries in the twentieth century. Recipient of the Nobel Peace Prize in 1979, Mother Teresa dedicated her life to helping the poor, the elderly, the sick, and the disabled in South Asia and the rest of the world. After joining the sisterhood in Ireland, she left the convent for missionary work in Calcutta, India. In 1948, she established the Order of the Missionaries of Charity in Calcutta. This organization established schools, refugee camps, hospitals, churches, and convents throughout the world. Clad in her iconic plain white sari with a blue border, Mother Teresa became famous for helping the downtrodden of the Third World. Millions lamented her death in 1997, knowing that they lost one of the most dedicated missionaries in modern history. Her work is as iconic as other social justice warriors such as Dr. Martin Luther King Jr. and Mohandas Gandhi.

Practice Questions

1. Which of the following civilizations developed the first democratic form of government?
    a. Roman Empire
    b. Ancient Greece
    c. Achaemenid Empire
    d. Zhou dynasty

2. Which of the following statements most accurately describes the Achaemenid Empire in Persia until the fourth century BC?
    a. Islam was the official religion.
    b. Achaemenid emperors constructed the entire Silk Road network.
    c. The Achaemenid Empire successfully conquered Greece.
    d. None of the above

3. The Silk Roads had which of the following results?
    a. Spread of Buddhism from India to China
    b. Resulted in the devastation of European economies
    c. Introduction of the Bubonic Plague to the New World
    d. Resulted in the Great War

4. What caused the end of the Western Roman Empire in 476 A.D.?
    a. Invasions by Germanic tribes
    b. The Mongol invasion
    c. The assassination of Julius Caesar
    d. Introduction of Taoism in Rome

5. Which of the following statements most accurately describes the Mongol Empire?
    a. The Mongol army was largely a cavalry force.
    b. Mongol rulers did not tolerate other religions.
    c. Mongol rulers neglected foreign trade.
    d. The Mongol Empire is known for its discouragement of literacy and the arts.

6. What social consequence(s) did the Black Death have in Europe?
    a. It gave birth to the concept of absolute monarchy.
    b. It ignited the Protestant Reformation.
    c. It eroded serfdom.
    d. It gave rise to Child Labor Laws in England.

7. Renaissance scholars and artists were inspired by which classical civilization?
    a. Ancient Greece
    b. Ancient Egypt
    c. The Zhou dynasty
    c. The Ottoman Empire

8. Nicolaus Copernicus was a key figure in which cultural phenomena?
    a. The Scientific Revolution
    b. The Age of Enlightenment
    c. The Renaissance
    d. The Protestant Reformation

9. Which of the following statements best describes King Louis XIV of France?
    a. He abdicated his throne during the French Revolution.
    b. He supported the American Revolution.
    c. He was the ultimate example of an absolute monarch.
    d. He created the concept of the Mandate of Heaven.

10. Which of the following resulted from the Age of Enlightenment?
    a. The discovery of the heliocentric theory
    b. The birth of Lutheranism
    c. The American Revolution
    d. The Renaissance

11. Which of the following consequences did NOT result from the discovery of the New World in 1492 A.D.?
    a. Proof that the world was round instead of flat
    b. The deaths of millions of Native Americans
    c. Biological exchange between Europe and the New World
    d. The creation of new syncretic religions

12. Which of the following statements best describes the relationship, if any, between the revolutions in America and France?
    a. The French Revolution inspired the American Revolution.
    b. The American Revolution inspired the French Revolution.
    c. They both occurred simultaneously.
    d. There was no connection between the French and American revolutions.

13. Which of the following was a consequence of industrialization in Europe during the 1800s?
    a. The birth of the working class
    b. The expansion of European empires in Africa and Asia
    c. Improved transportation and economic efficiency
    d. All of the above

14. Which of the following was a consequence of increasing nationalism in Europe in the 1800s?
    a. The unification of Spain
    b. The unification of France
    c. Increasing competition and tension between European powers
    d. More efficient trade between nations

15. Which of the following military technologies did NOT play a role in World War I from 1914 to 1918?
    a. The atomic bomb
    b. Poison gas
    c. Armored tanks
    d. Aircraft

16. Which of the following statements best describes international affairs between World War I and World War II?

    a. A lenient World War I peace treaty for Germany delayed the start of World War II.

    b. The policy of appeasement only encouraged further aggression by Hitler.

    c. A powerful League of Nations fostered increased cooperation and negotiation.

    d. Tensions grew between Germany and Japan.

17. Which of the following was a consequence of World War II?

    a. The collapse of British and French empires in Asia and Africa

    b. A Communist revolution in Russia

    c. The end of the Cold War

    d. The death of Franz Ferdinand, the Archduke of Austria

18. Which of the following trends did NOT occur after the end of the Cold War in 1991?

    a. A decrease in nationalistic tension

    b. An increase in cultural and economic globalization

    c. An increase in religious fundamentalism

    d. An increase in environmentalism

19. What impact, if any, did the introduction of the movable type printing press have in Europe?

    a. It increased the cost of books because the process was labor intensive.

    b. It led to an increase in literacy.

    c. The Catholic Church used it to effectively suppress the Protestant Reformation.

    d. It led to the Dark Ages.

20. In which phase(s) of the Space Race did the United States achieve victory over the USSR?

    a. Putting the first satellite into orbit

    b. Putting the first man into space

    c. Putting the first man on the moon

    d. All of the above

21. Which of the following is NOT a sect of Islam?

    a. Shinto

    b. Sunni

    c. Shi'a

    d. Sufi

22. Which form of economic exchange allowed the Chinese to maintain political control over their empire?

    a. Potlatches

    b. Tribute

    c. Bartering

    d. All of the above

Answer Explanations

1. B: Ancient Greeks created many of the cultural and political institutions that form the basis of modern western civilization. Athens was an important Greek democracy, and all adult men could participate in politics after they had completed their military service. The Roman Empire, Choice *A*, evolved from the Roman Republic, but it was not democratic. The Achaemenid Empire and Zhou Dynasty, Choices *C* and *D*, were imperial monarchies that did not allow citizens to have much, if any, political voice.

2. D: During the Achaemenid Empire, Persians practiced the Zoroastrian faith and worshipped two gods. Islam only came about one thousand years later. The Achaemenids built a Royal Road that stretched across their empire, but the Silk Roads expanded throughout Asia. The Achaemenids twice tried to conquer Greece but failed both times.

3. A: The Silk Roads were a network of trade routes between Asia and the Mediterranean. Merchants and Pilgrims traveled along the Silk Roads and brought new ideas and technologies, as well as trade goods. For example, Buddhism spread from India to China. Chinese technologies also spread westward, including gunpowder and the printing press. The Silk Roads also spread the Bubonic Plague to Europe, but it did not arrive in the New World until Columbus landed there in 1492.

4. A: Invasions by Germanic tribes. Large numbers of Franks, Goths, Vandals, and other Germanic peoples began moving south in the fifth century A.D.. They conquered Rome twice, and the Western Roman Empire finally disintegrated. The Mongol invasion, Choice *B*, pushed westward in the thirteenth century, long after the western Roman Empire was gone. The assassination of Julius Caesar, Choice *C*, led to the end of the Roman Republic and the birth of the Roman Empire. Taoism never spread to Rome, making Choice *D* incorrect.

5. A: The Mongol army was largely a cavalry force. The Mongols were a nomadic people who trained as horsemen from a young age. They used their highly mobile army to build a huge empire in Asia, the Middle East, and Eastern Europe. Mongol rulers were relatively tolerant of other religions because they wanted to reduce conflict within their empire, making Choice *B* incorrect. They also encouraged trade because they produced few of their own goods, making Choice *C* incorrect. The Mongol rulers also encouraged literacy and appreciated visual art, making Choice *D* incorrect.

6. C: It eroded serfdom. Millions of people died during the Black Death, but those who survived found that their standard of living had improved, especially serfs. Before the Black Death, serfs had few rights and were expected to work without pay for their lord. Because labor was in such short supply after the Black Death, serfs found they were in a much better bargaining position. The Protestant Reformation was a cultural phenomenon, and the rise of absolutism was a political change. Neither had any connection to the Black Death, making Choices *A* and *B* incorrect. Choice *D* is also incorrect; although Child Labor Laws came after the Black Death in the early 1800s, they weren't a direct result of the Black Death.

7. A: Renaissance scholars and artists sought to emulate classical Greek and Roman culture. They translated Greek and Roman political philosophers and literature. They also copied classical architecture. Europeans had little direct contact with China until the thirteenth century, which was long after the Zhou Dynasty collapsed, making Choice *C* incorrect.

8. A: Copernicus exemplified the key techniques of the Scientific Revolution, including an emphasis on empirical data and the scientific method. He carefully observed the movement of the planets and found that his data did not match the contemporary geocentric theory, which stated that the earth was the center of the universe. He found that his data indicated that the planets revolved around the sun instead.

9. C: Louis the XIV was an absolute monarch who ruled during the sixteenth century. He concentrated power on the throne by forcing nobles to spend most of their time at the royal court. The French Revolution occurred about two hundred years after he died. Absolute monarchs like Louis the XIV bolstered their prestige by claiming they were appointed by God. The Mandate of Heaven was a similar concept, but it was developed by the Zhou Dynasty in China about two thousand years before Louis XIV was born.

10. C: The Age of Enlightenment in the eighteenth century focused on political and economic philosophy as opposed to scientific discoveries. English philosopher John Locke introduced the concept of a social contract between the ruler and his subjects. His ideas helped inspire revolutions in the British colonies in North America and later France. Choice *A* is incorrect; the discovery of the heliocentric theory happened in 1543. Luther began to criticize the Catholic Church about two hundred years before the Age of Enlightenment began, making Choice *B* incorrect. Choice *D* is also incorrect, as the Renaissance happened before the Age of Enlightenment from approximately 1300-1600.

11. A: Most scholars already knew the world was round by 1492. On the other hand, the arrival of Europeans in North and South America introduced deadly diseases that killed millions of native peoples. Europeans had developed immunity to diseases such as smallpox, while Native Americans had not. In addition, Europeans introduced a number of new plants and animals to the New World, but they also adopted many new foods as well, including potatoes, tomatoes, chocolate, and tobacco. Finally, Europeans tried to convert Native Americans to Christianity, but Indians did not completely give up their traditional beliefs. Instead, they blended Christianity with indigenous and African beliefs to create new syncretic religions.

12. B: The American Revolution occurred first in 1775, and a number of European soldiers fought for the patriots. The American Revolution, in part, inspired the French Revolution. The Marquis de Lafayette came to America in 1777 and was wounded during the Battle of Brandywine. He returned to France after the American Revolution and became a leader in the French Revolution in 1789.

13. D: The Industrial Revolution is probably one of the most important turning points in world history. The United States and Western Europe, especially Britain, were the first areas to industrialize. Steam engines were used to improve economic and transportation efficiency. They also gave western empires a military advantage over less developed countries in Asia and Africa. Finally, industrialization required large amounts of unskilled labor, which created the working class.

14. C: In the 1800s, nationalists in different parts of Europe encouraged their countrymen to take pride in their shared backgrounds. This led to tension between different nations, as each sought to increase its status and prestige. The French and British nearly came to blows in Africa, and nationalism ultimately led to World War I in 1914. However, France and Spain were unified several centuries before the 1800s.

15. A: The atomic bomb was created during World War II (1939-1945). Scientists and engineers did develop a number of other weapons in order to break through the heavily entrenched front lines during World War I. Poison gas killed or injured millions of men between 1914 and 1918. Aircraft were used to observe enemy positions and bombard enemy troops. Armored tanks were able to crush barbed wire fences and deflected machine gun bullets.

16. B: Eager to avoid another global conflict, European leaders tried to appease Hitler by letting him occupy Austria and Czechoslovakia. This policy failed because it only emboldened Hitler, and he invaded Poland in 1939. Rather than receiving leniency after World War I, Germany was forced to sign a humiliating peace treaty. Furthermore, the League of Nations failed to prevent conflict because it lacked any real power. This encouraged continued aggression from Italy, Germany, and Japan, which culminated in World War II.

17. A: Devastated by World War II, Britain and France were unable to maintain their empires. Japan and Germany were also weak, which left only the United States and USSR as superpowers. The Russian Revolution had occurred during World War I, in 1917, making Choice *B* incorrect. Ideological and economic conflict between the U.S. and the USSR led to the start of the Cold War shortly after World War II ended, making Choice *C* incorrect. Choice *D* is also incorrect; the death of Franz Ferdinand marked the beginning of World War I.

18. A: Nationalism remains a powerful force to this day. Nationalism drove conflict in Ireland, Spain, Yugoslavia, and elsewhere. However, the end of the Cold War removed many of the political barriers that had prevented interaction between the western and Communist blocs. In addition, religious fundamentalism became an increasingly common response to the rapid changes that occurred during the late twentieth and early twenty-first centuries. There was also a rise in cultural and economic globalization, as well as in environmentalism.

19. B: The printing press was much more efficient than previous methods, which required a single scribe to copy text by hand. This made books much more affordable and encouraged the growing middle class to read. No church or organization had a monopoly on the technology, so many different writers used it to spread the ideas of the Reformation, as well as the Renaissance, Scientific Revolution, and Age of Enlightenment.

20. C: The USSR put Sputnik, the first satellite into orbit, in 1951. They also claimed victory when the Soviet cosmonaut Yuri Gagarin went into space in 1961. The United States only surpassed the USSR by sending the Apollo 11 crew to the moon in 1969.

21. A: The schism between Sunnis and Shi'as began shortly after the Islamic prophet Muhammad died in 632 A.D.. Sunnis and Shi'a disagreed over who should have become Muhammad's successor. Sufism emerged about eighty years after Muhammad died, and they focused on perfecting their faith through meditation. Shintoism is a traditional polytheistic faith that is practiced mainly in Japan.

22. B: The Chinese required other countries to pay tribute in order to establish trade relations. Foreign emissaries also had to prostrate themselves before the Chinese emperor. Potlatches, Choice *A*, were a Native American form of gift giving. Bartering, Choice *C*, was a common form of economic exchange, but it had no political significance.

U.S. History

Exploration and Colonization

European Exploration and Colonization of North America

When examining how Europeans explored what would become the United States of America, one must first examine why Europeans came to explore the New World as a whole. In the fifteenth century, tensions increased between the Eastern and Mediterranean nations of Europe and the expanding Ottoman Empire to the east. As war and piracy spread across the Mediterranean, the once-prosperous trade routes across Asia's Silk Road began to decline, and nations across Europe began to explore alternative routes for trade.

Italian explorer Christopher Columbus proposed a westward route. Contrary to popular lore, the main challenge that Columbus faced in finding backers was not proving that the world was round. Much of Europe's educated elite knew that the world was round; the real issue was that they rightly believed that a westward route to Asia, assuming a lack of obstacles, would be too long to be practical. Nevertheless, Columbus set sail in 1492 after obtaining support from Spain and arrived in the West Indies three months later.

Spain launched further expeditions to the new continents and established *New Spain*. The colony consisted not only of Central America and Mexico, but also the American Southwest and Florida. France claimed much of what would become Canada, along with the Mississippi River region and the Midwest. In addition, the Dutch established colonies that covered New Jersey, New York, and Connecticut. Each nation managed its colonies differently, and thus influenced how they would assimilate into the United States. For instance, Spain strove to establish a system of Christian missions throughout its territory, while France focused on trading networks and had limited infrastructure in regions such as the Midwest.

Even in cases of limited colonial growth, the land of America was hardly vacant, because a diverse array of Native American nations and groups were already present. Throughout much of colonial history, European settlers commonly misperceived native peoples as a singular, static entity. In reality, Native Americans had a variety of traditions depending on their history and environment, and their culture continued to change through the course of interactions with European settlers; for instance, tribes such as the Cheyenne and Comanche used horses, which were introduced by white settlers, to become powerful warrior nations. However, a few generalizations can be made: many, but not all, tribes were matrilineal, which gave women a fair degree of power, and land was commonly seen as belonging to everyone. These differences, particularly European settlers' continual focus on land ownership, contributed to increasing prejudice and violence.

Colonial Society and Interactions Among Europeans, Africans, and American Indians

Native Americans played an important role in the early history of Britain's North American colonies. Squanto was an Algonquian Indian who helped English settlers in Massachusetts survive by teaching them how to plant native crops. Some Native American tribes were friendly towards the colonists and traded with them.

However, Native Americans and Europeans often came into conflict, frequently over land disputes. The Native Americans and Europeans had very different concepts of land use and ownership. Native

Americans did not understand the concept of landownership or sale. When they entered into agreements with the colonists, Native Americans thought they were allowing the settlers to farm the land temporarily, rather than retain it in perpetuity. On the other hand, colonists were frustrated when Native Americans continued to hunt and fish on lands they had "sold." These, and other disagreements, eventually led to bloody conflicts that gradually weakened Native American tribes.

Native Americans were also vulnerable to diseases to which the Europeans had developed immunity. These diseases included bubonic plague, cholera, chicken pox, pneumonic plague, influenza, measles, scarlet fever, typhus, smallpox, and tuberculosis. These diseases killed millions of Native Americans and were sometimes used as a biological weapon. Historians estimate that as much as 80 percent of the Native American population died through disease and warfare.

The southern colonies, including Virginia, Maryland, the Carolinas, and Georgia, were also organized by county. The southern economy focused on labor-intensive crops such as tobacco and rice, and as a result, landowners relied on indentured servants and African slaves. Slaves were present in most colonies, but were more common in the south.

Thirteen Colonies

News of Columbus's success sparked a number of other expeditions and the British, French, Dutch, Spanish, and Portuguese all eventually laid claim to lands in the New World. Columbus himself made three more voyages to the Americas. The French and Dutch focused mostly on the lucrative fur trade in North America. The Spanish and Portuguese sought gold in Central and South America but also tried to convert Native Americans to Christianity. British settlers also sought economic opportunity and created the first British colony at Jamestown, Virginia, in 1607. However, the Puritans who landed at Plymouth Rock in 1620 left for the New World in order to establish their ideal religious community.

Connecticut, New Hampshire, Massachusetts, and Rhode Island were considered the "New England colonies." The settlements in New England were based around an economy focused on fishing and lumber. These colonies maintained puritanical and Congregationalist religious beliefs. While English Puritans mostly settled in New England, a wide variety of colonists settled in the mid-Atlantic region. English, Scottish, Dutch, and Swedish settlers came to Delaware, New York, New Jersey, and Pennsylvania. As a result, the mid-Atlantic colonies were more religiously diverse and tolerant than the settlements in New England. Agriculture was the foundation of the economy in mid-Atlantic colonies. This meant that settlements were more dispersed. Government and administration were based on counties instead of towns.

Political power was also distributed differently among the colonies. Some colonies, such as New York and Virginia, were royal colonies ruled directly by the king. Pennsylvania was a proprietary colony—the king allowed William Penn to appoint officials and govern the colony as he saw fit. Corporate colonies, such as Rhode Island and Connecticut, were administered by a group of investors. But, by the early 1700s, the king had revoked the charters of most proprietary and corporate colonies and assumed direct control himself.

Foundations of Representative Government in the United States

Virginia House of Burgesses
The Virginia House of Burgesses, which convened for the first time in 1619, became the first elected assembly ever established in the English colonies. The House of Burgesses only elected white landowners. Moreover, the Virginia Company and the Virginia governor reserved the right to nullify any

policy passed by the House. Although the House of Burgesses was, therefore, far from democratic in character, it still established a precedent for assembly-style government within the English colonies in North America and later the independent United States of America.

Mayflower Compact

On November 21, 1620, before landing on the coast of present-day Massachusetts, forty-one male Puritans drafted and signed a document that became known as the Mayflower Compact. The Mayflower Compact represents one of the first attempts at self-government in the English colonies of North America. These Separatist Puritans—sometimes referred to as "pilgrims"—wanted to establish their own basic laws and social rules. They believed these laws should be devised by the colonists themselves rather than the English Crown (though the compact did honor the colony's relationship with the king). The founding principles of the Mayflower Compact referenced basic Christian values such as justice and covenantal agreements with neighbors and God. The document also highlights notions of equality, which became even more prevalent during the heart of the Enlightenment in the 1700s. These foundational values served as a source of information for later representative government documents such as colonial charters, the Declaration of Independence, state constitutions, the Articles of Confederation, and the U.S. Constitution.

Iroquois Confederacy

Although not a primary shaper of the Articles of Confederation or U.S. Constitution, the governmental structure of the Iroquois Confederacy did influence some of the political principles of the Founding Fathers. The Iroquois Confederacy, much like the U.S. government, was federal in nature. The Iroquois Confederacy comprised five or six Native American tribes that worked together to resolve diplomatic issues with an overarching government. Much like the states within the Union, the tribes within the Confederacy maintained local self-government while addressing issues of common importance at a federal level. Some historians even believe the Iroquois system of government employed basic tenets of representational democracy. Other historians believe it acted more like the United Nations than the United States of America. Nevertheless, the Iroquois Confederacy should not be downplayed as a foundational contributor to the democratic-republican values of the Early Republic—the Iroquois Confederacy, much like the Mayflower Compact and the Plymouth Colony, served as a historical example of a unique governing body the Founding Fathers could draw inspiration from.

Fundamental Orders of Connecticut

The Fundamental Orders of Connecticut, written by Thomas Hooker in 1639, established basic principles of democratic rule in the English colonies, paving the way to the democratic character of future government documents in the United States of America. The Fundamental Orders of Connecticut expanded the right to vote in Connecticut by offering suffrage to men who did not belong to the church. Hooker's gradual expansion of voting rights preceded later democratic milestones such as the constitutional extension of voting rights to working-class men (the Age of Jacksonian Democracy), black men (post–Civil War), and women's suffrage (1920s). Early documents such as state constitutions, the Articles of Confederation, and the U.S. Constitution employed Hooker's methods by extending voting rights to all secular, landowning men.

Development of Colonial Society

Situated on the Atlantic Coast, the Thirteen Colonies that would become the United States of America constituted only a small portion of North America. Even those colonies had significant differences that stemmed from their different origins. For instance, the Virginia colony under John Smith in 1607 started with male bachelors seeking gold, whereas families of Puritans settled Massachusetts. As a result, the

Thirteen Colonies—Virginia, Massachusetts, Connecticut, Maryland, New York, New Jersey, Pennsylvania, Delaware, Rhode Island, New Hampshire, Georgia, North Carolina, and South Carolina— had different structures and customs that would each influence the United States.

Britain continued to hold onto its other colonies, such as Canada and the West Indies, which reflects the continued power of multiple nations across North America, even as the United States began to expand across the continent. Many Americans advocated expansion regardless of the land's current inhabitants, but the results were often mixed. Still, events both abroad and within North America contributed to the growth of the United States. For instance, the rising tumult in France during the French Revolution and the rise of Napoleon led France to sell the Louisiana Purchase, a large chunk of land consisting not only of Louisiana but also much of the Midwest, to the United States in 1803. Meanwhile, as Spanish power declined, Mexico claimed independence in 1821, but the new nation became increasingly vulnerable to foreign pressure. In the Mexican-American War from 1846 to 1848, Mexico surrendered territory to the United States that eventually became California, Nevada, Utah, and New Mexico, as well as parts of Arizona, Colorado, and Wyoming.

Even as the United States sought new inland territory, American interests were also expanding overseas via trade. As early as 1784, the ship *Empress of China* traveled to China to establish trading connections. American interests had international dimensions throughout the nation's history. For instance, during the presidency of Andrew Jackson, the ship *Potomac* was dispatched to the Pacific island of Sumatra in 1832 to avenge the deaths of American sailors. This incident exemplifies how U.S. foreign trade connected with imperial expansion.

This combination of continental and seaward growth adds a deeper layer to American development, because it was not purely focused on western expansion. For example, take the 1849 Gold Rush; a large number of Americans and other immigrants traveled to California by ship and settled western territories before more eastern areas, such as Nevada and Idaho. Therefore, the United States' early history of colonization and expansion is a complex network of diverse cultures.

Revolutionary Era and the Early Years of the Republic

U.S. Society During the Revolutionary Era and Early Years of the Republic

The French colonies in Canada also threatened the British settlements. France and Britain had been enemies for centuries. Religious differences reinforced their hostility; the British were Protestant and the French were mostly Catholic. Far fewer colonists settled in "New France," but they often clashed with the British, especially over the lucrative fur trade. Both the British and French sought to dominate the trade in beaver pelts, which were used to make hats in Europe. The British and French fought a series of colonial wars between 1689 and 1748 that failed to resolve the struggle for dominance in North America.

Eventually, the contest culminated in the French and Indian War (also known as the Seven Years' War), which ended in 1763. The French initially enjoyed the upper hand because they were able to persuade more Native American tribes to support them. The Native Americans felt the French were less likely to encroach on their territory than the land-hungry British. The Native Americans launched devastating raids along the British colonial frontier. However, the British eventually emerged victorious after they blockaded the French colonies in Canada. This prevented the French from bringing in reinforcements or from resupplying their Native American allies with gunpowder and ammunition. Native American raids subsided and eventually the French surrendered almost all of their colonial possessions in North

America. Some historians consider this war the first global conflict because battles were also fought in Europe, Asia, and Africa.

The French defeat radically altered the balance of power in North America. Previously, Native Americans had been able to play the French and British against each other, but now they were without many of their French allies. In addition, the French and Indian War also set the stage for the American Revolution. Although victorious, the British monarchy spent an enormous amount of money and the war doubled the national debt. In order to pay off the debts, King George III began imposing taxes upon the North American colonies, which eventually led to revolution.

The Molasses Act in 1731 was another outgrowth of mercantilism. This law imposed a higher tax on the molasses that colonists purchased from the Dutch, French, or Spanish colonies. The tax was unpopular with the colonists and British imperial officials eventually decided not to enforce the tax. The Molasses Act had threatened to disrupt the pattern of triangular trade that had emerged in the Atlantic world. First, ships from Britain's North American colonies carried rum to Africa where it was traded for slaves and gold. Then, the ships took the slaves to French and Spanish colonies in the Caribbean and exchanged them for sugar or molasses. In the last part of the triangular trade system, merchants sailed back to North America where the sugar and molasses was used to make rum, and the cycle could start over again.

In addition to economic connections, many other bonds also bridged the Atlantic Ocean. Most colonists shared a common language, common religion, and common culture. However, as the colonies grew in population, they began to develop local institutions and a separate sense of identity. For example, it became common for ministers to receive their education at seminaries in North America rather than Britain. Newspapers also began to focus on printing more local news as well. Perhaps most importantly, the colonies began to exercise more control over their own political affairs. The British government retained control over international issues, such as war and trade, but the colonists controlled their own domestic affairs. Colonies began to form their own political assemblies and elect landowners who represented local districts. In addition, communications between the colonies and Britain were very slow because it took months for a ship to cross the Atlantic and return with a response.

American Revolution

Competition among several imperial powers in eastern areas of North America led to conflicts that would later bring about the independence of the United States. The Seven Years' War from 1756 to 1763, also known as the French and Indian War, ended with Great Britain claiming France's Canadian territories as well as the Ohio Valley. The same war was costly for all the powers involved, which led to increased taxes on the Thirteen Colonies. In addition, the new lands to the west of the colonies attracted new settlers, and they came into conflict with Native Americans and British troops that were trying to maintain the traditional boundaries. These growing tensions with Great Britain, as well as other issues, eventually led to the American Revolution, which ended with Britain relinquishing its control of the colonies.

A number of political acts by the British monarchy also led to more discontent among the colonies. After the French and Indian War ended in 1763, the king declared that the colonists could not settle west of the Appalachian Mountains. This was known as the Proclamation of 1763. Many colonists were frustrated because they had expected this territory would be open for expansion after the French had been defeated.

Additionally, taxes were imposed in an effort to help reduce the debt Britain amassed during the French and Indian War. In 1764, Parliament passed the Sugar Act, which reduced the tax on molasses but also provided for greater enforcement powers. Some colonists protested by organizing boycotts on British goods. One year later, in 1765, Parliament passed the Quartering Act, which required colonists to provide housing and food to British troops. This law was also very unpopular and led to protests in the North American colonies.

The Stamp Act of 1765 required the colonists to pay a tax on legal documents, newspapers, magazines and other printed materials. Colonial assemblies protested the tax and petitioned the British government in order to have it repealed. Merchants also organized boycotts and established correspondence committees in order to share information. Eventually, Parliament repealed the Stamp Act but simultaneously reaffirmed the Crown's right to tax the colonies.

In 1767, Parliament introduced the Townshend Acts, which imposed a tax on goods the colonies imported from Britain, such as tea, lead, paint, glass, and paper. The colonies protested again and British imperial officials were assaulted in some cases. The British government sent additional troops to North America to restore order. The arrival of troops in Boston only led to more tension that eventually culminated in the Boston Massacre in 1770, where five colonists were killed and eight were wounded. Except for the duty on tea, most of Townshend Act taxes were repealed after the Boston Massacre.

Parliament passed the Tea Act in 1773 and, although it actually reduced the tax on tea, it was another unpopular piece of legislation. The Tea Act allowed the British East India Company to sell its products directly, effectively cutting out colonial merchants and stirring more Anglo-American anger and resentment. This resulted in the Boston Tea Party in 1773, an incident in which colonial tea merchants disguised themselves as Indians before storming several British ships that were anchored in Boston harbor. Once aboard, the disguised colonists dumped more than 300 chests of tea into the water.

Because the British government was unable to identify the perpetrators, Parliament passed a series of laws that punished the entire colony of Massachusetts. These acts were known as the Coercive or Intolerable Acts. The first law closed the port of Boston until the tea had been paid for (an estimated $1.7 million in today's currency). The second act curtailed the authority of Massachusetts' colonial government. Instead of being elected by colonists, most government officials were now appointed by the king. In addition, the act restricted town meetings, the basic form of government in Massachusetts, and limited most villages to one meeting per year. This act angered colonists throughout the thirteen colonies because they feared their rights could be stripped away as well. A third act allowed for British soldiers to be tried in Britain if they were accused of a crime. The fourth act once again required colonists to provide food and shelter to British soldiers.

Colonists responded by forming the First Continental Congress in 1774, and all the colonies except for Georgia sent delegates. The delegates sought a compromise with the British government instead of launching an armed revolt. The First Continental Congress sent a petition to King George III affirming their loyalty but demanding the repeal of the Intolerable Acts. The delegates organized a boycott of imports from and exports to Britain until their demands were met.

The colonists began to form militias and gather weapons and ammunition. The first battle of the revolution began at Lexington and Concord in April 1775 when British troops tried to seize a supply of gunpowder and were confronted by about eighty Minutemen. A brief skirmish left eight colonists dead and ten wounded. Colonial reinforcements poured in and harassed the British force as they retreated to Boston. Although the battle did not result in many casualties, it marked the beginning of war.

A month later, the Second Continental Congress convened in Philadelphia. The delegates formed an army and appointed George Washington as commander in chief. Delegates were still reluctant to repudiate their allegiance to King George III and did not do so until they issued the Declaration of Independence on July 4, 1776. The Declaration drew on the ideas of the Enlightenment and declared that the colonists had the right to life, liberty, and the pursuit of happiness. The Declaration stated that the colonists had to break away from Britain because King George III had violated their rights.

After the Battle of Lexington and Concord, British troops retreated to Boston and the colonial militias laid siege to the city. Colonists built fortifications on Bunker Hill outside the city and British troops attacked the position in June 1775. The colonists inflicted heavy casualties on the British and killed a number of officers. However, the defenders ran out of ammunition and British troops captured Bunker Hill on the third assault. Although it was a defeat for the colonists, the Battle of Bunker Hill demonstrated that they could stand and fight against the disciplined and professional British army.

The British army initially had the upper hand and defeated colonial forces in a number of engagements. The Americans did not achieve a victory until the Battle of Trenton in December 1776. Washington famously crossed the Delaware River on Christmas Day and launched a surprise attack against Hessian mercenaries. They captured more than 1,000 soldiers and suffered very minimal casualties. The victory at Trenton bolstered American morale and showed that they could defeat professional European soldiers.

The Battle of Saratoga in New York in the fall of 1777 was an important turning point in the American War for Independence. American troops surrounded and captured more than 6,000 British soldiers. This victory convinced the French king to support the revolutionaries by sending troops, money, weapons, and ships to the American continent. French officers who fought alongside the Patriots brought back many ideas with them that eventually sparked a revolution in France in 1789.

Revolutionary Era

Navigation Acts
Since 1651, the British crown had tried to control trade within its empire, which eventually led to tension and discontent in the North American colonies. That year, the monarchy introduced the Navigation Acts, which prevented the North American colonies from trading directly with other European powers—all goods had to be shipped to Britain first. This was an attempt to keep wealth within the British Empire and to prevent other empires from profiting from their colonies. This was an example of mercantilism—an economic policy that formed the foundation of Britain's empire. Mercantilism called for government regulation in the form of tariffs, a tax on imports from other countries. This raised prices on foreign goods and encouraged British imperial subjects to purchase goods made in Britain or the colonies. This reduced imports and maximized exports, thus enriching the British Empire.

Treaty of Paris of 1783
French support was very important in the last major battle of the revolution at Yorktown, Virginia, in 1781. American troops laid siege to General Cornwallis's British forces at Yorktown. The French fleet defeated a British naval squadron sent to relieve Cornwallis. French and American troops began attacking the British fortifications in Yorktown; a sustained artillery bombardment by American guns eventually forced Cornwallis to surrender. This ended the Revolutionary War, and in 1783 the British

signed the Treaty of Paris. Britain recognized the United States as an independent country and set the Mississippi River as the nation's western border. However, British troops continued to occupy several forts in the Great Lakes region.

In addition, tens of thousands of colonists who remained loyal to the British Empire fled the United States after the war. They were known as loyalists and many thousands had joined militias and fought against the patriots. Some loyalists fled to Canada or Britain but many remained in the United States. Many Native American tribes had sided with the British as well in an attempt to curb western expansion. No Native American leaders signed the Treaty of Paris and they refused to give up their territories, which led to further conflict as the new American nation began to expand westward.

Foundations of Representative Government in the United States

America's first system of government was actually laid out in the Articles of Confederation, and not the Constitution. The Articles of Confederation were ratified during the Revolutionary War and went into effect in 1781. The Articles of Confederation created a relatively weak central government and allowed individual states to retain most of the power. Under this system, the national government did not have a president or judiciary. Each state had only one vote in the Confederation Congress and most major decisions required unanimous approval by all thirteen states. Despite this requirement, the Confederation Congress did pass some important legislation, including the Northwest Ordinance, which organized the land west of Appalachian Mountains. The territories eventually became the states of Ohio, Indiana, Michigan, Illinois, Wisconsin, and Minnesota. However, Congress did not have the power to tax and could only request money from the states without any way to enforce its demands. A Revolutionary War veteran named Daniel Shays led an armed insurrection in western Massachusetts in 1787. Although Shay's Rebellion was defeated, it drew attention to the weaknesses of the Articles of Confederation.

The Constitutional Convention met in Philadelphia a few months after the rebellion in order to create a stronger federal government. However, delegates disagreed over how to structure the new system. The Virginia Plan was one proposal that included a bicameral legislature where states were awarded representation based on their population size. This would benefit more populous states at the expense of smaller states. The other main proposal was the New Jersey Plan, which retained many elements of the Articles of Confederation, including a unicameral legislature with one vote per state. This plan would put states on an equal footing regardless of population.

Eventually, delegates agreed to support the Connecticut Compromise (also known as the Great Compromise), which incorporated elements from both the Virginia and New Jersey Plans. Under the new Constitution, Congress would be a bicameral body. In the House of Representatives, states would be allocated seats based on population, but in the Senate each state would have two votes. The Constitution also included a president and judiciary that would each serve to check the power of other branches of government. In addition, Congress had the power to tax and had more enforcement powers.

Slavery was another contentious issue during the Constitutional Convention. Slavery was more common in the Southern states and less common in the North. The Southern states wanted slaves to be counted when calculating representation in Congress but not when it came to assessing taxes. Northern states wanted the opposite and eventually the two sides agreed to the Three-Fifths Compromise where slaves were counted as three-fifths of a person for the purposes of both taxation and representation. The

Constitution also included a provision that allowed slave owners to recover slaves who had escaped and permitted the international slave trade to continue until 1808.

Once the Constitution had been drafted, nine of the thirteen states had to ratify it. Vigorous debate erupted over whether or not the Constitution should be approved. Two different political factions emerged. The Federalists supported the Constitution because they felt a stronger central government was necessary in order to promote economic growth and improve national security. Several leading federalists, including Alexander Hamilton, John Jay, and James Madison, published a series of articles urging voters to support the Constitution. However, the Anti-Federalists, including Thomas Jefferson and Patrick Henry, felt that the Constitution took too much power away from the states and gave it to the national government. They also thought there weren't enough protections for individual rights and lobbied for the addition of a Bill of Rights that guaranteed basic liberties. Ultimately, the Constitution was ratified in 1788 and the Bill of Rights was approved a year later.

The Electoral College unanimously elected George Washington as the nation's first president in 1789. Despite this appearance of unity, deep political divisions led to the formation of the nation's first party system. Washington supported the Federalist ideology and appointed several Federalists to his cabinet, including Alexander Hamilton as secretary of the treasury. The Anti-Federalist faction evolved into the Democratic-Republican Party and favored stronger state governments instead of a powerful federal government. As settlers moved into the new Northwest Territories, Washington helped pacify Indians who opposed further expansion. He also successfully put down a rebellion in western Pennsylvania by farmers opposed to a federal tax on whiskey.

Washington declined to seek a third term and another Federalist, John Adams, became our second president. Adams signed the Alien and Sedition Acts, which made it a criminal offense to criticize the government, and allowed the president to deport aliens suspected of treason. Adams and the Federalists argued that the laws were necessary in order to improve security as Europe became embroiled in a war against the new French republic. Jefferson and the Democratic-Republicans said the laws restricted free speech. Jefferson made the acts an important topic in 1800 when he successfully ran for president.

Jefferson's victory marked a turning point in the political system because the Democratic-Republicans gained more power while the Federalists went into decline. He repealed the Alien and Sedition Acts when he was elected. The Federalists were further weakened when Hamilton was killed in a duel in 1804.

Jefferson accomplished several significant achievements during his presidency, and one of the most important was the Louisiana Purchase in 1803. For $15 million, Jefferson bought French territory west of the Mississippi River that doubled the size of the United States. He then appointed Meriwether Lewis and William Clark to lead an expedition to explore the vast new territory and study its geography, vegetation, and plant life. Clark also brought his African-American slave, York, on the journey. York helped hunt and even saved Clark's life during a flood. The expedition was also aided by Sacagawea, a Shoshone woman, who acted as a guide and interpreter. The explorers also established relations with Native American tribes and set the stage for further western expansion in the 1800s.

American Political System and Political Parties

The Founding Fathers of the United States opposed the divisiveness they associated with political parties, and President George Washington railed against the evil of political parties in his Farewell Address. However, the ratification of the Constitution led to the creation of the first two American political parties, the Federalists and the anti-Federalist Democratic-Republican Party. When Andrew Jackson became the seventh president of the United States as a Democrat, his opposition organized under the Whig Party. The Whigs asserted Congress' supremacy over the president and primarily focused on economic concerns, like banking and violations.

A number of different issues divided the Federalists and the Democratic-Republicans, including the French Revolution, which began in 1789. Initially, many Americans supported the French effort to replace their monarchy and create a republican government. However, the French Revolution quickly became more violent, as thousands of suspected opponents of the revolution were executed during the Reign of Terror. The Federalists, including Washington, were horrified by the violence, while Jefferson and the Democratic-Republicans thought the United States should help its former ally. Washington ensured that the country remain officially neutral.

Early Years of the Republic and the Age of Jackson

Following the fervor of the American Revolution, political leaders from across the newly founded United States joined together to discuss the governmental frameworks of the new nation. In many cases, these political leaders did not come to a consensus; they debated basic principles regarding the role of the federal, state, and local governments. Additionally, they debated what economic programs, tariffs and taxes, court systems, and foreign policies to employ. When the Second Continental Congress met in 1775, it drafted a governing document that became known as the Articles of Confederation. The Articles of Confederation mandated the creation of a Congress that would possess limited federal powers. The Articles of Confederation provided states with more power than the federal government—each state had its own militia, dissolving any remnants of a national revolutionary army. In its weakened state, the new federal government faced great threats from its former colonial enforcer, Great Britain. British soldiers posted in Canada threatened the safety and security of the United States of America.

The British also tried to "squeeze" the United States economically by enforcing high tariffs on the new nation. The British closed off markets in the West Indies, which negatively affected the domestic economy of the United States of America. Under the Articles of Confederation, the United States could not regulate interstate economy; moreover, the excessive printing of bank notes during the Revolution led to years of postwar inflation. The loss of trade, the increase in tariffs, and the minimal commercial regulations eventually thrust the United States into a depression. This depression led to social division, paving the way to heavy farming debts, rising domestic taxes, and the ensuing Shays' Rebellion. Although the rebellion failed, it had a lasting effect on the political conscience of the country. Many political leaders inaugurated a call for change that culminated in the ratification of the current U.S. Constitution.

After months of debate and compromise, the Constitution was created at the Constitutional Convention of 1787. Delaware became the first state to ratify the Constitution in December 1787, and Rhode Island was the last state to ratify the Constitution in 1790. In the years that followed the ratification of the Constitution, debates continued to wage on about the role of the federal government and economy in American life. Perhaps the most famous of these debates was the one between Thomas Jefferson and Alexander Hamilton. Jefferson opposed the creation of a national bank, and Hamilton supported its creation. Eventually, Hamilton's view took precedence with the creation of the first national bank in 1791. During the Age of Jackson, following the election of 1824, the expansion of the American frontier bolstered sectional differences, paving the way to debates over Indian removal and slavery/abolition. The era of Jackson also witnessed the democratization of voting in America with the extension of voting rights to working-class white men who did not own land.

<u>Indian Removal</u>

The Cherokee, Chickasaw, Choctaw, Creek, and Seminole tribes of the Southeastern United States were known as the "Five Civilized Tribes" because they had developed a written language and many members had become Christians. Nevertheless, Andrew Jackson signed the Indian Removal Act of 1830, which gave him the power to continue buying land from various tribes. The Cherokee filed a lawsuit to protect their territory and won their arguments before the Supreme Court. However, President Andrew Jackson ignored the ruling and eventually used troops to force many tribes off their land and sent them west to Oklahoma during the 1830s. This was known as the "Trail of Tears" because thousands of Native Americans died from starvation, exposure, and disease along the way.

Westward Expansion, the Civil War, and Reconstruction

Westward Expansion

Constant immigration meant that land prices in the eastern United States rose, and people sought new economic opportunities on the frontier where land was cheaper. The United States government tried purchasing land from Native Americans, but most refused to relinquish their territories. Native Americans continued to defend their land until Tecumseh was defeated in the War of 1812. This defeat helped secure the Northwest Territory, and more settlers began pouring in. After the Louisiana Purchase, Lewis and Clark paved the way for expansion into the Great Plains and further west.

Several important laws also stimulated western expansion during the second half of the 19th century. Congress passed the Homestead Act in 1862, which allowed citizens to claim 160 acres for only $1.25 per acre. The settler also had to live on the land for five years and make improvements. That same year, Congress also passed the Pacific Railroad Act, which supported the construction of a transcontinental railroad. The United States government provided land and financial support to railroad companies and the first transcontinental link was established in 1869. This facilitated trade and communication between the eastern and western United States.

As Americans poured westward, conflict again broke out between settlers and Native Americans. The discovery of gold in the Black Hills of South Dakota caused prospectors to flood into the area although the U.S. government had recognized the territory belonged to the Sioux. General George Armstrong Custer brought in troops to try and take possession of the Black Hills. This led to disaster when Custer and more than 250 soldiers died at the Battle of Little Big Horn in 1876.

The U.S. government continued its efforts to control Native American tribes. The Dawes Act of 1887 encouraged Native Americans to settle on reservations and become farmers in exchange for U.S. citizenship. Chief Joseph was a leader of the Nez Perce tribe who refused to live on a reservation and tried to flee to Canada. However, the U.S. captured Chief Joseph and his tribe and forced them onto a reservation. Reformers also required Native Americans to send their children to boarding schools where they had to speak English and dress like Caucasians instead of maintaining their traditional culture. The schools were often crowded, and students were also subjected to physical and sexual abuse.

In 1890, the Lakota Indians tried to preserve their traditional beliefs by performing a special ceremony called a Ghost Dance. U.S. government officials felt threatened and sent soldiers to try and disarm the Lakota. This led to the Massacre at Wounded Knee in 1890 where at least 150 Lakota, including many women and children, were slaughtered. It was the last major conflict between Native Americans and U.S. forces.

Manifest Destiny

The concept of Manifest Destiny emerged during the 1800s and introduced the idea that God wanted Americans to civilize and control the entire continent. This led to conflict when the province of Texas declared its independence from Mexico and asked to be annexed by the United States. President James K. Polk tried to buy Texas, but when Mexico refused, he sent troops into the disputed territory. Mexican troops responding by attacking an American unit, which led to war in 1846.

Manifest Destiny also sparked a desire to expand American influence into Central and South America. Adventurers launched several unsuccessful attempts to invade Nicaragua and Cuba.

Territorial Acquisitions

The United States purchased Alaska from Russia in 1867 for $7.2 million. At the time, the purchase was unpopular with the public, but seal hunting became very profitable and gold was discovered in 1896. Alaska became a state in 1959.

In 1893, American businessmen launched an armed coup, overthrew the queen of Hawaii, and asked Congress to annex Hawaii. The businessmen owned sugar plantations and feared the queen's attempts to enact reform would threaten their political influence. Hawaii became a U.S. territory in 1898 and a state in 1959.

The last phase of American territorial expansion occurred as a result of the Spanish-American War in 1898. New ideas arose in the late 19th century that helped justify further expansion. Some intellectuals applied Charles Darwin's ideas of "survival of the fittest" to the human race and called this new concept Social Darwinism. They used this idea to justify why stronger groups of people colonized and exploited weaker groups. In addition, imperialists also used the idea of the White Man's Burden to justify further expansion. They claimed that Caucasians were obligated to civilize and govern groups thought to be less advanced.

These ideas were used to justify America's new status as a colonial power as a result of the Spanish-American War. Although Spain had once been a powerful empire, it had been in decline. The United States went to war against Spain in 1898 when the American battleship USS Maine exploded in Havana Harbor and killed more than 250 sailors. The U.S. Navy defeated the Spanish fleet in several engagements and then the Army followed up with a victory at San Juan Hill, which included the famous charge by Teddy Roosevelt and the Rough Riders.

The war lasted less than four months and made the United States a world power. The U.S. also acquired several Spanish colonies, including Puerto Rico, Guam, and the Philippines. Guam became an important refueling station for American naval forces in the Pacific and remains a U.S. territory today, along with Puerto Rico. When the United States occupied the Philippines, the Filipino people launched a rebellion in order to obtain their independence. The U.S. Army put down the insurrection, but in doing so, they committed many atrocities against the Filipino people. The Philippines would remain an American territory until 1946.

United States-Mexican War

In the Mexican-American War, American troops won several battles although the Mexican army usually outnumbered them. The Mexican troops were poorly armed and trained, but, on the other hand, the Americans made use of their highly skilled artillery force. They eventually captured Mexico City and forced the Mexican government to sign the Treaty of Guadalupe-Hidalgo in 1848. The treaty recognized American control over Texas and also ceded California, Utah, Colorado, Arizona, New Mexico, and Nevada in exchange for $15 million. Tens of thousands of prospectors flooded into California when gold was discovered there in 1849. The prospectors often encroached on Native American lands, which led to further conflict. In 1854, the United States also acquired additional territories as part of the Gadsden Purchase. The acquisition of so much new territory sparked a debate over whether the land would be open or closed to slavery.

Sectionalism and the Civil War

In the early 1800s, political and economic differences between the North and South became more apparent. Politically, a small but vocal group of abolitionists emerged in the North who demanded a complete end to slavery throughout the United States. William Lloyd Garrison edited the abolitionist newspaper *The Liberator* and vehemently denounced the brutality of slavery. His criticism was so vicious that the legislature of Georgia offered a $5,000 bounty to anyone who could capture Garrison and deliver him to state authorities. Other activists participated in the Underground Railroad—a network that helped fugitive slaves escape to the Northern United States or Canada.

Economic differences emerged as the North began to industrialize, especially in the textile industry where factories increased productivity. However, the Southern economy remained largely agricultural and focused on labor-intensive crops such as tobacco and cotton. This meant that slavery remained an essential part of the Southern economy. In addition, the North built more roads, railroads, and canals, while the Southern transportation system lagged behind. The Northern economy was also based on cash, while many Southerners still bartered for goods and services. This led to growing sectional tension between the North and South as their economies began to diverge further apart.

These economic differences led to political tension as well, especially over the debate about the expansion of slavery. This debate became more important as the United States expanded westward into the Louisiana Purchase and acquired more land after the Mexican-American War. Most Northerners were not abolitionists. However, many opposed the expansion of slavery into the western territories because it would limit their economic opportunities. If a territory was open to slavery, it would be more attractive to wealthy slave owners who could afford to buy up the best land. In addition, the presence of slave labor would make it hard for independent farmers, artisans, and craftsman to make a living, because they would have to compete against slaves who did not earn any wages. For their part, Southerners felt it was essential to continue expanding in order to strengthen the southern economy and ensure that the Southern way of life survived. As intensive farming depleted the soil of nutrients, Southern slave owners sought more fertile land in the west.

Both the North and South also feared losing political power as more states were admitted to the nation. For example, neither side wanted to lose influence in the United States senate if the careful balance of free and slave state representation was disrupted. Several compromises were negotiated in Congress, but they only temporarily quieted debate. The first such effort, called the Missouri Compromise, was passed in 1820, and it maintained political parity in the U.S. Senate by admitting Missouri as a slave state and Maine as a free state. The Missouri Compromise banned slavery in the portion of the Louisiana Purchase that was north of the 36°30' parallel and permitted slavery in the portion south of that line as well as Missouri.

However, the slavery debate erupted again after the acquisition of new territory during the Mexican-American War. The Compromise of 1850 admitted California as a free state and ended the slave trade, but not slavery itself, in Washington D.C., in order to please Northern politicians. In return, Southern politicians were able to pass a stronger fugitive slave law and demanded that New Mexico and Utah be allowed to vote on whether or not slavery would be permitted in their state constitutions. This introduced the idea of popular sovereignty where the residents of each new territory, and not the federal government, could decide whether or not they would become a slave state or a free state. This essentially negated the Missouri Compromise of 1820. The enhanced fugitive slave law also angered many Northerners, because it empowered federal marshals to deputize anyone, even residents of a free state, and force them to help recapture escaped slaves. Anyone who refused would be subject to a $1,000 fine (equivalent to more than $28,000 in 2015).

The debate over slavery erupted again only a few years later when the territories of Kansas and Nebraska were created in 1854. The application of popular sovereignty meant that pro- and anti-slavery settlers flooded into these two territories to ensure that their faction would have a majority when it came time to vote on the state constitution. Tension between pro- and anti-slavery forces in Kansas led to an armed conflict known as "Bleeding Kansas."

John Brown was a militant abolitionist who fought in "Bleeding Kansas" and murdered five pro-slavery settlers there in 1856. He returned to the eastern United States and attacked the federal arsenal at Harper's Ferry, Virginia, in 1859. He hoped to seize the weapons there and launch a slave rebellion, but federal troops killed or captured most of Brown's accomplices and Brown was executed. The attack terrified Southerners and reflected the increasing hostility between North and South.

The sectional differences that emerged in the last several decades culminated in the presidential election of 1860. Abraham Lincoln led the new Republican Party, which opposed slavery on moral and economic grounds. The question of how best to expand slavery into new territories split the Democratic Party into two different factions that each nominated a presidential candidate. A fourth candidate also ran on a platform of preserving the union by trying to ignore the slavery controversy.

Lincoln found little support outside of the North but managed to win the White House since the Democratic Party was divided. Southern states felt threatened by Lincoln's anti-slavery stance and feared he would abolish slavery throughout the country. South Carolina was the first Southern state to secede from the Union and ten more eventually followed. Lincoln declared that the Union could not be dissolved and swore to defend federal installations. The Civil War began when Confederate troops fired on Fort Sumter in Charleston in 1861.

Civil War

The First Battle of Bull Run (also known as the First Battle of Manassas) in 1861 was the first major infantry engagement of the Civil War. Both the Northern and Southern troops were inexperienced and although they had equal numbers, the Confederates emerged victorious. Many had thought the war would be short, but it continued for another four years.

The Union navy imposed a blockade on the Confederacy and captured the port of New Orleans in 1862. The Union navy was much stronger than the Confederate fleet and prevented the Southern states from selling cotton to foreign countries or buying weapons.

In 1862, Union forces thwarted a Confederate invasion of Maryland at the Battle of Antietam. This engagement was the single bloodiest day of the war and more than 23,000 men on both sides were killed or wounded. Union troops forced the Confederates to retreat, and that gave Lincoln the political capital he needed to issue the Emancipation Proclamation in 1863. This declaration did not abolish slavery, but it did free slaves in Southern territory. It also allowed African Americans to join the Union navy and about 200,000 did so. The 54th Massachusetts Infantry was a famous unit of African American soldiers who led an assault on Fort Wagner in South Carolina in 1863. Although the attack failed, the 54th Massachusetts witnessed African American troops fighting bravely under fire.

The Siege of Vicksburg in 1863 was a major Union victory because they gained control of the Mississippi River and cut the Confederacy in half. This made it difficult the Confederacy to move troops around and communicate with their forces. Grant commanded the Northern forces in the siege and eventually became the Union army's top general.

The Battle of Gettysburg in 1863 marked the turning point of the Civil War. Robert E. Lee led Confederate troops into Pennsylvania, but in three days of heavy fighting, the Union army forced them to retreat. The victory bolstered Northern morale and weakened Southern resolve. Never again would Confederate forces threaten Northern territory.

In 1864, Union general William T. Sherman captured Atlanta and then marched more than 200 miles to Savannah. Along the way, he destroyed anything that could support the Southern war effort, such as railroads and cotton mills. At this point, the Southern economy was beginning to collapse. The North had more manpower than the South and could afford to sustain more casualties. The North also had more industrial capacity to produce weapons and supplies and more railroads to transport men and equipment.

Eventually, Robert E. Lee surrendered to Ulysses S. Grant at Appomattox, Virginia, on April 9, 1865. Five days later, John Wilkes Booth assassinated Lincoln in Washington D.C. Vice President Andrew Johnson, a Democrat, succeeded him and soon came into conflict with Republicans in Congress about how to reintegrate Southern states into the nation. This process was known as Reconstruction and lasted from 1865 to 1877.

Reconstruction

Johnson opposed equal rights for African Americans and pardoned many Confederate leaders. However, many Congressional Republicans wanted to harshly punish Southerners for their attempts to secede from the Union. They were known as Radical Republicans because they also wanted to give former slaves equal rights.

Johnson vetoed bills that were designed to protect the rights of freed slaves, but Congress overrode his vetoes. This led to increasing conflict between Johnson and Congress, which eventually caused Radical Republicans to impeach him. Although Johnson was acquitted in 1868, he had very little power, and Radical Republicans took control of the Reconstruction process.

Republicans passed three important constitutional amendments as part of the Reconstruction process. The 13th amendment was ratified in 1865, and it abolished slavery throughout the country. The 14th Amendment was ratified in 1868 and gave equal rights to all citizens. The 15th Amendment was ratified in 1870 and specifically granted all men the right to vote regardless of race.

Southerners resisted these demands and passed laws that prohibited freed slaves from owning weapons or testifying against whites. They also formed militias and vigilante groups, such as the Ku Klux Klan, in order to intimidate African Americans who tried to vote. Congress sent federal troops into Southern states in order to enforce the law and prevent vigilante violence.

After the much-disputed election of 1876, the Democrats offered to let the Republicans have the White House if they agreed to end Reconstruction. After the Republicans agreed, federal troops were withdrawn and African Americans in the South were subjected to discrimination until the Civil Rights movement of the 1960s. Scholars often consider the Reconstruction era the beginning of Jim Crow and a transition into a new form of "institutionalized racism" that still pervades much of modern U.S. society.

The United States as a World Power

Emergence of the United States as a World Power Between 1898 and 1920

The United States gained prestige and international status after the Spanish-American War of 1898, because the United States defeated Spain and acquired several colonies. American participation in World War I made the United States an economic and financial leader as well. The United States loaned money to Britain and France and supplied weapons and equipment that helped the Triple Entente achieve victory. The United States and USSR emerged from World War II as the only surviving superpowers because so much of the rest of the world had been devastated. This system was described as bipolar because there were two centers of power.

The United States was the leader of the free world during the Cold War and formed military and economic alliances with other nations. With the collapse of the USSR in 1991, the United States was the only surviving world power. This era was a unipolar system because there were no other major powers that could rival the United States.

How National and International Conflicts Between World War I and World War II Affected the United States

World War I began in 1914 with the assassination of Franz Ferdinand, the apparent heir of the Austro-Hungarian Empire. A network of secret alliances meant that most European nations were quickly drawn into the conflict, although President Woodrow Wilson initially tried to keep the United States neutral. The war involved two major European alliances: the Triple Entente of Britain, France, and Russia, and the Central Powers, which included Germany and Austria-Hungary. The British implemented a naval blockade that was very successful, and the Germans retaliated by launching submarine attacks. German submarines attacked any ship carrying supplies to the Triple Entente, including the passenger ship RMS Lusitania in 1915. About 1,200 people died, including more than 100 Americans. The Germans temporarily halted their unrestricted submarine campaign, but eventually resumed the attacks in 1917. In addition, in 1917, Germany asked Mexico to attack the United States in a communiqué known as the Zimmerman telegram. These events led the United States to join the Triple Entente in 1917, although significant numbers of American troops did not arrive in Europe until 1918. American reinforcement helped the British and French, who had been fighting continuously since 1914, launch a final offensive that defeated Germany in 1918. American forces suffered about 320,000 casualties. World War I also led to significant changes on the home front as women took on new responsibilities, and thousands of African Americans migrated north in search of work. World War I also led to a communist revolution that transformed Russia into the USSR in 1922.

After Germany was defeated in 1918, Wilson made a proposal known as the Fourteen Points and argued that the best way to resolve the conflict was by promoting free trade and democracy. For instance, Wilson wanted nations to respect the right to navigate in international waters and create a League of Nations that would resolve future disputes. Some of his suggestions, such as the League of Nations, were adopted, but many were not. In 1919, Germany was forced to sign the Treaty of Versailles, which imposed harsh economic penalties and restricted the German military. Ultimately, the Treaty of Versailles created resentment in Germany that lead to World War II. America emerged as an important player in world affairs after World War I because the American economy had supplied the Triple Entente with arms and equipment and American soldiers helped to achieve victory.

How National and International Conflicts from World War II to the Present Have Affected the United States

In the period between the world wars, fascism became popular in many European countries that were ravaged by the Great Depression. Fascism is a political ideology that advocates for a dictatorship in order to provide stability and unity. Adolf Hitler emerged as a prominent fascist leader in Germany and eventually brought the Nazi party to power in 1933. Germany, Italy, and Japan formed an alliance called the Axis and began to threaten other countries. The League of Nations could not diffuse the conflict. World War II broke out when Germany invaded Poland in 1939. Hitler quickly conquered most of Europe, except for Britain, and attacked the USSR in 1941. The United States sent military equipment and weapons to Britain and the USSR, but did not formally join the war until the Japanese attacked Pearl Harbor on December 7, 1941. Again, women played an important role on the home front by working in factories to build guns, tanks, planes, and ships. African Americans, Native Americans, and Japanese Americans also contributed by fighting on the front lines.

American forces first landed in North Africa where they, along with British and French troops, defeated German and Italian forces in 1942. In 1943, Allied forces invaded Italy, and Soviet troops began to push the German army back out of the USSR. Allied troops landed in France in 1944 and the Soviets began to advance on Germany as well. By May 1945, Hitler had committed suicide and Germany had been defeated.

This also brought about an end to the Holocaust. The Holocaust was a genocide committed by Hitler's Nazi Germany and collaborators that resulted in the deaths of more than 6 million Jews and 5 million Romans, gypsies, Afro-Europeans, disabled citizens, and homosexuals. A network of facilities in Germany and its territories were used to house victims for slave labor and mass murder, among other heinous crimes. The Nuremberg trials were part of the aftermath of the Holocaust, which served to prosecute important members of Nazi Germany leadership.

In the Pacific theater, American naval forces defeated the Japanese fleet in several key engagements, including the battle of Midway in 1942. American troops began recapturing territory in the Pacific as well and eventually pushed the Japanese back to their home islands in 1945. The Japanese refused to surrender until American planes dropped atomic bombs on the cities of Nagasaki and Hiroshima in August 1945.

Because World War II devastated most of Europe, the United States and the USSR emerged as the only superpowers when it ended. However, the erstwhile allies were suspicious of each other, which led to the Cold War.

Significant Individuals Who Shaped U.S. Foreign Policy from 1898 to the Present

Alfred Thayer Mahan
Alfred Thayer Mahan was a U.S. naval officer and historian who became famous after publishing a book titled *The Influence of Sea Power Upon History, 1600–1783* (1890). Mahan is famous for extending America's "Manifest Destiny" beyond its coasts and into the seas. Mahan believed that the future of world dominance and democratic hegemony rested upon the creation of a strong navy. He thus

encouraged the United States to carry out its imperial dreams on the high seas, paving the way to the aggressive expansionist initiatives of the U.S. government in the late 1800s.

Theodore Roosevelt

President Theodore Roosevelt, who led the nation between 1901 and 1909, is famous for bringing the United States of America into modernity through a series of modernization and conservation projects. Roosevelt is famous for enthusiastically offering the Panamanian governor $10 million per year to build and operate the Panama Canal. Operating under U.S. leadership between 1914 and 1999, the Panama Canal remained a last symbol of Roosevelt's diplomatic legacy in Latin America. The canal is a beacon of the United States' strong-armed diplomatic influence in Latin America during the years of the "Roosevelt Corollary." The unilateral diplomatic tactics hashed out by the Roosevelt Corollary stated that the United States had the right, as military leader of the Western Hemisphere, to act as the "international police force" of the region. The Roosevelt Corollary, backed by an impressive U.S. Navy, allowed the United States to have unchecked power in Latin America for decades after the Roosevelt administration. During Roosevelt's presidency, the United States occupied many Latin American countries for self-serving reasons. Nevertheless, not all of Roosevelt's policies were as self-serving—the rough-and-tumble president is also responsible for establishing the National Park System in the United States and setting aside hundreds of thousands of acres of land for conservation.

Woodrow Wilson

President Woodrow Wilson declared war on Germany on April 2, 1917. American troops helped defeat the German army in September 1918. Fighting ended in November of that year after Germany signed a peace agreement. President Woodrow Wilson's plan for peace was the League of Nations, which was adopted as part of the Treaty of Versailles in 1919, but then rejected by the U.S. Senate.

Franklin D. Roosevelt

Democratic candidate Franklin D. Roosevelt was elected president in 1932 on his promise to help the economy recover by increasing government spending. After taking office in 1933, Roosevelt introduced a barrage of proposals, called the New Deal, that he hoped would boost employment, stimulate demand, and increase government regulation. Some elements of the New Deal were temporary, such as the Civilian Conservation Corps, which put young men to work improving parks between 1933 and 1942. Other New Deal programs endure to this day, such as the Social Security Administration, which has provided pensions to retirees, temporary payments to unemployed workers, and benefits to handicapped individuals since 1935. In addition, the Securities and Exchange Commission was created in 1934 and continues to regulate stock markets and investment companies. The Wagner Act of 1935 was also an important part of the New Deal because it guaranteed the right of workers to unionize and go on strike. The 21st Amendment was ratified in 1933 and repealed Prohibition, which had been hard to enforce and was unpopular. Roosevelt also hoped it would create jobs and stimulate spending. The New Deal helped reduce unemployment, but the economy did not completely recover until America entered World War II and production increased in order to support the war efforts.

Henry Kissinger

Henry Kissinger is a Jewish refugee who fled Hitler's Nazi Germany in 1938. Kissinger rose to prominence as a foreign diplomat and political scientist for the United States of America. He is best known for his tenure as a secretary of state and national security advisor during the Nixon and Ford administrations. Between 1969 and 1977, Kissinger gained notoriety as a Cold Warrior who supported *Realpolitik* and *détente* approaches to Cold War diplomacy with the Soviet Union. He is renowned as the secretary of state who assisted President Richard Nixon in opening relations with China. He won a Nobel Peace Prize in 1973 for orchestrating a cease-fire in Vietnam. Opinions regarding his work as secretary of state are often divided. Some point to his practical approach to the Cold War; others condemn him for his support of controversial CIA missions in foreign nations.

Significant Events that Shaped U.S. Foreign Policy from 1898 to the Present

Marshall Plan
After World War II, the United States offered European countries the Marshall Plan—a grant of American subsidies to help Europe and Japan recover economically. The largest recipients were England, France, and West Germany. Aside from sincere humanitarian desires, the Marshall Plan also served the interests of the United States by ensuring that Europe's citizens did not resort to Communism out of desperation. In turn, the Soviet Union developed their own plan, the Molotov Plan, to help their Communist Allies' recovery.

NATO
NATO (North Atlantic Treaty Organization) is an organization of states from North America and Europe, led by the United States. This organization was formed after the end of World War II to counter the Soviet Union and Warsaw Pact's efforts to spread Communism across the world.

Berlin Airlift
Following the Second World War, France, Great Britain, and the United States began occupying Berlin, Germany, in hopes of rebuilding Europe and providing stability to the region. The USSR also encroached on the territory, specifically West Germany, hoping to weaken the former Nazi stronghold and strengthen their western military front. In 1948, the former Allies—France, Great Britain, and the United States—tried to withdraw their forces from Berlin, allowing their three occupation zones to unite. The USSR responded to the West's withdrawal by holding the western side of Berlin hostage. Much like Germany at large, the capital city of Berlin was previously divided into four sections following the war. In a strategic attempt to declare dominance over the former Nazi capital, the USSR's military blockaded the highways, waterways, and railways leading into West Berlin. The leader of the USSR—Joseph Stalin— believed the blockade would intimidate the former allies. Stalin's blockade forced many West Berliners into starvation. To prevent starvation, the American and British air forces flew over the blockade on a regular basis, dropping supplies to West Berlin. In a little over a year, the allied air forces made 277,000 flights over West Berlin. This strategy—known as the Berlin Airlift—eventually forced Stalin and the USSR to lift the blockade in May 1948.

McCarthyism
McCarthyism is a term in history and political science used to describe a period in American history that witnessed Wisconsin senator Joseph McCarthy lead the charge in a series of accusatory investigations and trials that sought to uncover and criminalize communist sympathies in U.S. society. Throughout the 1950s, McCarthy, who was elected to the Senate in 1946, rose to prominence in the 1950s when he made unsubstantiated claims about over 205 communists infiltrating the State Department. These claims led to a series of investigations and public hearings, which reached their peak in 1954 with thirty-six days of televised hearings. These hearings also symbolized the beginning of the end for McCarthyism. McCarthy's claims remained unsubstantiated despite their publicity, and by 1957 he had been censored by the Senate. McCarthyism is now a term that has become synonymous with Cold War fears and any type of public defamation or indiscriminate allegations.

Korean War
When Communist North Korea invaded South Korea in June 1950, the U.N. sent a group of troops led by the U.S. to help South Korea. This action led to a three-year conflict that ended in a cease-fire in 1953.

Although war was never officially declared and neither side won, the fighting showcased President Truman's hard stance against Communism.

Vietnam War

In 1954, rebels seized control of Vietnam from France. The country was split into two regimes with the northern part under Communist leadership. As the threat of communism continued to loom, the U.S. sent advisors and weapons to South Vietnam beginning in 1955. The U.S. got more directly involved in the 1960s during the presidency of Lyndon B. Johnson, who sent troops in great numbers to help South Vietnam win the fight. Many Americans opposed the war, which caused anti-war protests and unrest. A cease-fire was signed in 1973, and the last U.S. forces pulled out in 1975.

Cuban Missile Crisis

The Cuban Missile Crisis in 1962 was sparked by the failed invasion of Cuba by the U.S. a year earlier. After the invasion, the Soviets placed nuclear missiles aimed at the U.S. in Cuba. However, when U.S. spy planes spotted them, President John F. Kennedy demanded the dismantling and removal of the missile sites, and as a concession agreed to go forward with the planned removal of U.S. missile sites in Turkey. A year later on November 22, 1963, President Kennedy was assassinated in Dallas by Lee Harvey Oswald.

Sputnik I

The Cold War prompted the *space race* between the U.S. and Soviets, each attempting to outdo the other with different space exploration milestones. In 1957, the Russians launched *Sputnik*, the first satellite, into space. This prompted President Eisenhower to establish the National Aeronautics and Space Administration (NASA) in 1958. Although the Soviets were also the first nation to send a human into space in 1961, the U.S. quickly caught up. President Kennedy vowed to land an American on the moon by 1969—a feat that was accomplished by astronaut Neil Armstrong on July 20, 1969.

Gulf War

In 1990, Iraqi dictator Saddam Hussein invaded Kuwait in order to take possession of the tiny country's huge oil fields. A few months later, U.S. President George H.W. Bush launched Operation Desert Storm with a coalition of several Middle Eastern and European countries. This Gulf War started with air bombings and ended in a five-day ground war that drove Hussein out.

Major Foreign Policy Issues Currently Facing the United States

Nearly sixteen years after the terrorist attacks on the World Trade Center in New York City, the United States is still entangled in the politics of the Middle East and still finding ways to cope with the ongoing threat of global terrorism. The events of September 11, 2011—often referred to simply as "9/11"—galvanized the United States of America into a self-declared war on terrorism. These events have, presumably, challenged and changed many relationships between the United States and the world while simultaneously extending the post-9/11 paradigm. Some scholars, for instance, saw the war on terrorism as the final blow to old Cold War politics. However, recent military events in Eastern Europe, Syria, and the broader Middle East indicate that the Cold War may be "heating up" again on the geopolitical stage.

U.S. economy remains the largest in the world, making it a strong contender to continue its role as "Leader of the Free World." Although U.S. economic hegemony has declined, relatively, in an era of globalization and North American Free Trade Agreement (NAFTA), the United States is poised to be an economic player in the coming decades.

Political, Economic, and Social Developments from 1877 to the Present

United States from 1877 to the Present

The post-World War II era led to a number of social, economic, and technological changes in the United States. The counter-culture phenomenon was one of the most powerful social movements in the latter half of the twentieth century in the U.S. The counter-culture movement challenged social norms and rejected traditional authority figures. The movement began in the 1950s with the beatniks, a group of non-conformist writers and artists who were dissatisfied with society. The beatniks sought inspiration in African and Asian cultures and many eschewed materialism.

Political Developments

President Franklin D. Roosevelt created the New Deal in order to stimulate the economy and improve government regulation. The New Deal also marked an important shift in American politics because the Democratic Party began to favor government intervention while Republicans opposed it. This was a reversal of the parties' previous platforms. The Democratic Party relied on a coalition of labor unions, Catholics, African Americans, and other minorities. The Republican Party included conservatives, evangelicals, and business leaders.

The Great Society was another major government program that the Democratic Party supported. President Lyndon B. Johnson sought to end poverty and improve education. For example, he raised the minimum wage and created programs to provide poor Americans with job training. The Great Society also implemented a number of Civil Rights laws that will be discussed in greater detail later.

The presidential election of 1980 was another watershed moment. Republican nominee Ronald Reagan carried forty-three states, and the Republicans won a majority in the U.S. Senate after twenty-eight years of Democratic control. Reagan presented an optimistic message and broadcasted a television advertisement that proclaimed "It's morning again in America." He promised to restore America's military power, cut government regulations, and reduce taxes. Reagan enjoyed the support of resurgent conservative Christian evangelicals, who wanted to restore morality to American society. They were particularly concerned about issues such as abortion. The Moral Majority, founded by Baptist minister Jerry Falwell in 1979, was one key group that helped Reagan win the election. This coalition helped realign party loyalties, as more liberal Republicans and conservative Democrats shifted their allegiance.

Economic Developments

America emerged as one of the most powerful economies in the world after 1945. The US economy, especially manufacturing, was very prosperous during the 1950s and 1960s. The economy successfully switched from wartime production, and consumer demand was very high. During the Great Depression, few families had disposable income. Although most workers earned good wages during World War II, they had little to spend it on because most goods were rationed. Once production of consumer goods resumed, families used their savings to buy cars, household appliances, and televisions. This was good for the economy, and unemployment remained below 5 percent for most of the 1950s and 1960s. However, during the latter part of the 20th century, the manufacturing base in the North and Midwest began to crumble and the area became known as the Rust Belt. Manufacturing jobs began to move from the North and Midwest to states in the South and West, known as the Sun Belt, where land was cheap and wages were low.

The world economy also became increasingly interconnected during the post-World War II era. This accelerated the process of globalization, which is the integration of ideas and products from different cultures. This benefitted the United States economically because businesses, such as McDonald's and Coca-Cola, found many consumers around the world who were eager to consume American goods. However, the process works both ways, and many aspects of foreign culture, such as Japanese cartoons and animation, have become very popular in the United States. Many critics also point out that globalization has hurt the American economy in recent decades because manufacturing jobs have gone overseas to countries in South America and Asia where wages are low.

Social Developments

Counter-Culture Movement

The counter-culture movement became more popular during the 1960s as millions of children from the Baby Boomers generation entered into adulthood. Veterans came home after World War II and started families, and, by the 1960s, many of these young adults also felt disaffected and rebellious. Their parents criticized them because they began to wear colorful clothing and the boys let their hair grow out. Many members of the counter-culture movement, now called hippies, inherited the beatnik's interest in African and Asian cultures. Writer Ken Kesey traveled around the country on a bus encouraging people to experiment with psychedelic drugs, such as LSD. The counter-culture movement influenced musicians and avant-garde artists.

The counter-culture movement was also closely connected to other protest movements during the 1960s, including the Civil Rights movement, which will be discussed later. Many members of the counter-culture movement during the 1960s also opposed the war in Vietnam. The Baby Boomers could be conscripted to fight in Vietnam whether they wanted to or not. In 1965, young men began burning their draft cards, which was a criminal offense, in protest. Massive demonstrations against the war occurred around the country, especially on college campuses, but many other people also refused to support the war effort, including clergymen and even some veterans who had fought in Vietnam. The counter-culture movement disappeared during the 1970s but had a lasting impact on the social and cultural history of the United States.

Race, Gender, and Ethnicity

Race, gender, and ethnicity have been important themes in American history from the colonial era to the present. Individuals from different races, ethnicities, and genders have had very different experiences throughout the same historical events or eras. It is important to distinguish between race and ethnicity: race refers to a group of people with common ancestry, while ethnicity refers to cultural background, such as language and tradition.

Race played an important part in colonial America because both Caucasians and Africans occupied positions of servitude. White immigrants who could not purchase passage to the New World sometimes agreed to become indentured servants. Their employers paid for their passage across the Atlantic, and in exchange, the indentured servant agreed to work without wages for at least five years. However, African slaves were rarely able to free themselves. The strong connection between slavery and race meant that all blacks, whether free or enslaved, were viewed as inferior. After the American Revolution, most free blacks, even those living in northern states, were denied the right to vote. Although the Civil Rights Movement in the 1960s made great gains, many activists claim more must be done in order to overcome the legacy of racial inequality in America.

Japanese Americans experienced discrimination during and after World War II, specifically with the implementation of Japanese internment camps in America. This forced 110,000 to 120,000 Japanese Americans into camps, 62 percent of which were United States citizens.

Discrimination against certain ethnicities is also prominent throughout American history as well. For example, many Americans resented the arrival of German and Irish immigrants during the 1800s because they spoke a different language or practiced different religions. Hispanics were also subject to discrimination, and in 1943, a number of Hispanic youths were attacked during the Zoot Suit Riots.

Gender differences in the United States have also been impossible to ignore. For example, until the 1840s, most married women in the United States were unable to enter into contracts, own property, or retain their own wages. Women were unable to vote until the 19th Amendment was ratified in 1920. The Women's Rights Movement in the U.S. ranged from 1848 to 1920. This movement called for a woman's right to vote, the right to bodily autonomy, freedom from sexual violence, the right to hold public office, the right to work, the right to fair wages and equal pay, and the right to own property and obtain an education. Women continue to demand change during the 21st century for reasons such as the gender wage gap, better resources for women's health, female reproductive rights, and for protection of basic human rights, such as bringing greater awareness to rape culture, violence against women, and protection against female sex trafficking.

Technological Changes
Several technological changes have had a significant impact on the U.S. economy as well. The Cold War led to advances in nuclear power and aerospace engineering. The development of computers, in particular, has helped accelerate the transition to a post-industrial economy where information technology and other services have replaced traditional manufacturing jobs. The first computers were used to break coded messages during World War II and had very limited computing power. The invention of transistor technology in 1947 made computers cheaper, smaller, and more reliable. The invention of integrated circuits in the 1960s and 1970s increased computing power and gave birth to the first personal computers. The Internet was created in 1969, but widespread use in business and academia did not begin until the 1980s. These developments have made it much easier to share information and have increased economic opportunities. But, the increasing use of robots, especially in the manufacturing industry, have also made the economy more efficient while also causing layoffs.

Third Party Movements

Populism
Populism advocates for incorporating advances in technology, social organization, science, and economics into the government to benefit society. It is fueled by the idea that social goals should be achieved by the actions of the people, and not the dominant elites. The term "populism" became popular in the 1890s by farmers and labor unions in reaction to the Gilded Age, and returned in the 1950s. Some populist political parties in the U.S. include Greenback Party, Progressive Party of 1912, Progressive Party of 1924, and the Share Our Wealth movement by Huey Long.

Progressive Era Reforms
The social inequalities and economic abuses of the Gilded Age did not go unnoticed, and in the 1890s many reformers began to demand change. This period was called the Progressive Era and included activists in both the Democratic and Republican parties. The Progressives wanted to use scientific methods and government regulation to improve society. For example, they advocated the use of initiative, referendum, and recall to make government more responsive to its citizens. Progressives also

argued that it was necessary to breakup large monopolies (known as trust busting) in order to promote equal economic competition. In 1911, Rockefeller's Standard Oil was split up into thirty-four different companies in order to promote competition, and the Federal Trade Commission was established in 1914 in order to prevent other monopolies from forming. Many Progressives also supported several constitutional amendments that were ratified in early 20th century, including the 17th amendment, which established the direct election of U.S. Senators in 1913 (previously state legislatures had elected senators). They also favored the Prohibition of alcohol that went into effect with the 18th Amendment in 1919. Progressives also advocated for women's rights and backed the 19th Amendment, which gave women the right to vote in 1920.

New Deal
In 1933, President Franklin D. Roosevelt introduced the New Deal, which was a series of executive orders and laws passed by Congress in response to the Great Depression. The programs focused on relief, recovery, and reform, and were enacted until 1938. The second New Deal from 1935-1938 promoted the Social Security Act, labor unions, and aided tenant farmers and migrant workers who were struggling from the economic devastation of the Great Depression.

Susan B. Anthony
Susan B. Anthony was a woman's rights activist who was committed to social equality during the women's suffrage movement. She advocated for women's rights as well as the abolition of slavery. Anthony is widely known for her involvement in the National American Woman Suffrage Association, as well as her conviction and subsequent fine for voting in her hometown of Rochester, New York in 1872.

W.E.B. Du Bois
Du Bois was one of the co-founders of National Association for the Advancement of Colored People (NAACP) and was a sociologist, civil rights activist, Pan-Africanist, author, and historian. Du Bois was the first African American to earn a Ph.D. from Harvard University in 1895. W.E.B. DuBois wrote several prolific works, including *The Souls of Black Folk*, and *Black Reconstruction in America*, a text that challenged the notion that the failures of the Reconstruction Eras were the faults of African Americans.

George Wallace
Running on a third-party platform, George Wallace entered the 1968 presidential election as an Independent who was a founder and card-carrying member of the far-right American Independent Party (AIP). Under the leadership of George Wallace, who was a former governor of Alabama, the AIP promulgated a segregationist political platform that called for the reinstatement of Jim Crow and an unraveling of civil rights progress across the United States. As a southern neo-Dixiecrat, Wallace lamented the social and political advances of the civil rights movement in the mid-1960s. Even years earlier, as an Alabama governor, he promised his voters that he stood for "segregation now, segregation tomorrow, [and] segregation forever." During his 1968 election against Richard M. Nixon and Hubert H. Humphrey, Wallace acquired a record five states as a third-party candidate: Georgia, Mississippi, Alabama, Louisiana, and Arkansas. The state of third-party politics has remained weakened since the 1968 election, and no other platform has ever gained as many electoral votes as Wallace's AIP.

Industrialization in the United States

After the end of the Civil War, America experienced a period of intense industrialization, immigration, and urbanization, and all three trends were interrelated. The process of industrialization had begun before the Civil War but expanded into more sectors of the economy in the later part of the century. This era is often called the Second Industrial Revolution and included growth in the chemical, petroleum, iron, steel, and telecommunications industries. For example, the Bessemer process made it much easier to produce high quality steel by removing impurities during the smelting process.

The writer Mark Twain called the late 19th century the Gilded Age because the era was also one of extreme social inequality. Some corporations expanded and began to control entire industries. For example, by 1890, the Standard Oil Company produced 88 percent of all the refined oil in the nation. This made a few individuals, such as John D. Rockefeller who owned Standard Oil, extremely wealthy. On the other hand, many workers earned low wages and began to form labor unions, such as the American Federation of Labor in 1886, in order to demand better working conditions and higher pay. Strikes were one of the most common ways workers could express their dissatisfaction, and the Pullman Strike of 1894 was one of the largest such incidents in the 19th century. Workers went on strike after the Pullman Company, which manufactured railroad cars, cut wages by about 25 percent. More than 125,000 workers around the country walked off the job and attacked workers hired to replace them. Federal troops were sent in to end the strike, and more than eighty workers were killed or wounded during confrontations. The strike was unsuccessful, but Congress passed a law making Labor Day a federal holiday in order to placate union members.

Immigration also played an important part in the economic and social changes that occurred during the late 19th century. Immigration patterns changed during this time and immigrants from Southern and Eastern Europe, such as Italy and Poland, began to surpass the number of arrivals from Northern and Western Europe. The immigrants sought economic opportunity in the United States because wages for unskilled workers were higher than in their home countries. Some Americans resented the influx of immigrants because they spoke different languages and practiced Catholicism. In 1924, Congress passed a law that restricted immigration from Southern and Eastern Europe.

Increased urbanization was the last factor that contributed to the rapid changes of the Gilded Age. Factories were located near cities in order to draw upon a large pool of potential employees. Immigrants flooded into cities in search of work, and new arrivals often settled in the same neighborhoods where their compatriots lived. Between 1860 and 1890, the urbanization rate increased from about 20 percent to 35 percent. Cities struggled to keep up with growing populations, and services such as sanitation and water often lagged behind demand. Immigrants often lived in crowded living conditions that facilitated the spread of diseases.

Significant Individuals from 1877 to the Present

Jane Addams
Jane Addams is known as one of the most prominent reformers of the Progressive Era. She was a pioneer in Social Work and advocated for the health of mothers, the needs of children, world, peace, and public health. She was also an activist, author, and leader in the women's suffrage movement. She was the first American woman to be awarded the Nobel Peace Prize in 1931.

Henry Ford
Henry Ford is famous for the development of the assembly line technique, which gave rise to mass production. Known best as an American industrialist, he founded the Ford Motor Company in 1903.

Franklin D. Roosevelt
FDR was the 32nd President of the United States, elected in 1933. He is widely known for his New Deal policy, which was a program of relief for the Great Depression. He also obtained approval for the declaration of War on Japan and on Germany, effectively entering the U.S. into World War II. FDR was

also known for his efforts at conservation of the environment, and created 140 national wildlife refuges. He also expanded and funded National Park and National Forest systems.

Martin Luther King Jr.

Martin Luther King Jr. was a Civil Rights leader and activist as well as a Baptist minister. King argued for nonviolent resistance during the Civil Rights movement, for which he won the Nobel Peace Prize in 1964. King was assassinated on April 4, 1968, in Memphis, Tennessee.

King gave his speech "I Have a Dream" as part of the 1963 March on Washington. Drawing on Lincoln's past speech at Gettysburg, King argued that America's journey to true equality was not over yet. His references to biblical passages gave the speech a spiritual tone, but he also mentioned specific locations across the nation to signify how local struggles were tied with national consequences. By emphasizing his optimism, King's speech reflects not only civil rights activism but also the American dream of freedom and progress.

Cesar Chavez

Cesar Chavez was a labor union activist who organized transient Hispanic agricultural workers in an effort to obtain better working conditions in the 1960s and 1970s. He co-founded the National Farm Workers Association. Chavez became a historical icon after his death and is famous for popularizing the slogan "Sí, se puede," or "Yes, it can be done."

Betty Friedan

Betty Friedan was an American feminist and writer in the second wave of feminism in the 1960s who was elected the first president of the Nation Organization for Women (NOW). Her book, *The Feminine Mystique,* is often credited with beginning this second wave. Friedan aimed to empower women to be in an equal partnership with men. She also led the Women's Strike for Equality in 1970, which advocated for equal opportunities for women in jobs and education.

Malcolm X

An African American human rights activist and Muslim minister, Malcolm X advocated for the rights of African Americans. He became a member of the Nation of Islam, and through that platform promoted the separation of black and white Americans and black supremacy. Malcolm X rejected the Civil Rights movement for its emphasis on integration as well as passive resistance. Malcolm X is known to his admirers as a courageous and important figure in African American history.

Significant Events from 1877 to the Present

In the late 1800s and early 1900s, the forces of urbanization and industrialization combined to create rampant urban plight across the metropolitan centers of the United States of America. During this era, many progressive political leaders and groups rose to power, opening the door to urban-based reforms in labor, health care, education, women's rights, and temperance. These reforms coalesced in what is now referred to by historians as a "Progressive Era."

Antitrust legislation appeared in the late 1800s and early 1900s in response to the unchecked creation of trusts—"legal arrangements in which one board of trustees controls a variety of companies"—and monopolies—"sole vertical and horizontal control of a field business." As a result of these trusts and monopolies, many U.S. citizens had to pay more for railroad transportation, oil and gas, and loans. In the late 1800s and early 1900s, many progressive legislators looked to "bust" these trusts and monopolies. The Sherman Act of 1890, the Clayton Act of 1914, and the Federal Trade Commission Act of 1914 are all examples of "trust-busting" legislation. Using the Sherman Act of 1890, President Theodore Roosevelt dissolved forty-four monopolies and became known as the trust-buster.

The late 1800s and early 1900s also witnessed increased restrictions in immigration. Passed by President Chester A. Arthur, the Chinese Exclusion Act of 1882 inaugurated a decade-long moratorium on Chinese labor immigration. Likewise, the Johnson-Reed Immigration Act of 1924 placed semi-permanent limitations on the number of immigrants who could enter the United States per year. The act established quotas based on national origin, limiting immigration from the Asia-Pacific Triangle. The act also placed quotas on European, African, and Middle Eastern immigration.

Some postwar reforms, however, have been more positively received by history. The GI Bill, for instance, provided returning World War II veterans with the money and support systems necessary to obtain work and/or a college education. The GI Bill has changed over the years based on unique postwar needs and contemporary sociohistorical contexts. Even the original GI Bill, however, has been criticized because of its marginalization of African Americans in a pre–civil rights movement world.

Ratification of the 19th Amendment
With the ratification of the 19th Amendment in 1920, women obtained the right to vote. This achievement was partly due to women's contributions on the home front during World War I. Women served as Army nurses and worked in factories to help produce weapons, ammunition, and equipment. As more women entered the workforce, they became more financially independent and began to socialize without being supervised by a chaperone, as was the norm during the 19th century. Overall, women during this period, known as "New Women," took on a more active role in public life, pursued higher education in greater numbers, and sought more sexual freedom. During the 1920s, women, known as "flappers," began to flaunt social conventions by wearing short skirts, bobbing hair, smoking cigarettes, and driving automobiles. Nevertheless, a "glass ceiling" still remains in place decades after women's suffrage in regards to a gender wage gap.

Great Depression
Stock market speculation increased during the 1920s, and investors borrowed money in order to purchase shares. This did not cause any concern as long as the stock market went up, but it led to disaster when stock prices fell sharply in October 1929 and investors were unable to repay their loans. The stock market crash may have triggered the Great Depression, but it did not cause it. The Great Depression spread around the globe as nations stopped trading with each other. In the United States, families lost their savings when banks failed because there was no federal insurance. The economy went into a downward spiral because as more people lost their jobs, they had little money to spend, which led to further layoffs and more economic contraction. Unemployment peaked at 25 percent between 1932 and 1933.

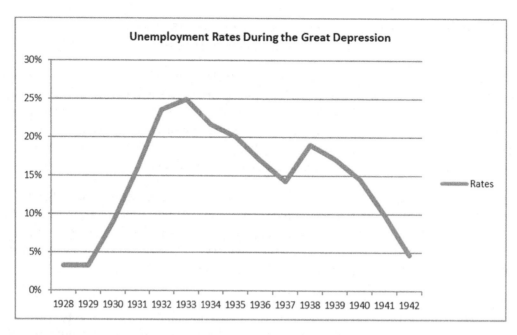

Unemployment Rates During the Great Depression

Civil Rights Act of 1964

When the Supreme Court ruled that school segregation was illegal in 1954 in the revolutionary case *Brown vs. the Board of Education*, the Civil Rights Movement was set in motion. This movement continued throughout the 1950s and 1960s and included dozens of nonviolent protests, such as the Montgomery bus boycott in Alabama. The boycott was organized after Rosa Parks was arrested because she refused to give up her seat on the bus to a white man. The Southern Christian Leadership Conference (SCLC) was soon formed as a way to bring African Americans together to help fight segregation in a peaceful way. The Reverend Dr. Martin Luther King, Jr. was its first president. Dr. King and his supporters kept up the fight throughout the 1960s, staging sit-ins at segregated lunch counters, *Freedom Rides* on segregated buses, and marches and protests in segregated cities, such as Birmingham, Alabama. The demonstrations often ended in violence and police brutality, which served to aid the cause and led to the passage of the Civil Rights Act in 1964.

Globalization

The twentieth century marked increasing globalization. The process had already been under way in the nineteenth century as technological improvements and imperial expansions connected different parts of the world, but the late twentieth century brought globalization to a new level. Trade became international, and local customs from different lands also gained prominence worldwide. Cultural exchanges occur on a frequent basis, and many people have begun to ponder the consequences of such rapid exchanges. One example of globalization was the 1993 establishment of the European Union—an economic and political alliance between several European nations.

Terrorism

Islamic fundamentalism often resorts to terrorism to fight against their conventionally more powerful enemies. The most infamous modern terrorist attack occurred on September 11, 2001, when terrorists associated with al-Qaeda hijacked four commercial airliners and flew the planes into the World Trade Center and Pentagon. The 9/11 attack initially led to the United States' invasion of Afghanistan and later contributed to the decision to invade Iraq. These wars heightened the interaction between the Western and Arab worlds, and fundamentalism has increased ever since. Jihadists and religious extremists have flooded the region to defend Islam against what they perceive as the invading West. Additionally, the Arab Spring created a spirit of unrest in many Middle Eastern countries with a history of authoritarian

76

rule. Following the Americans' withdrawal from Iraq and uprisings in neighboring Syria, the religious extremists declared an Islamic State in the region, known as the *Islamic State of Iraq and Levant*, ensuring the proliferation of Islamic fundamentalism and terrorism for the foreseeable future.

Civil Rights Movements

Although the Declaration of Independence declared "all men are created equal," blacks, women, and other minorities struggled for more than a century to make this dream a reality. The U.S. Constitution legalized slavery, and it was not abolished until the 13th Amendment was ratified in 1865. The 14th Amendment, ratified in 1868, granted African Americans citizenship, and the 15th Amendment, ratified in 1870, explicitly granted them the right to vote. However, white Southerners passed laws, known as the Jim Crow system, that prevented blacks from exercising their rights and, when that failed, they relied on violence and intimidation to oppress African Americans. For example, many Southern states required voters to pass literacy tests and used them to prevent blacks from casting a ballot. Whites were either exempt from the test or were held to much lower standards. Blacks who protested their oppression could be assaulted and even killed with impunity. In the 1896 decision *Plessy vs. Ferguson*, the U.S. Supreme Court ruled that "separate but equal" schools for white and black students were permissible. In reality, black schools were almost always inferior to white schools.

The emergence of the Civil Rights Movement after World War II finally destroyed the Jim Crow system. In the 1954 decision *Brown vs. Board of Education*, the Supreme Court reversed the "separate but equal" doctrine and declared that separate schools were inherently unequal because they stigmatized African American students. In 1957, President Dwight D. Eisenhower used federal troops to force the high school in Little Rock, Arkansas, to integrate and accept nine black students. This encouraged civil rights activists to demand additional reforms. In 1955, Rosa Parks refused to give up her seat on a bus in Montgomery, Alabama, which led to a boycott. Martin Luther King Jr. led the bus boycott and became a national leader in the Civil Rights Movement. In 1960, four students in Greensboro, North Carolina, launched a peaceful sit-in at a segregated lunch counter, which sparked similar protests around the country. White activists from the North went south to help blacks register to vote, and in 1964 three activists were murdered in Mississippi. That same year, King led 250,000 protesters in a march on Washington D.C. where he delivered his famous "I Have a Dream Speech."

Although King advocated for peaceful protests, many other civil rights activists disagreed with him. For example, Malcolm X believed that blacks should use violence to defend themselves. Furthermore, King worked with white activists while Malcom X rejected any cooperation. Malcolm X was assassinated in 1965, and, despite his reputation as a non-violent leader, King was also gunned down in 1968.

Under mounting pressure, Congress passed several important pieces of legislation. The 1964 Civil Rights Act banned discrimination based on race, color, religion, sex, or national origin. The Voting Rights Act of 1965 prohibited the use of poll taxes or literacy tests to prohibit voting. The Civil Rights Act of 1968 banned housing discrimination. In 1967, Carl Stokes became the first black mayor of a major American city, Cleveland. That same year, Thurgood Marshall became the first African American to serve on the Supreme Court. President Gerald Ford declared February to be black history month. In 1989, Colin Powell became the first black chairman of the Joint Chiefs of Staff. Despite these reforms, activists claim institutional racism is still a problem in the 21st century. The Civil Rights movement inspired women, Latinos, and other groups to make similar demands for equal rights.

Women

In 1776, Abigail Adams urged her husband, founding father John Adams, to advocate for women's rights, but it would take more than a century before women could vote. In 1848, activists organized a convention in Seneca Falls, New York, to organize the women's suffrage movement, and their efforts slowly gained momentum. The ratification of the 19th Amendment in 1920 finally gave women the right to vote.

Although women had achieved political equality, they continued to demand reform throughout the 20th century. In the early 1900s, Margaret Sanger provided women with information about birth control, which was illegal at the time. Women entered the industrial workforce in large numbers during World War II, but when the war ended, they were fired so that veterans would have jobs when they came home. Many women were frustrated when told they had to return to their domestic lives. Simone de Beauvoir, a French writer, published her book "The Second Sex" after World War II, and an English translation was published in 1953. It highlighted the unequal treatment of women throughout history and sparked a feminist movement in the United States. In 1963, Betty Friedan published a book, called "The Feminine Mystique," that revealed how frustrated many suburban wives were with the social norms that kept them at home. During the 1960s, women participated in the sexual revolution and exerted more control over their own sexuality. In 1972, Congress passed Title IX, which prohibited sexual discrimination in education and expanded women's sports programs. In the 1970s, women's rights activists also pushed for greater access to birth control, and in 1973 the Supreme Court issued the controversial decision *Roe vs. Wade* which removed many barriers to abortion services. Women also demanded greater protection from domestic abuse and greater access to divorce.

During the 20th century, many American women made notable achievements, including Amelia Earhart, who was the first woman to cross the Atlantic in an airplane in 1928. In 1981, Sandra Day O'Connor became the first woman to serve on the Supreme Court. In 1983, Sally Ride became the first female astronaut. In 1984, Geraldine Ferraro became the first woman to run for vice-president, although she was unsuccessful. However, many activists continue to demand reform in the 21st century. For example, women only account for 20 percent of the U.S. Senate and House of Representatives. Furthermore, women only earn 79 percent of what men in similar jobs are paid. In 1980, President Jimmy Carter declared March to be women's history month.

Hispanics

After World War II, many Hispanics also began to demand greater equality. In 1949, veterans protested a refusal by a Texas town to bury a Mexican American soldier, who died during World War II, in the local cemetery, because only whites could be buried there. Activists called themselves Chicanos, a term that previously was used as a pejorative to describe Mexican Americans. Cesar Chavez was a labor union activist who organized transient Hispanic agricultural workers in an effort to obtain better working conditions in the 1960s and 1970s. Activists encouraged a sense of pride in Chicano identity, especially in arts and literature. In 1968, President Lyndon B. Johnson declared National Hispanic Heritage Month would run from mid-September to mid-October.

In 1959, biochemist Severo Ochoa became the first Hispanic to win a Nobel Prize. Franklin Chang-Diaz became the first Hispanic astronaut in 1986, and he flew a total of seven space shuttle missions. In 1990, Oscar Hijuelos became the first Hispanic American to win the Pulitzer Prize. Sonja Sotomayor became the first Hispanic to serve on the Supreme Court in 2009.

Native Americans

Native Americans suffered centuries of oppression at the hands of European colonists, and later American settlers as they pushed further west. Native Americans resisted attempts to encroach on their lands but were pushed onto smaller and smaller reservations. The Massacre at Wounded Knee in 1890 was the last major conflict between Native Americans and U.S. forces. However, American officials continued to try and force Native Americans to assimilate into white culture.

In 1968, a group of Native Americans formed the American Indian Movement in order to combat racism and demand greater independence. Between 1969 and 1971, a group of Native American activists occupied the federal prison on Alcatraz Island near San Francisco, although it had been closed since 1963. The activists offered to buy back the island for $9.40 in order to draw attention to how the federal government had forced tribes to sell their lands at low prices. Other activists disrupted Thanksgiving Day ceremonies aboard a replica of the Mayflower in Boston in 1970. In 1971, Native American activists also occupied Mount Rushmore, which is located on ground the Native Americans consider sacred. Violence broke out between activists and law enforcement officials in 1973 when Native Americans occupied the town of Wounded Knee, sight of the famous massacre.

In 1970, President Richard Nixon granted Native American tribes more autonomy. In 1978, Congress passed the American Indian Religious Freedom Act, which guaranteed Native Americans' rights to practice their religious ceremonies and visit sacred sites. In 1990, President George H.W. Bush declared November Native American History Month. In 1969, Navarre Scott Momaday became the first Native American to win a Pulitzer Prize for his book "House Made of Dawn." In 2014, Diane Humetewa, a member of the Hopi tribe, became the first Native American woman to serve as a federal judge. However, many Native American communities still suffer from high rates of unemployment, alcoholism, and domestic abuse.

Asian Americans

Asian Americans also faced discrimination throughout American history and in 1882, Congress passed a law banning all Chinese immigrants. During World War II, more than 100,000 Japanese Americans were interned in concentration camps. In 1982, two American autoworkers beat Vincent Chin to death with a baseball bat because his assailants blamed him for the loss of jobs in the automotive manufacturing industry.

In the 1960s, activists demanded that the term "Asian American" replace the word "oriental," because it carried a stigma. Asian Americans also promoted a sense of pride in their cultural identity and successfully pushed for the creation of ethnic studies programs. Ellison Onizuka became the first Asian American astronaut in 1985, although he perished in the space shuttle Challenger disaster. In 1990, President George H.W. Bush declared May Asian Pacific American Heritage Month and Sheryl WuDunn became the first Asian American to win a Pulitzer Prize that same year.

Practice Questions

1. Which of the following documents outlawed slavery throughout the United States?
    a. U.S. Constitution
    b. Compromise of 1850
    c. Emancipation Proclamation
    d. 13th Amendment

2. What were the consequences of the Spanish-American War?
    a. The U.S. acquired colonies in the Caribbean and Pacific oceans.
    b. The U.S. acquired large swaths of territory in the Southwestern United States.
    c. It led to the formation of the League of Nations.
    d. It ended the Great Depression.

3. Which constitutional amendment gave women the right to vote in the United States?
    a. 15th
    b. 18th
    c. 19th
    d. 20th

4. What consequences did the Great Migration have?
    a. It led to conflict with Native Americans in the West in the 1800s.
    b. It led to increased racial tension in the North in the early 1900s.
    c. It led to increased conflict with Mexican immigrants in the 1900s.
    d. It led to increased conflict with Irish and German immigrants in the 1800s.

5. Which Supreme Court decision struck down the "separate but equal" doctrine?
    a. *Roe vs. Wade*
    b. *Brown vs. Board of Education*
    c. *Plessy vs. Ferguson*
    d. *Marbury vs. Madison*

6. Which of the following led to the American Revolution?
    a. The Stamp Act
    b. The Boston Massacre
    c. The Boston Tea Party
    d. All of the above

7. Which event(s) contributed to increasing sectional tension before the Civil War?
    a. Malcom X's death
    b. The "Bleeding Kansas" conflict
    c. The 13th Amendment
    d. Shay's Rebellion

8. Which of the following caused America to join World War I in 1917?
    a. Germany's unrestricted submarine warfare
    b. The destruction of the USS Maine
    c. The Japanese attack on Pearl Harbor
    d. Franz Ferdinand's death in 1914

9. What consequences did World War II have?
    a. It led to the creation of the League of Nations.
    b. It led to a communist revolution in Russia.
    c. It made the U.S. the only superpower in the world.
    d. None of the above.

10. Which event was the last major armed conflict between U.S. forces and Native Americans?
    a. Trail of Tears
    b. Tecumseh's War
    c. Massacre at Wounded Knee
    d. Battle of the Little Big Horn

11. What consequences did the Neolithic Revolution have?
    a. Native Americans domesticated cattle and horses.
    b. Native Americans began to grow crops.
    c. Native Americans developed steel weapons and tools.
    d. Native Americans began to emigrate to Canada.

12. Which document established the first system of government in the United States?
    a. Declaration of Independence
    b. Constitution
    c. Articles of Confederation
    d. Bill of Rights

13. What consequences did the New Deal have?
    a. It established a number of federal agencies and programs that continue to function in the 21st century.
    b. It led to a third political party.
    c. It established a two-term limit in the White House.
    d. It led to the Great Depression.

14. What is one advantage that the North had over the South during the Civil War?
    a. The North was defending their homes from damage.
    b. The North had free labor at home.
    c. The North had a larger navy.
    d. The North had more experienced military leaders.

15. In which of the following areas did the United State achieve victory during the Cold War?
    a. The Korean War
    b. The Space Race
    c. The Vietnam War
    d. The Battle of Gettysburg

16. The presidential cabinet has which of the following duties?
    a. Advise the president.
    b. Act as spokesperson for the U.S. government administration.
    c. Solicit donations for the president's re-election campaign.
    d. Preside over the Senate.

17. What organization helped Ronald Reagan win the White House in 1980?
    a. Great Awakening
    b. Moral Majority
    c. Know-Nothings
    d. Anti-Defamation League

18. Since 1965, most immigrants to the United States have come from what region(s)?
    a. Central and South America and Asia
    b. Australia
    c. Europe
    d. Antarctica

19. Which event helped sparked the gay and lesbian rights movement in 1969?
    a. The Stonewall Inn Riot
    b. The murder of Matthew Shepard
    c. The murder of Vincent Chin
    d. The emergence of AIDS

20. Which of the following were characteristics of the Gilded Age?
    a. Social inequality
    b. Increasing urbanization
    c. Expanding industrialization
    d. All of the above.

21. Which of the following were characteristics of the American political environment in the early 1900s?
    a. The Federalists and the Democratic Republicans
    b. The Populist Party and Progressive Reformers
    c. The Whig Party and the Democrat Party
    d. National Union Party and the Democrat Party

22. Which of the following motivated Christopher Columbus to sail across the Atlantic Ocean?
    a. A desire to establish a direct trade route to Asia.
    b. A desire to confirm the existence of America.
    c. A desire to prove the world was round.
    d. A desire to spread Judaism.

23. Which battle of the Revolutionary War was a key turning point in 1777 because it brought France into the war?
    a. The Battle of Lexington and Concord
    b. The Battle of Saratoga
    c. The Battle of Trenton
    d. The Battle of Bunker Hill

24. What did Radical Republicans hope to accomplish during Reconstruction?
    a. Equal rights for freed slaves.
    b. Leniency for former Confederates.
    c. Acquittal of President Johnson during impeachment.
    d. Effective segregation laws.

25. Which of the following were characteristics of the American economy after World War II?
    a. A return to the Great Depression.
    b. Increased use of computers.
    c. The decline of the Sun Belt.
    d. The fall of the stock market.

26. Which of the following agreements allowed territories to vote on whether or not they would become free or slave states?
    a. The Connecticut Compromise
    b. The Missouri Compromise
    c. The Compromise of 1850
    d. The Three-Fifths Compromise

27. Which of the following sets comprises a primary cause and effect of the American Revolution?
    a. A cause was the taxation of the colonies, and an effect was the civil rights movement.
    b. A cause was the Declaration of Independence, and an effect was the Constitution.
    c. A cause was the French and Indian War, and an effect was the Bill of Rights.
    d. A cause was the debate over slavery, and an effect was the Seven Years' War.

28. Which of the following statements about the U.S. Constitution is true?
    a. It was signed on July 4, 1776.
    b. It was enacted at the end of the Revolutionary War.
    c. New York failed to ratify it, but it still passed by majority.
    d. It replaced the Articles of Confederation.

Answer Explanations

1. D: 13th Amendment. The U.S. Constitution, Choice *A*, actually legalized slavery by counting slaves as three-fifths of a person. The Compromise of 1850, Choice *B*, banned the slave trade in Washington D.C. but also created a stronger fugitive slave law. The Emancipation Proclamation, Choice *C*, only banned slavery in the Confederacy. The 13th Amendment finally banned slavery throughout the country.

2. A: The Spanish-American War of 1898 made the U.S. a colonial power because it acquired many former Spanish colonies. The Mexican-American War of 1846-48 led to the acquisition of California, Nevada, Utah, Arizona, and New Mexico, Choice *B*. World War I led to the formation of the League of Nations in 1919, Choice *C*. The Great Depression ended when Americans joined World War II in 1941, Choice *D*.

3. C: The 19th amendment gave women the right to vote. The 15th Amendment, Choice *A*, gave blacks the right to vote. The 18th Amendment, Choice *B*, introduced alcohol prohibition. The 20th amendment, Choice *D*, repealed prohibition.

4. B: More than one million African Americans in the South went north in search of jobs during and after World War I. The Great Migration led to increased racial tension as blacks and whites competed for housing and jobs in northern cities. The Great Migration also led to the Harlem Renaissance.

5. B: *Brown vs. Board of Education* ruled that separate schools for blacks and whites were inherently unequal and sparked demands for more civil rights. *Roe v. Wade* in 1973, Choice *A*, increased access to abortion. *Plessy vs. Ferguson*, Choice *C*, established the "separate but equal" doctrine. *Marbury vs. Madison* in 1803, Choice *D*, established the doctrine of judicial review.

6. D: All three events led to increasing tension and conflict between the colonists and the British government, which finally exploded at the Battle of Lexington and Concord in 1775. The Stamp Act of 1765 imposed a tax on documents. It was repealed after colonists organized protests. The Boston Massacre resulted in the death of five colonists in 1770. The Boston Tea Party was a protest in 1773 against a law that hurt colonial tea merchants. The British responded to the tea party by punishing the colony of Massachusetts, which created fear among the other colonies and united them against the British government.

7. B: The "Bleeding Kansas" conflict contributed to sectional tension before the Civil War. The application of popular sovereignty in Kansas led to conflict as free-soil and pro-slavery forces rushed into the territory. Malcolm X's death, Choice *A*, was in 1965, almost 100 years after the Civil War ended. The 13th Amendment, Choice *C*, was ratified in 1865 and was approved at the very end of the Civil War. Shay's Rebellion, Choice *D*, was an uprising during 1786 and 1787 in Massachusetts.

8. A: Because the British naval blockade during World War I was so effective, Germany retaliated by using submarines to attack any ship bound for Britain or France. This led to the sinking of the RMS Lusitania in 1915, which killed more than 100 Americans. The destruction of the USS Maine, Choice *B*, sparked the Spanish-American War in 1898. The Japanese attack on Pearl Harbor in 1941, Choice *C*, brought America into World War II, not World War I. Franz Ferdinand's death in 1914, Choice *D*, sparked the outbreak of World War I, but America did not join the war until 1917.

9. D: World War I led to the League of Nations and the communist revolution in Russia, Choices *A* and *B*. The USSR and U.S. both emerged as two rival superpowers after World War II. It was thus a bipolar, rather than unipolar, world. The tension and mistrust between the U.S. and USSR eventually led to the Cold War, which ended in 1991.

10. C: Massacre at Wounded Knee. The Massacre at Wounded Knee in 1890 left at least 150 Native Americans dead, including many women and children, and was the last major engagement between Indians and American soldiers. The Trail of Tears, Choice *A*, involved the forced relocation of tribes from the American Southeast in the 1830s. Although thousands of Native Americans died along the way, it was not a battle. Tecumseh launched his uprising in 1811, Choice *B*, and conflict between Native Americans and U.S. soldiers would continue for decades as the country expanded further west. The Battle of Little Big Horn in 1876, Choice *D*, was a great Native American victory that led to the death of General Custer and more than 200 men.

11. B: Native Americans began to grow crops. During the Neolithic Revolution, Native Americans began to cultivate beans, squash, chilies, and other vegetables. However, they did not domesticate many large animals, Choice *A*—only the dog in North America and the llama in Central America. Horses and cattle only arrived in North America as a result of European exploration. Native Americans also did not develop steel or iron, Choice *C*—Native Americans only obtained these items by trading with Europeans. Despite these limits, Native Americans did develop a semi-sedentary lifestyle, formed social hierarchies, and created new religious beliefs.

12. C: Articles of Confederation. Issued in 1776, the Declaration of Independence, Choice *A*, explained why the colonists decided to break away from England but did not establish a government. That was left to the Articles of Confederation, which were adopted in 1781. The Articles of Confederation established a very weak central government that was replaced by the Constitution, Choice *B*, in 1789. It established a stronger executive branch. In 1791, the Bill of Rights, Choice *D*, amended the Constitution by guaranteeing individual rights.

13. A: The New Deal introduced a number of programs designed to increase regulation and boost the economy. Many of them remain in effect today, such as the Social Security Administration and the Securities and Exchange Commission. The New Deal also led to the Republican and Democratic parties to reverse their ideological positions on government intervention. It did not lead to a third party, Choice *B*. President Franklin D. Roosevelt was actually elected to four terms in office and the official two-term limit was not established until the 22nd Amendment was ratified in 1951. Until then, the two-term limit had been an informal custom established by President George Washington when he left office in 1797. Thus, Choice *C* is incorrect. Choice *D* is also incorrect. The Great Depression led to the New Deal, and not the other way around.

14. C: The North had a population of about 18.5 million while the South had only 5.5 million citizens and 3.5 million slaves. This meant the Union could more easily replace men while the Confederacy could not. The South was defending their homes from damage, since most of the war happened in the South, so Choice *A* is incorrect. Choice *B* is incorrect—the South had free labor at home, so they didn't have to worry about leaving their farms to go to war. Finally, Choice *D* is incorrect; the South had more experienced military leaders due to their participation in the Mexican-American War.

15. B: Although the United States initially lagged behind the Soviets, the U.S. successfully landed the first man on the Moon in 1969. However, the Korean War resulted in a stalemate in 1953, leaving Choice *A* incorrect. The Vietnam War, Choice *C*, was a defeat for U.S. forces. Despite sending more than 500,000 troops to Vietnam, the Vietnam War became increasingly unpopular and the United States eventually withdrew in 1973. The communist North Vietnamese eventually captured the southern capital of Saigon in 1975. Choice *D*, Battle of Gettysburg, is part of the Civil War.

16. D: Although the Constitution makes no provisions for a presidential cabinet, President George Washington created one when he took office. Members of the cabinet advise the president on a wide variety of issues including, but not limited to, defense, transportation, and education. The White House Press Secretary acts as spokesperson for the U.S. government administration, Choice *B*. The cabinet members are not required to raise money for the president's re-election effort, Choice *C*. The Vice President, not the cabinet, is who presides over the Senate, Choice *D*.

17. B: Conservative evangelicals formed the Moral Majority in 1979 in an effort to address issues like abortion. Their enthusiasm helped carry Reagan into the White House and bring the U.S. Senate under Republican control for the first time in twenty-eight years. The First Great Awakening, Choice *A*, occurred in the 1700s and the Second Great Awakening began in the 1800s. These movements encouraged Protestants to have a more personal connection to Christ. The Know-Nothings, Choice *C*, opposed Catholic immigration during the 1800s. The Anti-Defamation League, Choice *D*, focused on combating anti-Semitism and Holocaust deniers.

18. D: Congress passed immigration reform in 1965 that made it much easier for immigrants from Central and South America, as well as Asia, to enter the United States. During the colonial period, most immigrants came from Britain. During the mid-1800s, Irish and German immigrants became more numerous. That changed again around 1900 when an influx of immigrants from Southern and Eastern Europe began.

19. A: The Stonewall Inn Riot in 1969 helped ignite the gay and lesbian rights movement when patrons fought back against a police raid. The site became a national monument in 2016. Although he became an icon of the gay and lesbian rights movement, Matthew Shepard was murdered in 1998. Thus, Choice *B* is incorrect. The murder of Vincent Chin, Choice *C*, in 1982, became a rallying cry for Asian American activists. The gay and lesbian rights movement was well established when activists campaigned to raise awareness of AIDS during the 1980s and 1990s, making Choice *D* incorrect.

20. D: Mark Twain called the late 1800s the Gilded Age because the appearance of extreme wealth covered up massive social inequality. While many wealthy industrialists became very rich, many workers worked in poor conditions for low wages. The onset of the Second Industrial Revolution led to an expansion of the chemical, telecommunications, and metallurgical industries. Urbanization also increased during this period as workers crowded into cities in search of work.

21. B: Progressive reformers sought to remedy some of the abuses that emerged during the Gilded Age. They wanted to break up monopolies that interfered with economic competition. Muckraking journalists, including Upton Sinclair and Jacob Riis, also exposed political corruption and social inequality. The Populist Party sought political reforms that would alleviate the plight of farmers and the working class, such as the abolition of national banks and government regulation of railroads.

22. A: King Ferdinand and Queen Isabella agreed to support his mission because he promised to establish a direct trade route to Asia that would allow European merchants to bypass Middle Eastern middlemen. Columbus had no idea that America existed, Choice *B*, and he believed he had landed in India when he arrived in the Caribbean. That's why he mistakenly called the natives *Indians*. It is a common myth that Columbus sought to prove experts wrong by showing them the world was round, not flat. Most European thinkers already knew the world was round, making Choice *C* incorrect. Choice *D* is also incorrect; Christopher Columbus practiced the Christian faith, not Judaism.

23. B: Battle of Saratoga. The Battles of Lexington and Concord marked the start of the American Revolution in 1775. The Battle of Bunker Hill in 1775 was a defeat for the Patriot cause but showed they could stand up to the British army. The Battle of Trenton in 1776 bolstered morale in the Continental army but was not as significant as the Battle of Saratoga in 1777. In this engagement, the Continental army captured thousands of British troops. This victory convinced the French king to support the Patriot cause and his military aid was an important factor in the success of the American Revolution.

24. A: Radical Republicans wanted to ensure that recently freed slaves had the economic and political rights that would enable them to achieve self-sufficiency in the post-Civil War era. Democrats, such as Andrew Johnson, preferred leniency towards the South while Radical Republicans wanted a harsher punishment, making Choice *B* incorrect. This led to conflict between Johnson and Radical Republicans who almost succeeded in having him impeached in 1868.

25. B: World War II brought about an end to the Great Depression by switching over to wartime production. After the end of World War II, consumer demand remained high and unemployment was usually low. Computers began to become more powerful, efficient, and inexpensive in the latter part of the 20th century, and they became more common in business. The Sun Belt actually expanded after World War II as the traditional manufacturing base in the North and Midwest fell into decline. Land was cheaper in the South and West and wages were also lower too, so these regions were very attractive to businesses.

26. C: The Compromise of 1850. The Connecticut Compromise, Choice *A*, formed the basis for the Constitution by proposing a bicameral Congress. The Missouri Compromise, Choice *B*, banned slavery north of the 36°30' parallel in the Louisiana Territory. The Compromise of 1850 essentially undid the Missouri Compromise by introducing popular sovereignty, which allowed voters in territories to decide whether or not the state constitution would ban slavery. The Three-Fifths Compromise, Choice *D*, counted slaves as three-fifths of a human being when allocating representatives.

27. C: The Declaration of Independence occurred during the American Revolution, so it should therefore be considered an effect, not a cause. Similarly, slavery was a cause for the later Civil War, but it was not a primary instigator for the Revolutionary War. Although a single event can have many effects long into the future, it is also important to not overstate the influence of these individual causes; the civil rights movement was only tangentially connected to the War of Independence among many other factors, and therefore it should not be considered a primary effect of it. The French and Indian War (also known as the Seven Years' War) and the Bill of Rights, on the other hand, were respectively a cause and effect from the American Revolution, making Choice *C* the correct answer.

28. D: The Constitution was signed in 1787; the Declaration of Independence was signed in 1776. It was successfully ratified by all the current states, including New York. Finally, the Articles of Confederation was established at the end of the American Revolution; the Constitution would replace the articles years later due to issues with the government's structure.

Texas History

Exploration and Colonization

Pre-Colonial Texas

Texas was home to Paleoindians during the prehistoric period. In fact, people have lived in Texas for over 12,000 years. Anthropologists and archaeologists working in Texas have discovered artifacts of the Clovis culture that developed in North America some 11,000-12,000 years ago. During the First Agricultural Revolution, many hunter-gatherers of nomadic Paleoindian groups began to settle permanently or semi-permanently in Texas. These earliest Native American groups included the Karankawas, the Coahuiltecans, the Caddos, the Witchitas, the Atakapas, the Jumanos, the Tonkawas, and the Apaches. Additionally, many Native Americans resettled in Texas during the era of Indian Removal and Manifest Destiny. These included the Comanches and Kiowas.

First Contact and Colonial Texas

In the 1500s, Spanish conquistadors and French settlers began exploring the Gulf Coast region. In 1519, Spanish explorer Alonso Alvarez de Pineda became one of the first conquistadors to probe the Texas coast. There is no evidence that he reached the Texas mainland, but his expedition increased Spanish interest in Texas. Spanish explorer Panfilo de Narvaez's expedition became the first to explore the Texas mainland, albeit accidentally. During this expedition, Narvaez's ships wrecked, and explorer Alvar Nunez Cabeza de Vaca was taken in by Karankawa Indians. This first contact, which occurred in 1528, encouraged Cabeza de Vaca to continue his travels, even after he was captured and placed in captivity by Coahuiltecan Indians. Between 1528 and 1536, Cabeza de Vaca and a band of other shipwrecked survivors wandered across Texas and modern-day Mexico. Eventually they reached Mexico City in 1536 with the help of Spanish soldiers they encountered on their journey.

Cabeza de Vaca later published an account of his expedition, which caught the attention of Spanish viceroys and explorers. This led conquistador Francisco Vasquez de Coronado to embark on a journey with a force of over 1,300 men in 1540 in search of gold. While Coronado never found gold, he and his men did become some of the first Europeans to see the Grand Canyon and travel through modern-day West Texas. By the 1600s, after years of expeditions, the Spanish colonial government began establishing missions along the frontiers of modern-day Mexico, New Mexico, California, and Texas. Some settlements sprouted up along the Rio Grande in South Texas. French explorer Robert de La Salle led several expeditions in East Texas in the 1680s. Control over East Texas shifted hands from the Spanish and French on multiple occasions in the late 1600s and early 1700s until Spain took possession due to the missionary efforts of men like Father Francisco Hidalgo, a Franciscan priest who established missions in East Texas for the Spanish crown. Throughout the 1700s, Spain continued to establish missions, presidios, and ranches throughout Texas. Life in Spanish Texas during this era was marked by extreme isolation, loose government control, and border skirmishes. The Spanish crown had a hard time controlling the region based on its remoteness and a lack of manpower.

The Mexican National Period

Following Mexican independence from Spain in September 1821, Texas became part of the new Republic of Mexico. Young Tejano ranchers, now generations removed from their grandparents' settlement in the region, became the new lifeblood of Texas under Mexican national rule. During this era, Texas became a key frontier for both Mexico and the United States. The Mexican government created plans to colonize the region while many Anglo-Americans also founded frontier homes on Mexican land. Catalyzed by the free labor of slaves, farming and ranching became the economic cornerstones of the regions. Gradually, Texans established a unique cultural identity that resisted the loose control of the Mexican Republic.

Revolution and the Republic of Texas

Eventually, Mexican and Texan identities became so distinct that the Texans decided to rebel against the centralist Mexican government. The ensuing Texas Revolution, which took place in 1835 and 1836, allowed Texas to declare independence from Mexico. A flood of United States volunteers assisted in helping Texans to found the Republic of Texas, which officially received its independence via the Consultation of 1836. The Republic of Texas was a short-lived nation because its people quickly accepted annexation by the United States of America in 1845.

U.S. Annexation and the Mexican-American War

President John Tyler initiated an annexation bill in March 1845, which President James K. Polk officially signed in December 1845. The Republic of Texas officially revoked its sovereignty, lawfully agreeing to become the 28th state of the Union in February 1846. The Mexican-American War (1846-1848), in many ways, was a direct response to President Polk's annexation of Texas. The war ended in the Treaty of Guadalupe, which resulted in a Mexican Cession that officially brought parts of Texas, New Mexico, Arizona, and California within the territory of the United States. One social impact of U.S. annexation and the Mexican-American War was increased political tensions over the role of slavery in new territories.

Independence, Statehood, Civil War Reconstruction, and Aftermath

Mexico Becoming an Independent Nation

When Mexico won independence from Spain in 1821, Texas—which used to be a frontier region in the Spanish colony—became part of the Mexican Republic. Few Mexican residents occupied this frontier region prior to independence, so there were not that many permanent settlements in Texas during the early Mexican Republic. The Mexican government understood that the climate and large amount of available space in Texas made it an ideal region for colonization and a budding ranching industry. Thus, the Mexican government encouraged people to migrate to Texas. Many of the immigrants who relocated to Texas were actually Anglo-Americans. These Anglo-American frontiersmen helped Mexico ward off attacks from the Native Americans. Moreover, they strengthened the local economy through ranching, farming, and paying taxes. The Mexican government created an *empresario* system to attract even more immigrants. *Empresarios* were land agents who helped settlers acquire land in Texas. Among these *empresarios* was future Texas revolutionary Stephen F. Austin. Austin persuaded Anglo-American settlers to move to the northern frontier of Mexico in exchange for large land acquisitions. These immigration policies laid the groundwork for the Texas Revolution. Many of the Anglo-American settlers ignored Mexican laws; others arrived illegally and maintained allegiances to the United States of America. The Mexican government tried to end immigration by passing the anti-immigration Law of April 6, 1830. Although the law did little to control illegal immigration, it did successfully instill discontent and distrust in the Anglo-American settlers of Texas. This discontent and distrust eventually led Texas to its independence.

Texas Revolution

By 1833, Anglo-American immigrants and their Tejano counterparts had begun to embody a growing sense of separateness along Mexico's frontier region in Texas. These settlers were grounded in revolutionary republican principles and became very independent minded when it came to their relationship with the federal government in Mexico City. These settlers disregarded many Mexican laws and capitalized on the fact that the federal government maintained little control over their territory. Prominent leaders in the region, such as David Burnet, called for the residents of Texas to separate from the Mexican Republic. Since the Mexican government hardly ever defended these frontiersmen, they were used to creating their own militias and defending themselves. Tejanos such as Juan Seguin and Ambrosio Rodriguez joined in the resistance, noting that the Law of April 6, 1830, not only threatened the liberty of Anglo-Americans in the region, but also the liberty of Tejanos.

As tensions increased, the Mexican government and military tried to assert greater control over the region. In September and October of 1835, the Mexican military arrived at the settlement of Gonzales to reclaim a cannon that was issued by the federal government. The ensuing skirmish between Mexicans and Texans over a government-issued cannon paved the way for the Texas Revolution. The Texans antagonized the Mexican military with the defiant slogan "Come and take it!" And as the Mexican army did, indeed, try to "take it" on October 2, 1835, Texas citizens fought back under the leadership of John Henry Moore. Shots were fired that day, making the Texas Revolution a violent reality. Following the events of Gonzales and the infamous Battle at the Alamo, fifty-nine Texan delegates gathered at Washington-on-the-Brazos for an assembly that would be remembered as the Convention of 1836. At this convention, on March 2, 1836, the fifty-nine delegates officially declared independence from the Mexican Republic. The Republic of Texas was born, but was not fully conceived until the final shots were fired at the Battle of San Jacinto on April 21, 1836. The Texans won this battle, bringing about an official end to the Texas Revolution.

Republic of Texas and Early Texas Statehood

The Republic of Texas only lasted a short ten years, from 1836 to 1846. However, these short years were rich with a unique history and culture. The Treaties of Valesco—which were signed on May 14, 1836—officially ended Texas's war with Mexico, at least in the eyes of the United States and Texas. Nevertheless, the Mexican government refused to initially recognize the terms of the treaties, stating that President Santa Anna was no longer an official representative of the federal government as a prisoner of war. Tensions, therefore, continued with Mexico, although the war remained behind both nations for nearly a decade. David G. Burnet—the interim president of the Republic of Texas—eventually stepped down as the nation's leader following the ratification of the Constitution of 1836 and the election of 1836. The constitutional committee elected Sam Houston as the first president and Mirabeau B. Lamar as the first vice president. The committee also debated U.S. annexation, with many delegates expressing a desire to make Texas a part of the United States of America.

For ten years, however, Texas remained its own independent nation. Following the revolution, the Republic of Texas faced new challenges under the leadership of its first and only presidents: Sam Houston, Mirabeau B. Lamar, and Anson Jones. Economically, the Republic of Texas struggled post independence. The war had accrued a large amount of debt. Texas was threatened on its borders by the expansionist policies of the U.S. government, Native American skirmishes, and the bitter sentiment of the Mexican government. The Republic of Texas opened its borders to thousands of immigrants from the United States and Mexico, which diversified its demographics. By December 29, 1845, this diversified body of Texas citizens decided that it was time for Texas to become the twenty-eighth state of the United States of America. Annexation presented new challenges, including a U.S. war with Mexico. The earliest years of statehood were therefore tied to war and transition, as the Republic of Texas evolved into the Lone Star State. During these early years of statehood, thousands of Americans flocked to the fertile soil and mild climates of the twenty-eighth state of the Union.

Civil War and Reconstruction in Texas

By 1860, cotton had become the leading crop in the Lone Star State. Texas helped cotton become king in the American South, shipping hundreds of thousands of cotton bales out of crucial gulf ports such as Houston and Galveston. From Houston and Galveston, the cotton bales set sail to the industrial northeast or Europe. Texas helped make cotton the "white gold" of America, but not without cost. The cotton industry was built on the backs of enslaved African Americans. These African Americans helped whites and Tejanos in Texas amass great fortunes on their vast Southern plantations. As the debate over slavery and abolition waged on in the late 1850s and early 1860s, most Texans concluded that slavery was a necessary and essential component to the booming Texas economy. These Texans saw abolition as a direct threat to their personal prosperity.

Following the election of Abraham Lincoln in 1860, the citizens and politicians of Texas voted to secede from the Union. Residents in Texas were overwhelmingly in support of Texas joining the Confederate States of America. The governor at that time—Sam Houston—openly lamented this decision. After he refused to take an oath of loyalty to the Confederate States of America, Texans removed him from office. Growing divisions over states' rights and slavery placed Texas right at the heart of the imminent American Civil War. During the Civil War, Texans participated in such key coastal battles as the Battle of Galveston and the Battle of Sabine Pass. These battles along the Gulf Coast placed Texas at the heart of the Confederacy's "cotton diplomacy," which used cotton shipments and boycotts to seduce the British as allies. Although this diplomacy essentially failed, Texas continued to use its cottonclads (ironclads used for cotton shipments) in naval battles. Texas maintained ties with the Confederacy all the way to the war's close in 1863, and some Texans declared their ties to the Confederacy well into the era of Reconstruction.

Effects of Reconstruction on Texas

Following the war, many Texans rebelled against Reconstructionist policies by joining such white-supremacist terrorist groups as the Ku Klux Klan (KKK). During postwar Reconstruction, the power of the KKK seeped into the governmental structures of Texas, forcing many politicians, such as Senators Matthew Gaines and George T. Ruby, to fight back against the crimes committed by KKK members and politicians. Prior to the Civil War, Democrats dominated Texas politics, but during the era of Reconstruction, radical Republicans held the most power in the Texas legislature. This temporary control, however, ended following the heated election of 1873. This election allowed Democrats, under the leadership of Governor Richard Coke, a former Confederate soldier, to regain Texas politics by a landslide. This election witnessed a dramatic sociocultural shift toward a staunchly segregationist Texas in the Jim Crow South. Economically speaking, this antiblack sentiment placed freed African Americans back into exploitative labor situations. Slavery gave way to tenant farming and sharecropping in the cotton fields of Texas. The tenant farming and sharecropping systems of agriculture placed many freed African Americans into substantial debt to large landowners. Essentially, although they were free, they became "waged slaves."

Expansion of Settlement Along the Frontier in Texas

Throughout the 1860s, many Native American groups along the frontiers of Texas took advantage of the absence of frontiersmen during the Civil War. The outbreak of the American Civil War offered an opportunity for many Plains Indians groups to reestablish their foothold in northern, central, and western Texas. Comanche groups raided settlements around the Fredericksburg region of Hill Country during this time. Once frontiersmen returned from battles in the Civil War, they often returned to violent fights with Native American groups. During this time, many former Union solders were also stationed in Texas to carry out Reconstructionist policies and protect the frontier. Between the 1860s and 1880s, several wars between the U.S. Army and Native Americans erupted across the landscape of Texas. The 1860s to 1880s witnessed several wars, battles, and raids such as the Elm Creek Raid (1864), the Salt Creek Raid (1971), the Mackenzie's Raids (1871), the Red River War (1874), the Battle of Adobe Walls (1874), and the Battle of Palo Duro Canyon (1874). This era also saw the creation of many treaties and peace policies that forced thousands of Native Americans onto reservations in the West. The expansionist efforts of settlers and troops in Texas assisted with the widespread slaughter of the buffalo. This slaughter angered Native American groups who depended on the buffalo for survival.

Economic and Technological Developments in Texas in the Period 1821 to 1900

The advent of steam power and steamboats in the early 1800s marked the beginning of a transportation revolution in Texas and the broader North American continent. These steam-powered ships were used not only to transport cotton across the rivers and along the coasts of Texas, but they were also used during the battles of the Civil War. Ironclads and cottonclads assisted the Confederate navy in its war with the Union. Steam, however, marked only the beginning of Texas's transportation revolution. The railroad boom, on the other hand, sent Texas and the United States of America chugging at Godspeed toward modernity. The railroad boom in Texas took place between 1870 and 1900. In the beginning, only around five hundred miles of tracks were laid. By the turn of the century, there were nearly ten thousand railroad tracks across the state. Locomotives brought travelers and settlers across the state. With the advent of electricity and electrical power plants in the 1880s, Texas also saw its fair share of electrified streetcars across the main streets of the Lone Star State. New technologies brought new industries to Texas, including an increasingly technological Texas agricultural industry. Commercial farming—a product of technological advancement—slowly became the economic backbone of the state. Mills, mines, meatpacking plants, and factories also sprouted up in Texas during the broader Industrial Revolution of the nineteenth century. But by the late 1800s, it became clear that Texas had found its new gold: oil. The budding automobile and gasoline industries of the late 1800s and early 1900s made Texas into the petroleum capital of the United States of America. Oil became big business in Texas, drawing thousands of workers and their families to the Lone Star State.

Geographic Features of Texas

The varied geographic landscapes of Texas state have impacted migration, settlement patterns, and economic development in different ways. Moreover, these varied landscapes have led to different methods for altering the natural environment. The plains in parts of west, central, and north Texas have lent themselves to agriculture and ranching throughout history. These plains have historically hosted the production of cotton, wheat, and sorghum. Additionally, they have become ranching and meatpacking centers. Ranches and farms in Texas are usually divided into large tracts of land, and at times, this can lead to land disputes. The rolling hills and valleys of Hill Country have made Texas a center for vineyards and wine making. Hill Country also produces peaches and pecans depending on the season. East Texas maintains more of a Gulf Coast climate, making it perfect for rice fields and oil refineries. Texas oil production has littered the Gulf Coast with large, mechanical refineries and plants. Cities like Dallas, Austin, San Antonio, and Houston maintain their own unique relationships with the land, setting aside large plots for urban infrastructure. These cities, which are currently experiencing a period of rapid growth, have ravaged the land for the sake of roadways, river walks, and railroads.

Cultural Developments in Texas in the Period 1821 to 1900

Between 1821 and 1900, Texas shifted its national identity on several occasions: It went from being a region in the Mexican Republic to its own Republic of Texas to part of the United States of America to part of the Confederate States of America and back to being part of the Union. It witnessed the collateral postwar years following the Mexican Revolution, the heart of the Texas Revolution and Mexican-American War, and the reverberations of the Civil War and the Spanish-American War. During this time, Texas's identity shifted with its national allegiances and its conflicts. Texas became a unified yet conflicted state. Its boundaries were formed and re-formed, and its identity was constantly in flux. Yet there remained a cultural strain through all these years of revolution and conflict: The Lone Star State became a symbol of American perseverance and diversity. Texas remains one of the most diverse states due to these historical foundations. Mexican and Southern culture still reign supreme. In these years, Texas also transitioned from being an agricultural state to an industrial hub. The discovery of oil in Texas made it one of the wealthiest industrializing beacons at the turn of the century. These cultural developments created a stubborn sense of independence in the state psyche, but they also tied Texas closer to the broader American Dream. Texas became the center of heated debates over war and peace, colonization and liberation, abolition and slavery, national progress and moral regression, state rights and federal rights, local control and federal power, and industrialization and deindustrialization. These cultural fibers made Texas into a cross-cultural and intercultural tapestry of the American psyche.

Texas in the 20th and 21st Centuries

Reform Movements in Texas in the Late Nineteenth and Twentieth Centuries

The Progressive movement in Texas was led by such reform-minded legislators as Alexander W. Terrell, the sponsor of the forward-looking Terrell Election Law of 1905. This law attacked election fraud and established primary elections to choose state, district, and county officials. The law of 1905 preceded such democratic federal voting changes as the Seventeenth Amendment (1913), which allowed for the direct election of U.S. senators by the American people. Progressives in Texas and beyond looked to also reform labor, education, urban planning, health care, women's rights/suffrage, and rampant alcoholism. The culminating reform of the Progressive movement was the passage of the Eighteenth and Nineteenth Amendments, which respectively instituted prohibition and mandated women's suffrage. These progressive reforms, however, also had their limits: The era witnessed a rise in poll taxes and interracial violence as many African Americans were either illegally, financially, or extralegally banned from the polls.

The failures of these reforms paved the way to the Long Civil Rights Movement that gained steam in the 1920s and reached its pinnacle in the 1960s. In Texas and beyond, the civil rights movement manifested itself most noticeably in the desegregation of public space and public schooling. The civil rights movement expanded to include rights in other communities such as the American Indian community, the Hispanic community, and the LGBTQ community. The civil rights fervor of the early to mid-1960s eventually led to race riots in the late 1960s, exposing the world to the necessity of even more reforms.

Impact of World War I, the Great Depression, World War II, and the Cold War on Texas

During World War I, Texas slowly urbanized as the Lone Star State's economy expanded to meet the needs of the United States' blossoming military-industrial complex. Throughout the Great War, Texans supplied U.S. forces with the oil, lumber, minerals, and agricultural products they needed to sustain military battles across the Atlantic Ocean. Wartime production inaugurated an economic boom that encouraged thousands of Texas farmers to borrow more land and equipment to create larger commercial farms. Texas transformed from a rural state to a largely urban state throughout the twentieth century.

The growing military-industrial complex encouraged many Texans to assume new jobs in factories, plants, and offices across the state. The booming oil and commercial farming industries brought hundreds of thousands of migrants and immigrants to Texas soil. These economic excesses paved the way to the economic busts and social unrests of the Great Depression. The postwar 1920s witnessed continued growth followed by a stark economic decline brought about by the stock market crash in 1929. The 1930s in Texas, like much of the United States, was marked by industry crises, rampant unemployment, and agricultural devastation brought on by the Dust Bowl. Some New Deal programs helped stave off hunger, unemployment, and economic devastation in Texas, but in reality, it was the wartime economy of the Second World War that brought Texas and the rest of the country out of the Depression.

Texas's budding aerospace industry thrived during World War II. The military-industrial complex in Texas expanded even more rapidly during World War II than it did during World War I. Texas also urbanized more rapidly in the years following the Second World War. The ensuing Cold War with the Soviet Union made Texas one of the country's postwar military-industrial juggernauts. The defense industry and the National Aeronautics and Space Administration (NASA) in Houston placed Texas at the epicenter of a global Space Race. High-tech industries flocked to Texas between 1950 and 1980, contributing to urban growth in the broader Sunbelt region of the South. Texas played a critical role in placing the first man on the moon and contributed to the scientific advances and technologies necessary to continue exploring space throughout the Cold War.

Major Events in Texas in the Latter Half of the Twentieth and Early Twenty-First Centuries

Following the boom and bust of the oil industry in the 1970s and 1980s, Texas and other states scrambled to diversify their economies. This diversification was built on the backs of the Richards, Bush, and Perry gubernatorial administrations. Texas, like much of the Sunbelt South, struggled to cope with the deindustrialized changes brought about by the passage of the North American Free Trade Agreement (NAFTA) in 1994. Unlike the Rust Belt North, however, Texas experienced a slight economic boom in the decades following the decline of industry. Cities like Dallas, Austin, and San Antonio became centers for a dramatic growth in telecommunications, computers, and high-tech manufacturing. NAFTA also catalyzed trade between these cities and Mexico to the South. During this time, Texas developed one of the United States' leading medical technology industries. Tourism and retail trade also became a cornerstone in the region, thanks to the influx of immigrants and visitors. As the economy diversified, so did the populace—thousands of immigrants and migrants flocked to the urban hubs of Texas to find new jobs in the booming economy.

Alteration of the Natural Environment from 1900 to the Present

The processes of industrialization, urbanization, and suburbanization throughout the early to mid-twentieth century inevitably affected the natural landscapes and environments of the Lone Star State.

The rapid urban growth of Texas cities in the earliest years of the twentieth century made it difficult for city governments to provide the necessary services to construct sewers and collect garbage. Some Texas cities grew at such a rapid rate that they were unable to provide basic infrastructure such as a sustainable water supply. Public health became a concern as poor infrastructure and pollution led to high rates of death from disease. Eventually, reforms and infrastructural changes helped alleviate Texas of these public health concerns, but continued population expansion over the last century has often come at the cost of the environment. To sustain the blossoming populations of Texas cities, many dams had to be built. These dams have helped supply thousands of residents with water, but often at the expense of local ecosystems. Plenty of plants and animals have had their natural habitats destroyed by the ever-growing force of Texas urbanization.

At first, urbanization in Texas was sustained by the forces of industrialization. Specifically, Texas cities have been able to grow, thanks to advances in industrial technologies. Electricity—which first came to Texas via the construction of an electric power plant in Galveston in the early 1880s—revolutionized the way Texans communicated, traveled, and manufactured goods. By the early 1920s, Texas became the leader in electric streetcar transit systems for states located west of the Mississippi River. These streetcars established Texas's first major suburbs. Electricity also lit up the budding skyscraper systems in cities such as Waco and Dallas.

The explosion of the petroleum and gasoline industry in Texas helped catalyze automobile manufacturing in the early 1900s. Eventually, rails gave way to paved roadways, as cities abandoned streetcars for Henry Ford's mass-produced Model T. As Texas became one of the oil capitals of the world throughout the twentieth century, it paved the way to the creation of suburbs and superhighways. These developments coincided with growth of the commercial agriculture industry in Texas. Electricity, oil, and gasoline fueled large-scale commercial farms that shipped produce, dairy, poultry, and meats from remote rural locations to thriving urban and suburban centers of development. The creation of suburbs and superhighways cut across the once-pristine prairies and hills of Texas, destroying the natural environment.

Eventually, manufacturing, commercial farming, and the oil industry packed their bags for foreign soil in the 1970s to 1990s, contributing to rampant deindustrialization. Texas, benefitting from the rise of the Sunbelt economy, was not delivered a direct blow by deindustrialization, but still felt the reverberations from America's Rust Belt. The result was a decrease in jobs and an increase in abandoned manufacturing sectors. Today, across Texas and most of the United States, one can still witness the aftermath of deindustrialization—dilapidated factories and farms pepper the natural American landscape with decaying scenes of the past.

Computer Technology, Transportation, and Medical Research in Texas

Thanks to its dedication to high-tech improvements in computer technology, transportation, and medical research, Texas experienced a slight economic boom in the decades following the decline of the oil industry. Cities like Houston, Dallas-Fort Worth, Austin, and San Antonio blossomed into southwestern hubs for the tech industries. The Dallas-Fort Worth metroplex, for instance, became one of the leading centers for the nation's growth in telecommunications, computers, and high-tech manufacturing. Hosting over five hundred tech companies, the Dallas-Fort Worth metroplex became a leader in telecommunications, employing nearly seventy thousand people in tech alone. Recently, Austin has also become a magnet for the tech industry. This has shifted the social demographics of the region, bringing in more young professionals, immigrants, and migrants. Medical research, in particular, has boomed alongside the tech industry, as places like Dallas, Austin, and Houston have become leaders in medical technology and health care.

Geography, Culture, and the Behavioral and Social Sciences

Physical Geography Concepts, Natural Processes, and Earth's Physical Features

Physical Region

Soils and River Systems

The Earth's surface, like many other things in the broader universe, does not remain the same for long; in fact, it changes from day to day. The Earth's surface is subject to a variety of physical processes that continue to shape its appearance. In each process, water, wind, temperature, or sunlight play a role in continually altering the Earth's surface.

Erosion can be caused by a variety of different stimuli including ice, snow, water, wind, and ocean waves. *Wind erosion* is a specific phenomenon that occurs in generally flat, dry areas with loose topsoil. Over time, the persistent winds can dislodge significant amounts of soil into the air, reshaping the land and wreaking havoc on those who depend on agriculture for their livelihoods. Erosion can also be caused by water and is responsible for changing landscapes as well. For example, the Grand Canyon was carved over thousands of years by the constant movement of the Colorado River. Over time, the river moved millions of tons of soil, cutting a huge gorge in the Earth along the way. In all cases, erosion involves the movement of soil from one place to another. In water erosion, material carried by the water is referred to as *sediment*. With time, some sediment can collect at the mouths of rivers, forming *deltas*, which become small islands of fertile soil. This process of detaching loose soils and transporting them to a different location where they remain for an extended period of time is referred to as *deposition*, and is the end result of the erosion process.

In contrast to erosion, *weathering* does not involve the movement of any outside stimuli. In this physical process, the surface of the Earth is either broken down physically or chemically. *Physical weathering* involves the effects of atmospheric conditions such as water, ice, heat, or pressure. Through the process of weathering over the course of centuries, large rocks can be broken down with the effects of icy conditions. *Chemical weathering* generally occurs in warmer climates and involves organic material that breaks down rocks, minerals, or soil. This process is what scientists believe led to the creation of fossil fuels such as oil, coal, and natural gas.

Climate

Weather is defined as the condition of the Earth's atmosphere at a particular time. *Climate* is different; instead of focusing on one particular day, climate is the relative pattern of weather in a place for an extended period of time. For example, the city of Atlanta is in the American South and generally has a humid subtropical climate; however, Atlanta also occasionally experiences snowstorms in the winter months. Despite the occasional snow and sleet storm, over time, geographers, meteorologists, and other Earth scientists have determined the patterns that are indicative to north Georgia, where Atlanta is located. Almost all parts of the world have predictable climate patterns, which are influenced by the surrounding geography.

The Central Coast of California is an example of a place with a predictable climate pattern. Santa Barbara, California, one of the region's larger cities, has almost the same temperature for most of the summer, spring, and fall, with only minimal fluctuation during the winter months. The temperatures there, which average between 75 and 65 degrees Fahrenheit daily regardless as to the time of year, are influenced by a variety of different climatological factors including elevation, location relative to the mountains and ocean, and ocean currents. In the case of Santa Barbara, the city's location on the Pacific Coast and its position near mountains heavily influences its climate. The cold California current, which sweeps down the west coast of the United States, causes the air near the city to be temperate, while the mountains trap cool air over the city and the surrounding area. This pattern, known as the *orographic effect*, or *rain shadow*, also affects temperatures on the leeward side of the mountains by blocking most of the cool air and causing dry conditions to dominate. Temperatures can fluctuate by more than 20 degrees Fahrenheit on opposite sides of the mountain.

Other factors affecting climate include elevation, prevailing winds, vegetation, and latitudinal position on the globe.

Physical Processes

Earth is a complex system of the atmosphere (air), hydrosphere (water), as well as continental land (land). All work together to support the biosphere (life).

The atmosphere is divided into several layers: the troposphere, stratosphere, mesosphere, and thermosphere. The troposphere is at the bottom and is about seven and a half miles thick. Above the troposphere is the 30-mile-thick stratosphere. Above the stratosphere is the mesosphere, a 20-mile layer, followed by the thermosphere, which is more than 300 miles thick.

The troposphere is closest to Earth and has the greatest pressure due to the pull of gravity on its gas particles as well as pressure from the layers above. 78 percent of the atmosphere is made of nitrogen. Surprisingly, the oxygen that we breathe only makes up 21 percent of the gases, and the carbon dioxide critical to insulating Earth makes up less than 1 percent of the atmosphere. There are other trace gases present in the atmosphere, including water vapor.

Although the stratosphere has minimal wind activity, it is critical for supporting the biosphere because it contains the ozone layer, which absorbs the sun's damaging ultra-violet rays and protects living organisms. Due to its low level of air movement, airplanes travel in the stratosphere. The mesosphere contains few gas particles, and the gas levels are so insignificant in the thermosphere that it is considered space.

Visible light is colors reflecting off particles. If all colors reflect, we see white; if no colors reflect, we see black. This means a colored object is reflecting only that color—a red ball reflects red light and absorbs other colors.

Because the thermosphere has so few particles to reflect light rays (photons), it appears black. The troposphere appears blue in the day, and various shades of yellow and orange at sunset due to the angle of the sun hitting particles that refract, or bend, the light. In certain instances, the entire visible spectrum can be seen in the form of rainbows. Rainbows occur when sunlight passes through water droplets and is refracted in many different directions by the water particles.

The hydrosphere, or water-containing portion of the Earth's surface, plays a major role in supporting the biosphere. In the picture below, a single water molecule (molecular formula H_2O) looks like a mouse head. The small ears of the mouse are the two hydrogen atoms connected to the larger oxygen atom in the middle.

Each hydrogen atom has one proton (positively charged, like the plus end of a magnet) in its nucleus (center), while oxygen has eight protons in its center. Hydrogen also has only one electron (negatively charged, like the minus end of a magnet) orbiting around the nucleus. Because hydrogen has only one proton, its electron is pulled more toward the oxygen nucleus (more powerful magnet). This makes hydrogen exist without an electron most of the time, so it is positively charged. On the other hand, oxygen often has two extra electrons (one from each hydrogen), so it is negatively charged. These bonds between the oxygen and hydrogen are called covalent bonds.

This charged situation is what makes water such a versatile substance; it also causes different molecules of water to interact with each other.

Water molecules in solid ice.   Water molecules in liquid water.   Water molecules in water vapour - a gas.

In a solid form (ice), water lines up in a crystal structure because the positive hydrogen atoms prefer to be next to the negative oxygen atoms that belong to other water molecules. These attractions are represented by the blue lines in the molecular picture of ice above. As heat is added and the ice melts, the water molecules have more kinetic energy and move faster; therefore, they are unable to perfectly arrange in the lattice structure of ice and turn into liquid. If enough heat is added, the water molecules will have so much kinetic energy they vaporize into gas. At this point, there are no bonds holding the water together because the molecules aren't close enough.

Notice how ice in its intricate arrangement has more space between the particles than liquid water, which shows that the ice is less dense than water. This contradicts the scientific fact that solids are denser than liquids. In water's case only, the solid will float due to a lower density! This is significant for the hydrosphere, because if temperatures drop to lower than freezing, frozen water will float to the surface of lakes or oceans and insulate the water underneath so that life can continue in liquid water. If ice was not less dense than liquid water, bodies of water would freeze from the bottom up and aquatic ecosystems would be trapped in a block of ice.

The hydrosphere has two components: seawater and freshwater (less than 5 percent of the hydrosphere). Water covers more than 70 percent of the Earth's surface.

The final piece of the biosphere is the lithosphere, the rocky portion of earth. Geology is the study of solid earth. Earth's surface is composed of elemental chunks called minerals, which are simply crystallized groups of bonded atoms. Minerals that have the same composition but different arrangements are called polymorphs, like graphite and diamonds. All minerals contain physical properties such as luster (shine), color, hardness, density, and boiling point. Their chemical properties, or how they react with other compounds, are also different. Minerals combine to form the rocks that make up Earth.

Earth has distinct layers—a thin, solid outer surface, a dense, solid core, and the majority of its matter between them. It is kind of like an egg: the thin crust is the shell, the inner core is the yolk, and the mantle and outer core that compose the space in between are like the egg white.

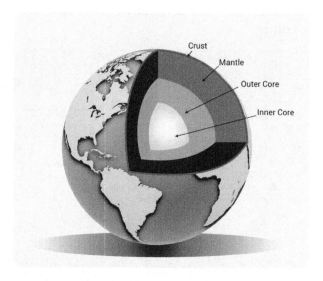

The outer crust of Earth consists of igneous or sedimentary rocks over metamorphic rocks (dense compacted rock underneath). The crust, combined with the upper portion of the mantle, forms the lithosphere, which is broken into several different plates, like puzzle pieces.

Earth-Sun Relationships

Other major lines of latitude and longitude exist to divide the world into regions relative to the direct rays of the sun. These lines correspond with the Earth's *tilt*, and are responsible for the seasons. For example, the northern hemisphere is tilted directly toward the sun from June 22 to September 23, which creates the summer season in that part of the world. Conversely, the southern hemisphere is tilted away from the direct rays of the sun and experiences winter during those same months.

The transitions from season to season involve two factors: the 23 ½ degree tilt of the Earth and the movement of the direct rays of the sun relative to the Earth's revolution. To clarify, the area between the *Tropic of Cancer* (23 ½ degrees north) and the *Tropic of Capricorn* (23 ½ degrees south) can be envisioned as the playing field for the direct rays of the sun. These rays never leave the playing field, and, as a result, the area between those two lines of latitude—the *tropics*—tends to be warmer and experience fewer variations in seasonal temperatures. In contrast, the area between the Tropic of Cancer and the *Arctic Circle* (66 ½ degrees north) is in the *middle latitudes*—the region where most of the Earth's population resides. In the Southern Hemisphere, the middle latitudes exist between the Tropic of Capricorn and the *Antarctic Circle* (66 ½ degrees south). In both of these places, indirect rays of the sun strike the Earth, so seasons are more pronounced and milder temperatures generally prevail. The final region, known as the *high latitudes*, is found north of the Arctic Circle and south of the Antarctic Circle. These regions generally tend to be cold all year, and experience nearly twenty-four hours of sunlight during their respective *summer solstice* and twenty-four hours of darkness during the *winter solstice*.

Regarding the seasons, it is important to understand that those in the Southern Hemispheres are opposite of those in the Northern Hemisphere, due to the position of the direct rays of the sun. When the sun's direct rays are over the Equator, it is known as an *equinox*, and day and night are almost of equal length throughout the world. Equinoxes occur twice a year; the fall, or autumnal equinox, occurs on September 22nd, while the spring equinox occurs on March 20th. Obviously, if seasons are opposite of one another depending on the hemisphere, the corresponding names flip-flop depending on one's location (i.e. when the Northern Hemisphere is experiencing summer, it is winter in the Southern Hemisphere).

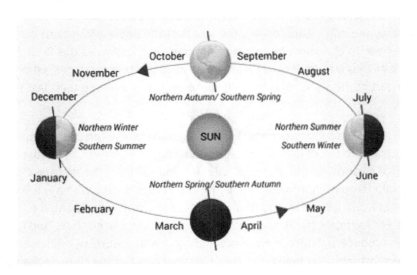

Climate, Vegetation, Soil, and Geology

Climate inevitably affects the vegetation, soil, and geology/geomorphology of particular regions around the globe. In terms of vegetation, the world can be divided into four major biomes: forest, savannah, grassland, and desert. These biomes produce different types of land vegetation. In a forest biome, trees form a continuous canopy. In a savannah biome, trees are with various grasses. In a grassland biome, the entire environment is covered in grass. In a desert biome, there is little to no land vegetation. Vegetation is both a product of the soil and a contributor to the soil. Erosion of the soil, for instance, can be minimized through planting crops and conserving the environment. The earth's geology/geomorphology is also fundamentally tied to vegetation and the soil. Different elevations and climates, for instance, produce different vegetation and soil. Likewise, the nutrients present in vegetation and the soil may affect the geological components of the earth.

Major Landforms, Climates, and Ecosystems

Earth is an incredibly large place filled with a variety of different land and water *ecosystems*. *Marine ecosystems* cover over 75 percent of the Earth's surface and contain over 95 percent of the Earth's water. Marine ecosystems can be broken down into two primary subgroups: *freshwater ecosystems*, which only encompass around 2 percent of the earth's surface; and *ocean ecosystems*, which make up over 70 percent. On land, *terrestrial ecosystems* vary depending on a variety of factors, including latitudinal distance from the equator, elevation, and proximity to mountains or bodies of water. For example, in the high latitudinal regions north of the Arctic Circle and south of the Antarctic Circle, frozen *tundra* dominates. Tundra, which is characterized by low temperatures, short growing seasons, and minimal vegetation, is only found in regions that are far away from the direct rays of the sun.

In contrast, *deserts* can be found throughout the globe and are created by different ecological factors. For example, the world's largest desert, the Sahara, is almost entirely within the tropics; however, other deserts like the Gobi in China, the Mojave in the United States, and the Atacama in Chile, are the result of the orographic effect and their close proximity to high mountain ranges such as the Himalayas, the Sierra Nevada, and the Andes, respectively. In the Middle Latitudes, greater varieties of climatological zones are more common due to fluctuations in temperatures relative to the sun's rays, coupled with the particular local topography. In the Continental United States, *temperate deciduous forest* dominates the southeastern portion of the country. However, the Midwestern states such as Nebraska, Kansas, and the Dakotas, are primarily *grasslands*. Additionally, the states of the Rocky Mountains can have decidedly different climates relative to elevation. In Colorado, Denver, also known as the "Mile High City," will often see snowfalls well into late April or early May due to colder temperatures, whereas towns and cities in the eastern part of the state, with much lower elevations, may see their last significant snowfall in March.

In the tropics, which are situated between the Tropics of Cancer and Capricorn, temperatures are generally warmer, due to the direct rays of the sun's persistence. However, like most of the world, the tropics also experience a variety of climatological regions. In Brazil, Southeast Asia, Central America, and even Northern Australia, tropical rainforests are common. These forests, which are known for abundant vegetation, daily rainfall, and a wide variety of animal life, are absolutely essential to the health of the world's ecosystems. For example, the *Amazon Rain Forest* is also referred to as "the lungs of the world," as its billions of trees produce substantial amounts of oxygen and absorb an equivalent amount of carbon dioxide—the substance that many climatologists assert is causing climate change or *global warming*. Unlike temperate deciduous forests whose trees lose their leaves during the fall and winter months, *tropical rain forests* are always lush, green, and warm. In fact, some rainforests are so dense with vegetation that a few indigenous tribes have managed to exist within them without being influenced by any sort of modern technology, virtually maintaining their ancient way of life in the modern era.

The world's largest ecosystem, the *taiga*, is found primarily in high latitudinal areas, which receive very little of the sun's indirect rays. These forests are generally made up of *coniferous* trees, which do not lose their leaves at any point during the year as *deciduous* trees do. Taigas are cold-climate regions that make up almost 30 percent of the world's land area. These forests dominate the northern regions of Canada, Scandinavia, and Russia, and provide the vast majority of the world's lumber.

Overall, it is important to remember that climates are influenced by five major factors: elevation, latitude, proximity to mountains, ocean currents, and wind patterns. For example, the cold currents off the coast of California provide the West Coast of the United States with pleasant year-round temperatures. Conversely, Western Europe, which is at the nearly the same latitude as most of Canada, is influenced by the warm waters of the *Gulf Stream*, an ocean current that acts as a conveyor belt, moving warm tropical waters to the icy north. In fact, the Gulf Stream's influence is so profound that it even keeps Iceland—an island nation in the far North Atlantic—relatively warm.

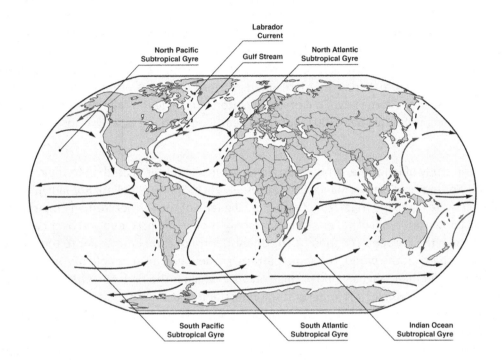

Global and Regional Patterns of Culture and Human Geography

Cultural Region

<u>Regions</u>
Geographers divide the world into regions in order to more fully understand differences inherent with the world, its people, and its environment. Lines of latitude such as the Equator, the Tropics, and the Arctic and Antarctic Circles already divide the Earth into solar regions relative to the amount of either direct or indirect sunlight that they receive. Although not the same throughout, the middle latitudes generally have a milder climate than areas found within the tropics. Furthermore, tropical locations are usually warmer than places in the middle latitudes, but that is not always the case. For example, the lowest place in the United States—Death Valley, California—is also home to the nation's highest-ever recorded temperature. Likewise, the Andes Mountains in Peru and Ecuador, although found near the Equator, are also home to heavy snow, low temperatures, and dry conditions, due to their elevation.

Formal regions are spatially defined areas that have overarching similarities or some level of *homogeneity* or *uniformity*. Although not exactly alike, a formal region generally has at least one characteristic that is consistent throughout the entire area. For example, the United States could be broken down into one massive formal region due to the fact that in all fifty states, English is the primary language. Of course, English isn't the only language spoken in the United States, but throughout that nation, English is heavily used. As a result, geographers are able to classify the United States as a formal region; but, more specifically, the United States is a *linguistic region*—a place where everyone generally speaks the same language.

Functional regions are similar to formal regions in that they have similar characteristics, but they do not have clear boundaries. The best way to understand these sorts of regions is to consider large cities. Each large city encompasses a large *market area,* whereby people in its vicinity generally travel there to conduct business, go out to eat, or watch a professional sporting event. However, once anyone travels farther away from that *primate city*, they transition to a different, more accessible city for their needs. The functional region, or *area of influence,* for that city, town, or sports team transitions, depending upon the availability of other primate cities. For example, New York City has two primary professional baseball, basketball, and football teams. As a result, its citizens may have affinities for different teams even though they live in the same city. Conversely, a citizen in rural Idaho may cheer for the Seattle Seahawks, even though they live over 500 miles from Seattle, due to the lack of a closer primate city.

Linguistics

Linguistics, or the study of language, groups certain languages together according to their commonalities. For example, the Romance Languages—French, Spanish, Italian, Romansh, and Portuguese—all share language traits from Latin, the language of the former Roman Empire. These languages, also known as *vernaculars*, or more commonly spoken *dialects*, evolved over centuries of physical isolation on the European continent. The Spanish form of Latin emerged into today's Spanish language. In other parts of the world, the same pattern is true. The Bantu people of Africa travelled extensively and spread their language, now called *Swahili*, which is the first Pan-African language. When thinking of the world as a whole, it is important to understand that thousands of languages exist; however, to interconnect the world, it is important to have a means of communication with which everyone is at least somewhat familiar. A *lingua franca* is essentially the language of business. In other words, when executives from multinational corporations need to communicate regarding business, they often communicate in English, which is considered to be the world's lingua franca, due to the economic dominance of the United States.

Religion

Religion has played a tremendous role in creating the world's cultures. Devout Christians crossed the Atlantic in hopes of finding religious freedom in New England, Muslim missionaries and traders travelled to the Spice Islands of the East Indies to teach about the Koran, and Buddhist monks traversed the Himalayan Mountains into Tibet to spread their faith. In some countries, religion helps to shape legal systems. These nations, termed *theocracies*, have no separation of church and state and are more common in Islamic nations such as Saudi Arabia, Iran, and Qatar. In contrast, even though religion has played a tremendous role in the history of the United States, its government remains *secular*, or nonreligious, due to the influence of European Enlightenment philosophy at the time of its inception. Like ethnicity and language, religion is also a primary way that people self-identify. As a result, religious influences can shape a region's laws, architecture, literature, and music. For example, when the Ottoman Turks, who are Muslim, conquered Constantinople, which was once the home of the Eastern Orthodox Christian Church, they replaced Christian places of worship with mosques. Additionally, different forms of Roman architecture were replaced with those influenced by Arabic traditions.

Economics

Economic activity also has a spatial component. For example, nations with few natural resources generally tend to import what they need from nations willing to export raw materials to them.

Furthermore, areas that are home to certain raw materials generally tend to alter their environment in order to maintain production of those materials. In the San Joaquin Valley of California, an area known for extreme heat and desert-like conditions, local residents have engineered elaborate drip irrigation systems to adequately water lemon, lime, olive, and orange trees, utilizing the warm temperatures to constantly produce citrus fruits. Additionally, other nations with abundant petroleum reserves build elaborate infrastructures in order to pump, house, refine, and transport their materials to nations who require gasoline, diesel, or natural gas. Essentially, different spatial regions on Earth create jobs, infrastructure, and transportation systems that seek to ensure the continued flow of goods, raw materials, and resources out of their location, so long as financial resources keep flowing into the area.

Innovation and Diffusion

Technological innovation in the earliest "hearths of domestication" allowed the regions to become centers for trade, government, art, science, language acquisition, writing systems, and specialized economic activities. Additionally, these agricultural hearths became epicenters for economic inequality and social stratification, as increases in the wealth of certain farmers and merchants inevitably led to financial strata in each hearth.

As the varying cultures residing in each of the earliest hearths of domestication developed and evolved via spontaneous ideological adaptations, inventive technological advancements, and self-perpetuating cycles of population growth, elaborate continental trading systems emerged. A larger process of cultural diffusion allowed disparate ideas, traditions, and practices to be outwardly spread and exchanged between groups. This transfer of culture and knowledge impacted the daily interactions of previously isolated groups, thrusting them into a new, broader world of complex, multilateral social exchange.

Major World Regions

Texas is in the Northern Hemisphere, the northern half of the Earth between the equator and the North Pole. Texas is located on the North American continent, a landmass in the Western Hemisphere that encompasses half of the Earth to the west of the prime meridian. Texas is part of the United States of America, and it's usually considered part of the Southwestern or Sunbelt regions. Texas is bordered by the states of Louisiana to the east, Oklahoma to the north, Arkansas to the northeast, and New Mexico to the west. Texas is also bordered by Mexico to the south and the Gulf of Mexico to the southeast. The Gulf of Mexico is a large body of saltwater that serves as a major port for international trade, making Texas a leader in the American shipping industry. The state of Texas, from Port Arthur (coastal east) to El Paso (mountainous west), spans nearly 773 miles.

How the Components of Culture Affect the Way People Live

Like any other animal, humans adapt to their environment; but, unlike other animals, humans also adapt their environment to suit their needs. For example, human social systems are created around the goal of providing people with access to what they need to live more productive, fulfilling, and meaningful lives. Sometimes, humans create systems that are destructive, but generally speaking, humans tend to use their environment to make their lives easier. For example, in warmer climates, people tend to wear more comfortable clothing such as shorts, linen shirts, and hats. Additionally, in the excessively sun-drenched nations of the Middle East, both men and women wear flowing white clothing complete with both a head and neck covering, in order to prevent the blistering effects of sun exposure to the skin. Likewise, the native Inuit peoples of northern Canada and Alaska use the thick furs from the animals they kill to insulate their bodies against the bitter cold.

Humans also adapt to their environment to ensure that they have access to enough food and water for survival. Irrigation, or the process of moving water from its natural location to where it's needed, is an example of how humans change their environment in order to survive. For example, the city of Los Angeles, America's second most populous city, did not have adequate freshwater resources to sustain its population. However, city and state officials realized that abundant water resources existed approximately three hundred miles to the east. Rather than relocating some of its population to areas with more abundant water resources, the State of California undertook one of the largest construction projects in the history of the world, the Los Angeles Aqueduct, which is a massive concrete irrigation ditch connecting water-rich areas with the thirsty citizens of Los Angeles.

The Los Angeles Aqueduct is just one example of a human-environment interaction. In other cases, humans utilize what nature provides in close proximity. For example, the very first permanent British Colony in North America, Jamestown, VA, was heavily influenced by its environment. In contrast to the Pilgrims who settled in Plymouth, Massachusetts, Jamestown settlers found themselves in a hot, humid climate with fertile soil. Consequently, its inhabitants engaged in agriculture for both food and profit. Twelve years after Jamestown's foundation in 1607, it was producing millions of dollars of tobacco each year. In order to sustain this booming industry, over time, millions of African slaves and indentured servants from Europe were imported to provide labor. Conversely, the poor soils around Plymouth did not allow for widespread cash crop production, and the settlers in New England generally only grew enough food for themselves on small subsistence farms. Furthermore, slavery failed to take a strong foothold in the New England states, thus creating significantly different cultures within the same country, all due in part to human interaction with the environment.

World Populations and Globalization

Two primary realms exist within the study of geography. The first realm, *physical geography*, essentially correlates with the land, water, and foliage of the Earth. The second realm, *human geography*, is the study of the Earth's people and how they interact with their environment. Like land and water on Earth, humans are also impacted by different forces such as culture, history, sociology, technological advancement and changes, and access to natural resources. For example, human populations tend to be higher around more reliable sources of fresh water. The metropolitan area of New York City, which has abundant freshwater resources, is home to nearly 20 million people, whereas Australia, both a continent and a country, has almost the same population. Although water isn't the only factor in this disparity, it certainly plays a role in a place's *population density*—the total number of people in a particular place divided by the total land area, usually square miles or square kilometers. Australia's population density stands at 8.13 people per square mile, while the most densely populated nation on Earth, Bangladesh, is home to 2,894 people per square mile.

Population density can have a devastating impact on both the physical environment/ecosystem and the humans who live within the environment/ecosystem of a particular place. For example, Delhi, one of India's most populated cities, is home to nearly five million gasoline-powered vehicles. Each day, those vehicles emit an enormous amount of carbon monoxide into the atmosphere, which directly affects the quality of life of Delhi's citizens. In fact, the problem of the smog and pollution has gotten so severe that many drivers are unable to see fifty feet in front of them. Additionally, densely populated areas within third-world nations, or developing nations, struggle significantly in their quest to balance the demands of the modern economy with their nation's lack of infrastructure. For example, nearly as many automobiles operate every day in major American cities like New York and Los Angeles as they do in Delhi, but they create significantly less pollution due to cleaner burning engines, better fuels, and governmental emission regulations.

Due to improvements in transportation and communication, the world has become figuratively smaller. For example, university students on the Indian Subcontinent now compete directly with students all over the world to obtain the skills employers desire to move their companies forward. Additionally, many corporations in developed nations have begun to *outsource* labor to nations with high levels of educational achievement but lower wage expectations. The process of opening the marketplace to all nations throughout the world, or *globalization*, has only just started to take hold in the modern economy. As industrial sites shift to the developing world, so does the relative level of opportunity for those nation's citizens. However, due to the massive amounts of pollution produced by factories, the process of globalization also has had significant ecological impacts. The most widely known impact, *climate change*, which most climatologists assert is caused by an increase of carbon dioxide in the atmosphere, remains a serious problem that has posed challenges for developing nations, who need industries in order to raise their standard of living, and developed nations, whose citizens use a tremendous amount of fossil fuels to run their cars, heat their homes, and maintain their ways of life.

Cultural Patterns and Characteristics in Various Regions

Although it's a significant factor, population density is not the only source of strain on the resources of a particular place. Historical forces such as civil war, religious conflict, genocide, and government corruption can also alter the lives of a nation's citizens in a profound manner. For example, the war-torn nation on the Horn of Africa, Somalia, has not had a functioning government for nearly three decades. As a result, the nation's citizens have virtually no access to hospital care, vaccinations, or proper facilities for childbirth. Due to these and other factors, the nation's *infant mortality rate*, or the total number of child deaths per 1,000 live births, stands at a whopping 98.39/1000. When compared to Iceland's 1.82/1000, it's quite evident that Somalia struggles to provide basic services in the realm of childbirth and there is a dire need for humanitarian assistance.

Literacy rates, like the infant mortality rate, are also an excellent indicator of the relative level of development in a particular place. Like Somalia, other developing nations have both economic and social factors that hinder their ability to educate their own citizens. Due to radical religious factions within some nations like Afghanistan and Pakistan, girls are often denied the ability to attend school, which further reduces the nation's overall literacy rate. For example, girls in Afghanistan, which spent decades under Taliban control, have a 24.2 percent literacy rate, one of the lowest rates of any nation on Earth that keeps records (Somalia's government is so dysfunctional records don't exist). Although literacy rates are useful in determining a nation's development level, high literacy rates do exist within developing nations. For example, Suriname, which has a significantly lower GDP (Gross Domestic Product) than Afghanistan, enjoys a nearly 96 percent literacy rate among both sexes. Utilizing this and other data, geographers can create questions regarding how such phenomena occur. How is Suriname able to educate its population more effectively with fewer financial resources? Is it something inherent within their culture? Demographic data, such as population density, the infant mortality rate, and the literacy rate all provide insight into the characteristics of a particular place and help geographers better understand the spatial world.

The demographic transition model is a concept that explains the pattern of population change by examining two key statistics of a country: birth rate and death rate. This model suggests that as a country becomes more developed, the birth and death rates move through a predictable cycle.

Importance of Place for Populations

<u>Place</u>
Both absolute and relative location help humans understand their sense of place. Place is a simple concept that helps to define the characteristics of the world around us. For example, people may create *toponyms* to further define and orient themselves with their sense of place. Toponyms are simply names given to locations to help develop familiarity within a certain location. Although not always the case, toponyms generally utilize geographical features, important people in an area, or even wildlife commonly found in a general location. For example, many cities in the state of Texas are named in honor of military leaders who fought in the Texas Revolution of 1836 (such as Houston and Austin), while other places, such as Mississippi and Alabama, utilize Native American toponyms to define their sense of place.

Historically, Mecca, Jerusalem, Cuzco, the Ganges River, and the Shrine of Guadalupe have all represented sacred places of pilgrimage or worship. All religious groups are influenced in some way by the physical environment around them—they sanctify significant persons, events, and calendar days by elevating the spaces/objects around them to a holy position. Two kinds of elements from the physical environment can be sanctified by religious groups: distinctive physical environments (mountains, rivers, forests, stones, etc.) and significant objects (shrines, temples, churches, etc.). In Islam, Mecca remains the holiest city for Muslims. Mecca is the birthplace of the prophet Mohammed. Mecca also contains one of the most sacred shrines of the major world religions—the Ka'bah. Believed to have been built by Ishmael, Abraham's biblical son, the Ka'bah has become the final destination of Muslims who take annual pilgrimages, known as a *hajj*. Likewise, Jerusalem remains one of the holiest cities in the Judeo-Christian tradition because it is the site of the First and Second Temples of Jewish antiquity. Jerusalem was also a site of early Christian proselytism. Even Muslims see Jerusalem as a holy city, making it the epicenter of many historical religious wars such as the Crusades. Cuzco was a sacred location for the ancient Incan civilization, and it still holds a spiritual value in modern-day Peru. The Ganges River is the holiest river in India; it is the focal point of Hindu purification. Millions of Hindus flock to the Ganges riverbanks each year to bathe in its holy waters. Lastly, the Shrine of Guadalupe is a Roman Catholic holy site located near Mexico City that commemorates a historical vision of the Blessed Mother, Mary. The Marian commemoration site is dedicated to the Blessed Mother's protection of the American continent.

Religion in the United States

Religion has also been an important, albeit divisive, theme in American history since the colonial period. The British colonies in North America attracted settlers from many different religions, including Catholics in Maryland, Quakers in Pennsylvania, Puritans in New England, and Anglicans in Virginia. This led to conflict and tension. For example, Puritans in New England expelled dissenters and even executed four Quakers between 1659 and 1661.

In the 1730s and 1740s, a religious revival known as the First Great Awakening swept through the British colonies in North America. This movement emphasized a more personal connection to Christ, and some Protestant preachers, such as Jonathan Edwards, began to present their sermons in a more passionate and emotional style. This "fire and brimstone" form of religious dissemination became the cornerstone of the First Great Awakening. These passionate sermons—and the emotions that they stirred—caused divisions within Protestant congregations. Those who supported the Great Awakening were known as New Lights while those who opposed it were called Old Lights. The Baptists and Methodists became more popular during the revival because they embraced this new style of preaching.

The Second Great Awakening occurred in the early 1800s and urged Protestants to work not only for their own salvation but for the salvation of others as well. This helped fuel a social reform movement that promoted the abolition of slavery, temperance, and prison reform. The question of slavery caused schisms in the Baptist and Methodist churches during the 1840s. The Second Great Awakening, much like the First Great Awakening, inaugurated the creation of several New Religious Movements (NRMs) in the United States, especially in the southern states.

A third revival occurred in the late 1800s that emphasized temperance. The religious right emerged after World War II and began to play an important part in American politics, especially during the election of President Ronald Reagan in 1980.

Although Catholics were a minority during the colonial period of American history, Catholicism has become the largest religious denomination in the United States. Many colonial governments actually banned Catholicism, but the American Revolution brought more toleration. However, anti-Catholic sentiment renewed in the 1800s as immigrants from Ireland and Germany, many of whom were Catholic, arrived in ever-increasing numbers. The arrival of Italian immigrants in the late 1800s and early 1900s also increased Protestant-Catholic tension in America. Many Americans feared that Catholic immigrants would be more loyal to Pope than they would be to the Constitution. This led to the creation of the Know-Nothings who sought to limit immigration and physically attacked Catholics. Anti-Catholic sentiment remained an issue even until the presidential election of 1960 when John F. Kennedy, a Catholic, won the Democratic nomination. Kennedy helped allay fears by promising to respect the separation of church and state. Since then, anti-Catholicism has largely disappeared.

Small numbers of Jews immigrated to the U.S. during the colonial period, but large numbers of Jews from Eastern Europe began to arrive in the late 19th and early 20th centuries. Jews contributed to the American economy in many different ways but drew criticism from anti-Semites because of their prominence in the financial industry. The Anti-Defamation League was founded in 1913 to combat anti-Semitic sentiments. In the 1920s, the resurgent Ku Klux Klan revived anti-Semitism. The Anti-Defamation League sponsored events after World War II to commemorate the Holocaust and repudiate Holocaust deniers. Anti-Semitism has declined, but the Anti-Defamation League reported that more than 900 anti-Semitic incidents occurred across the country in 2014.

Muslim immigration in the 1800s remained modest. The first mosque was not constructed in the United States until the 20th century. In the latter part of the 20th century, more Muslims, especially from Pakistan, began arriving in the United States. In the wake of the 9/11 attacks, Islamophobic incidents increased, and Muslims were victims of harassment, intimidation, and assaults. The United States' current battle with ISIS in the Middle East, North Africa, and Europe has also increased Islamophobia.

Arts in the United States and World Areas

It's also important to study different time periods of art and architecture. In the Classical period, Greek artists focused on physical beauty and the human form, paying particular attention to Olympian gods and their idealized proportions in their works. The Medieval period that occurred in Europe from 500 to 1400 CE saw a flourish of Romanesque style art that shifted the emphasis from portraying realism to conveying a message, particularly symbolic Christian ideals. Students should also learn about the history of art in other countries such as China, with its jade, pottery, bronze, porcelain, and calligraphy. Educators should focus on how various influences over time affected the predominant artwork each period. For example, Buddhism in the early first century BCE increased calligraphy on silks, the Song dynasty created landscape paintings that were popular, and the Ming and Qing dynasties developed color painting and printing with an evolution towards individualism. As China became increasingly influenced by Western society in the nineteenth and early twentieth centuries, social realism predominated. In addition to covering other Asian nations, educators should expose students to traditional African art, which generally demonstrates moral values, focuses on human subjects, and seeks to please the viewer. Educators can also introduce art from the American Indians such as woodcarving, weaving, stitchery, and beading. Art in American Indian populations varies widely from tribe to tribe but tends to beautify everyday objects and create items of spiritual significance. Students should be exposed to music and theater from other cultures and observe the costumes, movements, instruments, and themes in performing arts from places like the Caribbean islands, Japan, Mexico, Australia, Africa, Italy, and Russia.

Throughout U.S. history, art has been created by individuals to communicate a social message. For example, the Harlem Renaissance used music, poetry, literature, and various iconography to depict the doings and sufferings of early 20th century African Americans. During WWII, the images of Rosie the Riveter were used to enlist women to support the war effort in industry. During the Cold War, the U.S. and the USSR utilized art/propaganda to win over adherents. Political commentary and satire have also been used throughout U.S. history, from Mark Twain to Stephen Colbert.

It can be argued that the primary functions of art are personal, social, and physical. When art is used personally, it can have a host of functions. An artist can create art for personal enjoyment, the refinement of a skill, aesthetic reasons, religious reasons, therapeutic reasons, political reasons, sensual reasons, and beyond. No matter an artist's intent, an artist's finished piece can be interpreted in a variety of ways—ways that the artist may not have intended.

Interactions Between Human Groups and the Physical Environment

The Physical Environment in Cultural and Technological Contexts

As civilizations blossomed globally in river valleys, disparate cultures such as the Israelites, Babylonians, and Egyptians entered into long-term, unofficial social contracts, forcing populations into a constant cultural dialogue with the processes of acculturation, assimilation, and ethnic genocide. In many ways, these complex, multilateral patterns of cultural diffusion marked the beginnings of the long process of globalization that has affected humanity's exchange of goods and ideas for centuries. Moreover, these cultural and technological changes inevitably had *natural* and/or *ecological* ramifications—as humanity shifted from nomadic to domesticated life, the earth was forever impacted by the transformative processes of domestication. At times, these processes have had a positive impact on global ecology and physical geography; in most cases, they have ravaged the land for the sake of human existence.

The microcosmic processes of war, trade, migration, drought, famine, personal contact, and mass communication catalyzed this larger process of cultural diffusion, forcing each civilization into a sort of cultural symbiosis with the other. Each burgeoning city-state relied on other city-states for obtaining new objects, ideas, and customs. The transformation from village to city-state—and the accompanying cultural diffusions that followed—spanned several generations, making it difficult for scholars to pinpoint the origins of many specific agricultural-based practices. The cultural diffusion spawned by the First Agricultural Revolution created a web of interrelated objects, ideas, and practices that multilaterally affected the social institutions and geographic dispositions of many of the world's first civilizations.

The diffusion and exchange of new tools (hoes, sickles, plow sticks) and new farming practices (slash-and-burn farming, terrace farming, animal husbandry) impacted not only the original "hearts of domestication" in the Fertile Crescent, but also the budding agricultural civilizations that came into contact with these hearths. The First Agricultural Revolution, which began in communities like Jarmo and Catal Huyuk, thus marked a dramatic change in the ways in which communities interacted with their neighbors. As small neighboring villages altered into elaborate collections of regional city-states, each budding civilization connected with its neighboring civilizations via the superstructural process of cultural diffusion. At times, cultural diffusion was a conscious process; in most cases, it was an unconscious aggregate of proximal interactions.

Interdependence of People, Places, and Environments

Like climate, *natural hazards* also affect human societies. In tropical and subtropical climates, hurricanes and typhoons form over warm water and can have devastating effects. Additionally, tornadoes, which are powerful cyclonic windstorms, are also responsible for widespread destruction in many parts of the United States and in other parts of the world. Like storms, earthquakes, usually caused by shifting plates along faults deep below the Earth's surface, also cause widespread devastation, particularly in nations with a poor or crumbling infrastructure. For example, San Francisco, which experiences earthquakes regularly due to its position near the San Andreas Fault, saw relatively little destruction and deaths (67 total) as a result of the last major earthquake to strike there. However, in 2010, an earthquake of similar magnitude reportedly killed over 200,000 people in the western hemisphere's poorest nation, Haiti. Although a variety of factors may be responsible for the disparity, modern engineering methods and better building materials most likely helped to minimize destruction in San Francisco. Other natural hazards, such as tsunamis, mudslides, avalanches, forest fires, dust storms, flooding, volcanic eruptions, and blizzards, also affect human societies throughout the world.

Processes of Settlement Development Over Time

Transportation Routes
From a geographer's point of view, the most important aspect of any geographic network is its connectivity attributes. Connectivity makes contact and interaction possible through communication and transportation. Connectivity also dictates the availability of resources, or accessibility. Accessibility is the opportunity to take advantage of certain resources from a given point or location. Although distance is only one aspect of accessibility, it is, perhaps, the most important aspect. Connectivity and the availability of resources throughout history have often been dictated by transportation routes. From the Nile River to the Silk Road to the Eisenhower Interstate System, human geographic settlement patterns have often depended on transportation routes. These transportation routes—especially in an increasingly technological and globalized world—have been crucial for cultural diffusion and human settlement. The oceanic transportation routes of the Age of Exploration, for instance, were crucial in developing a Triangle Trade System that forced cultures into economic, cultural, and social change.

Migration
Migration is governed by two primary causes: *push factors*, which are reasons causing someone to leave an area, and *pull factors*, which are factors luring someone to a particular place. These two factors often work in concert with one another. For example, the United States of America has experienced significant *internal migration* from the industrial states in the Northeast (such as New York, New Jersey, Connecticut) to the Southern and Western states. This massive migration, which continues into the present-day, is due to high rents in the northeast, dreadfully cold winters, and lack of adequate

retirement housing, all of which are push factors. These push factors lead to migration to the *Sunbelt*, a term geographers use to describe states with warm climates and less intense winters.

In addition to internal migrations within nations or regions, international migration also takes place between countries, continents, and other regions. The United States has long been the world's leading nation in regard to *immigration*, the process of having people come into a nation's boundaries. Conversely, developing nations that suffer from high levels of poverty, pollution, warfare, and other violence all have significant push factors, which cause people to leave and move elsewhere. This process, known as *emigration*, is when people in a particular area leave in order to seek a better life in a different—usually better—location.

Demography, or the study of human populations, involves a variety of closely related stimuli. First, economic factors play a significant role in the movement of people, as do climate, natural disasters, or internal unrest. For example, in recent years, millions of immigrants from the war-torn country of Syria have moved as far as possible from danger. Although people are constantly moving, some consistencies remain throughout the world. First, people tend to live near reliable sources of food and water, which is why the first human civilizations sprung up in river valleys like the Indus River Valley in India, the Nile River Valley in Egypt, and the Yellow River Valley in Asia. Second, extreme temperatures tend to push people away, which is why the high latitudinal regions near the North and South Poles have such few inhabitants. Third, the vast majority of people tend to live in the Northern Hemisphere, due to the simple fact that more land lies in that part of the Earth. In keeping with these factors, human populations tend to be greater where human necessities are easily accessible, or at least more readily available. In other words, such areas have a greater chance of having a higher population density than places without such characteristics.

Demographic patterns on earth are not always stagnate. In contrast, people move and will continue to move as both push and pull factors fluctuate along with the flow of time. For example, in the 1940s, thousands of Europeans fled their homelands due to the impact of the Second World War. Today, thousands of migrants arrive on European shores each month due to conflicts in the Levant and difficult economic conditions in Northern Africa. Furthermore, people tend to migrate to places with a greater economic benefit for themselves and their families. As a result, developed nations such as the United States, Germany, Canada, and Australia have a net gain of migrants, while developing nations such as Somalia, Zambia, and Cambodia generally tend to see thousands of their citizens seek better lives elsewhere.

It is important to understand the key variables in changes regarding human population and its composition worldwide. Religion and religious conflict play a role in where people choose to live. For example, the Nation of Israel won its independence in 1948 and has since attracted thousands of people of Jewish descent from all over the world. Additionally, the United States has long attracted people from all over the world, due to its promise of religious freedom inherent within its own Constitution. In contrast, nations like Saudi Arabia and Iran do not typically tolerate different religions, resulting in a decidedly uniform religious—and oftentimes ethnic—composition. Other factors such as economic opportunity, social unrest, and cost of living also play a vital role in demographic composition.

Physical and Human Geographic Factors

Dust Bowl
One need not look further than the United States' Dust Bowl example in the 1930s to envision the detrimental effects human development and agricultural overproduction can have on the soils of

nutrient-rich regions. Crops such as wheat and barley tend to deplete the soil of its nutrients. In the late 1920s and 1930s, agricultural overproduction in the Heartland of the United States of America depleted the soil to the point that it was arid. The arid nature of the soil created a so-called Dust Bowl, a series of devastating dust storms that destroyed rural agricultural communities and forced families to migrate. Many families died as a result of the ecological impact of the Dust Bowl; they died from the starvation and disease that stemmed from poor environmental conditions. The Dust Bowl not only affected the health of human beings in the Heartland, but it also completely transformed the political, social, cultural, technological, and economic character of the entire region. For decades, families uprooted themselves from the region over fear that history would repeat itself and once again they would be forced into economic tatters.

Panama Canal

The building of the Panama Canal revolutionized global travel and trade and is largely considered one of the greatest feats in modern engineering. The construction of the 51-mile canal was mired in geopolitical controversy even before the first ditch was dug by the United States of America. The French had previously tried to build a canal through Central America, but failed. The United States went as far as to assist Panamanians in fighting for independence from Colombia to make the impressive construction project a reality. In 1903, President Theodore Roosevelt deployed the U.S. Navy to assist the Panamanian province in its revolution against Colombia. Economics also drove the geographic development of the Panama Canal—Roosevelt promised to pay Panama $10 million per year to build the canal and maintain ownership over it.

The United States of America benefitted heavily from the canal once it was completed. The United States controlled the tollgate, making money off the thousands of ships that used the Panama Canal to expedite travel between the Atlantic and Pacific Oceans. At its peak, the Panama Canal brought in $340 million each year for the U.S. government. The building and operation of the canal, however, did not come without its own costs. Many Americans and Panamanians lost their lives building and operating the canal, thanks to floods, heat, and disease-carrying mosquitoes. Many workers lost their lives to yellow fever and malaria. The canal became a cross-cultural phenomenon, as over seventy nations utilized its waterways each year. The construction of the Panama Canal, however, did strain relationships between the United States and Latin America. The United States controlled the waterways of the canal until December 31, 1999. On this date, the U.S. government handed over the canal to the Panamanians. Nonetheless, many Latin American countries still lament the U.S. exploitative involvement in the creation of Panama and its world-famous canal. Over the years, technological advances in dam construction, lockbuilding, and shipbuilding adapted to fit the needs of the unique structures of the Panama Canal. Thus, the Panama Canal was not only an agent of change in politics and economics, but also in maritime technological advances and human engineering.

Suez Canal

The construction of the Suez Canal, much like the construction of the Panama Canal, was marred in political and economic controversy. Egyptians began building the Suez Canal under the modernization efforts of Isma'il Pasha, who is often referred to by Egyptian historians as Ismail the Magnificent. Isma'il Pasha was the grandson of former Ottomon leader Mohammed Ali Pasha. Much like his grandfather, Isma'il wanted to modernize Egypt for the growing global economy. He decided to build a canal that cut through the Isthmus of Suez and connected the Red Sea and the Mediterranean Sea. Isma'il tapped into French money and labor to make the public works project a success. In 1969, the Suez Canal opened with a grand international celebration. The project, however, proved to be extremely expensive. Egypt accrued $450 million in debt to fund canal construction; they consequently owed European bankers, making them financially indebted to colonial governments such as the British Empire. Noticing an opportunity to take advantage of the poor financial choices of the Egyptians, the British government assumed control over the canal in 1882 as they began to occupy Egypt. The Suez Canal expedited travel between Europe, the Middle East, and South Asia, but it remained the focal point of anti-colonial protest and geopolitical conflict well into the twentieth century.

Neolithic Agricultural Revolution

Agriculture is essential to human existence. The *Neolithic Revolution*, or the use of farming to produce food, had a profound effect on human societies. Rather than foraging and hunting for food, human societies became more stable and were able to grow due to more consistent food supplies. In modern times, farming has changed drastically in order to keep up with the increasing world population.

Until the twentieth century, the vast majority of people on Earth engaged in *subsistence farming*, or the practice of growing only enough food to feed one's self, or one's family. Over time, due to inventions such as the steel plow, the mechanical reaper, and the seed drill, farmers were able to produce more crops on the same amount of land. As food became cheaper and easier to obtain, populations grew, but rather than leading to an increase in farmers, fewer people actually farmed. After the advent of mechanized farming in developed nations, small farms became less common, and many were either abandoned or absorbed by massive commercial farms producing both foodstuffs, staple crops, and cash crops.

In recent years, agricultural practices have undergone further changes in order to keep up with the rapidly growing population. Due in part to the *Green Revolution*, which introduced the widespread use of fertilizers to produce massive amounts of crops, farming techniques and practices continue to evolve. For example, *genetically modified organisms*, or *GMOs*, are plants or animals whose genetic makeup has been modified using different strands of DNA in hopes of producing more resilient strains of staple crops, livestock, and other foodstuffs. This process, which is a form of *biotechnology*, attempts to solve the world's food production problems through the use of genetic engineering. Although these crops are abundant and resistant to pests, drought, or frost, they are also the subject of intense scrutiny. For example, the international food company, Monsanto, has faced an incredible amount of criticism regarding its use of GMOs in its products. Many activists assert that "rewiring" mother nature is inherently problematic and that foods produced through such methods are dangerous to human health. Despite the controversy, GMOs and biotechnologies continue to change the agricultural landscape by changing the world's food supply.

Like Monsanto, other agribusinesses exist throughout the world. Not only do these companies produce food for human consumption, but they also provide farming equipment, fertilizers, agrichemicals, and breeding and slaughtering services for livestock. While these companies are found all over the world, they are generally headquartered near the product they produce. For example, General Mills, a cereal manufacturer, is headquartered in the Midwestern United States, near its supply of wheat and corn—the primary ingredients in its cereals.

Population Growth and Modernization

Population growth and modernization, sparked by the technological transformations of the Industrial Revolution, forever changed the physical environment of the earth, catalyzing the growth of urban centers. Mechanical inventions, medical advances, and agricultural transformations helped human beings live longer and reproduce more. As a result, more infrastructure was built to maintain growing civilizations in industrialized countries. Modernity became synonymous with pollution, animal extinction, and ecological devastation. The advent of locomotive and automobile transportations

114

allowed for greater human connections, but they often came at the expense of the earth. Railroads and roadways swiftly carved up the landscape of burgeoning countries such as the United States and Russia/USSR in the late 1800s and early 1900s.

Fossil fuels began to dominate, leading to the devastation of mountainous regions such as Appalachia. An increased need for timber, ore, and stone also tore up the ground in the name of extravagant buildings and skyscrapers. Modernity ravaged the physical environment of most industrial countries, powering the way to urban decay and suburban sprawl. By the 1950s to 1980s, many industrial nations had their fair share of environmental catastrophes. With the advent of the nuclear age, these environmental issues became even more evident across the globe. The dropping of the atomic bombs on Hiroshima and Nagasaki made the remnants of these former Japanese hubs look like the apocalypse. Nuclear meltdowns in places like Chernobyl, Russia, and Three Mile Island, Pennsylvania, poisoned the surrounding earth and air. Population growth and modernization also led to the construction of large agribusinesses and meatpacking plants that laid waste to the environment much like an Upton Sinclair novel.

Management of Key Natural Resources

When gas prices are high, prices on virtually everything increase. After all, there are very few products that humans can buy that are not transported by either a gasoline- or diesel-powered engine. As a result, an increase in fuel prices leads to an increase in the price of food, goods, or other cargo. Recently, there has been considerable debate regarding the reliance on *nonrenewable resources* like oil, natural gas, and coal. These resources, which are also known as *fossil fuels*, are quite common throughout the world and are generally abundant, and cheaper to use than *renewable resources* like solar, wind, and geothermal energy. While solar energy is everywhere, the actual means to convert the sun's rays into energy is not. Conversely, coal-fired power plants and gasoline-powered engines, which are older technologies in use during the industrial revolution, remain quite common throughout the world. In fact, reliance on non-renewable resources continues to grow, due to the availability coupled with the existing infrastructure. However, use of renewable energy is increasing, as it becomes more economically competitive with nonrenewable resources.

In addition to sources of energy, nonrenewable resources also include anything that can be exhausted. These can include precious metals like gold, silver, and platinum, freshwater underground aquifers, and precious stones such as diamonds, emeralds, and opals. Although abundant, most nonrenewable sources of energy are not sustainable because their creation takes so long. Renewable resources are sustainable, but must be properly overseen so that they remain renewable. For example, the beautiful African island of Madagascar is home to some of the most amazing rainforest trees in the world. As a result, logging companies cut, milled, and sold thousands of them in order to make quick profits without planning how to ensure the continued health of the forests. As a result of severe deforestation on the island, mudslides became more and more common as the forests gradually shrank from widespread logging. In this case, renewable resources were mismanaged, and thus essentially became nonrenewable, due to the length of time for growth for the replacement of rainforest trees. In the United States, paper companies harvest pine trees to create paper; and because it can take almost twenty years for a pine tree to reach maturity, most of the companies utilize planning techniques to ensure that mature pine trees will always be available. In this manner, these resources remain renewable for human use in a sustainable fashion.

Renewable sources of energy are relatively new in the modern economy. Even though electric cars, wind turbines, and solar panels are becoming more common, they still do not provide enough energy to power the world's economy. As a result, reliance on older, reliable forms of energy continues, which has a devastating effect on the environment. Beijing, China, which has seen a massive boom in industrial jobs, is also one of the most polluted places on Earth. Furthermore, developing nations with very little modern infrastructure also rely heavily on fossil fuels, due to the ease in which they are converted into usable energy. Even the United States, which has one of the most developed infrastructures in the world, still relies almost exclusively on fossil fuels, with only ten percent of the required energy coming from renewable sources.

Physical and Human Geographic Factors, Political Divisions, Relationships, and Policies

Nations, states, and nation-states are all terms with very similar meanings, but knowing the differences aids in a better understanding of geography. A nation is an area with similar cultural, linguistic, and historical experiences. A state is a political unit with sovereignty, or the ability to make its own decision in a particular area; and a nation-state is an entity that combines states into one, singular government system. For example, in the United States, the state of Texas is not an independent nation-state. Instead, it is part of the United States and thus, is subject to its laws. In a similar fashion, the United Kingdom encompasses four member states: England, Wales, Northern Ireland, and Scotland. Although people in those states may consider themselves to be *sovereign*, or self-governing, the reality is that those states cannot make decisions regarding international trade, declarations of war, or other important decisions regarding the rest of the world. Instead, they are *semi-autonomous*, meaning that they can make some decisions regarding how their own state is run, but must yield more major powers to a centralized authority. In the United States, this sort of system is called *Federalism*, or the sharing of power among Local, State, and Federal entities, each of whom is assigned different roles in the overall system of government.

Nation-states, and the boundaries that define where they are, are not always permanent. For example, after the fall of the Soviet Union in 1991, new nations emerged that had once been a part of the larger entity called the Union of Soviet Socialists Republics. These formerly sovereign nations were no longer forced to be a part of a unifying communist government, and as a result, they regained their autonomy and became newly independent nations that were no longer *satellite nations* of the Soviet Union. In a historical sense, the United States can be seen as a prime example of how national boundaries change. After the conclusion of the American Revolution in 1781, the Treaty of Paris defined the United States' western boundary as the Mississippi River; today, after a series of conflicts with Native American groups, the Mexican government, Hawaiian leadership, the Spanish, and the purchase of Alaska from the Russians, the boundaries of the United States have changed drastically. In a similar fashion, nations in Europe, Africa, and Asia have all shifted their boundaries due to warfare, cultural movements, and language barriers.

In the modern world, boundaries continue to change. For example, the Kurds, an ethnic minority in the Middle East, are still fighting for the right to control their people's' right to *self-determination*, but have not yet been successful in establishing a nation for themselves. In contrast, the oil-rich region of South Sudan, which has significant cultural, ethnic, and religious differences from Northern Sudan, successfully won its independence in a bloody civil war, which established the nation's newest independent nation. In recent years, Russia has made the world nervous by aggressively annexing the Crimean Peninsula, an area that has been part of the Ukraine since the end of the Cold War. Even the United Kingdom and Canada have seen their own people nearly vote for their own rights to self-determination. In 1995, the French-speaking Canadian province of Quebec narrowly avoided becoming a sovereign nation through a tightly contested referendum. In a similar fashion, Scotland, which is part of the UK, also voted to remain a part of the Crown, even though many people in that state see themselves as inherently different from those in other regions within the nation.

Political geography is constantly changing. Boundaries on maps from ten years ago are not consistent with those of 2016 and beyond. Simply looking at a map of Africa from 1950 can give one a sense of the level of change that takes place in a lifetime. For example, a map of Africa before 1950 looks completely different than a map of Africa from 2016. There are fewer European nations in the names on the 2016 map. *Decolonization*, or the removal of dependency on colonizers, has altered the political landscape of Africa, allowed more autonomy for the African people, and has forever redefined the boundaries of the entire continent.

Sociological, Anthropological, and Psychological Concepts and Processes

Role of Culture

Human behavior is influenced by culture and cultural changes, human adaptation, and diversity. Every person is different. People are born into different types of families, religions, geographic areas, and other circumstances. These differences affect how people act. Respecting differences is key to influencing human behavior.

Culture and Culture Change
Culture derives from the beliefs, values, and behaviors of people in a community. These beliefs, values, and behaviors tend to be passed from one generation to the next. Culture can change over time and from generation to generation.

All people are born into a certain culture, which can be embedded within families, schools, businesses, social classes, and religions. Within these cultural institutions, people learn positive and negative reinforcement, dialect and slang, diet, acceptable and unacceptable practices of society, and many more societal norms.

The social class that people are born into also influences their behavior. A social class is determined by someone's social and economic status and can change over time. Indicators of social class include wealth, education level, job perspectives, marital status, and standard of living. Some living in poverty may strive to attain a higher education level to find a better job and become upwardly mobile. However, others living in poverty may continue to support themselves day to day and use government assistance funds. The culture in which one was raised will influence how a person lives their life. As a person's social class changes, they will adapt their behavior to new situations.

Human Adaptation and Diversity
Over time, the environment in which a person lives changes. Humans adapt their behaviors to fit the needs of their new environment, as well as their own needs. Every person adapts to situations in a unique way simply because everyone is different. Diversity accounts for differences in race, gender, sexual orientation, economic status, and language. Culture creates a set of "norms" to compare what is considered different or diverse within a given culture. In every culture, there is a minority and majority group. The majority of the culture typically sets the "norm" and then influences people's behaviors within the society.

Race and Gender Relations in the United States

Over the course of its history, the United States has experienced a multicentury democratization process that has reinforced diversity and promoted equality among the various racial, ethnic, religious, and gender groups within its citizenship. In terms of race and gender, the culture of the United States has not always been a beacon of equality. Slavery and patriarchy have dominated the social, political, and economic institutions of the country since its inception. Beginning with abolition in the 1860s and women's suffrage in the 1920s, the United States has gradually progressed from a staunchly racist and sexist republic to a more open-minded limited democratic-republic. The moral victories won by the nonviolent protests of the women's rights and civil rights movement have brought about positive democratic change. The nature of race and racism in the United States is a far cry from slavery, and the nature of gender roles is a far cry from Victorian values. Nevertheless, racism and gender-based forms of discrimination still exist in the United States in the form of segregation and economic ceilings. Although people of color and women are earning more, as respective groups, than they ever have in U.S. history, white men continue to earn more on average. The women's rights and civil rights movements in this country have, therefore, had to adapt to new challenges that have formed since the peak of the Cultural Revolution in the 1960s. Today, these movements live on in modern-day feminist movements and the Black Lives Matter movement.

How Cultures and Societies Both Change and Maintain Continuity

<u>Modernization</u>
Developing nations are nations that are struggling to modernize their economy, infrastructure, and government systems. Many of these nations may struggle to provide basic services to their citizens like clean water, adequate roads, or even police protection. Furthermore, government corruption makes life even more difficult for these countries' citizens. In contrast, *developed nations* are those who have relatively high *Gross Domestic Products (GDP)*, or the total value of all goods and services produced in the nation in a given year. To elucidate, the United States, which is one of the wealthiest nations on Earth when ranked by overall GDP, has nearly a 19 trillion dollar GDP; while Haiti, one of the poorest nations in the Western Hemisphere, has nearly a nine billion dollar GDP. This is a difference of almost seventeen trillion dollars. This is not to disparage Haiti or other developing nations; the comparison is simply used to show that extreme inequities exist in very close proximity to one another, and it may be difficult for developing nations to meet the needs of their citizens and move their economic infrastructure forward toward modernization.

In the modern world, industrialization is the initial key to modernization and development. For developed nations, the process of industrialization took place centuries ago. England, where the *Industrial Revolution* began, actually began to produce products in factories in the early 1700s. Later, the United States and some nations of Western Europe followed suit, using raw materials brought in from their colonies abroad to make finished products. For example, cotton was spun into fabric on elaborate weaving machines that mass-produced textiles. As a result, nations that perfected the textile process were able to sell their products around the world, which produced enormous profits. Over time, those nations were able to accumulate wealth, improve their nation's infrastructure, and provide more services for their citizens. Similar to the events of the eighteenth and nineteenth centuries, nations throughout the world are undergoing the same process in today's world. China exemplifies this concept. In China, agriculture was once the predominant occupation, and although it is true that agriculture is still a dominant sector of the Chinese economy, millions of Chinese citizens are flocking to major cities like Beijing, Shanghai, and Hangzhou, due to the availability of factory jobs that allow its workers a certain element of *social mobility*, or the ability to rise up out of one's socioeconomic situation.

Theoretical Foundations of Sociology

A group consists of people who interact with one another on a consistent basis based on their shared and/or intersecting interests, values, or norms. Group membership is contingent upon a willingness to affirm the interests, values, and norms of a group for the sake of remaining in good standing. When a person subscribes as a member of a particular group, they yield to others the right to judge his or her behaviors.

Roles are the behaviors, obligations, and privileges assigned to a particular person at birth as a result of status. The difference between a status and a role is that people *play* roles, but *occupy* statuses in society. Roles are significant in sociology because they establish expectations for people. An entire matrix of roles form society at large.

Status refers to the position that someone occupies within society. There are ascribed statuses and achieved statuses. Ascribed statuses are inherited; achieved statuses are earned/accomplished. One may be born into a lower socioeconomic status but achieve wealth throughout their life.

Statuses, specifically socioeconomic statuses, usually create some sort of stratification in society. Socioeconomic stratification is part of types of governments and economic systems. In some societies, stratification may be based on religious caste, as in India.

Values are the glue that holds groups together. Values are the belief systems, world views, and ethical frameworks that inform a person's identity and group membership.

A variety of theories have been used to explain different aspects of sociology. Functionalism focuses on the structure of society and is based on the idea that the different sections of society work together to create a functioning whole. Each part of society, often represented by social institutions, serve different purposes to meet the needs of the larger group.

Conflict theory, as proposed by Karl Marx, suggests that society is based on a power struggle predicated by competition for a restricted supply of resources. Limited resources include food, housing, and education.

Symbolic interactionism is a theory that hinges on the communication and relationships among individuals in society. Words and symbols that individuals use to define and understand the world around them shape the larger society.

Social Institutions

Society refers to the community in which people live together. Human behavior is greatly influenced by society. People may feel pressure to live by certain standards or act in a specific way. Certain societal "norms" influence a person's behavior in both positive and negative ways.

Additionally, groups can influence how people behave. Peer pressure and the pressure to conform to certain group norms are present throughout life. Peer pressure is often greatest during adolescence, where young people seek the approval of those around them and are willing to do nearly whatever it takes to get their peers' approval. Opinions on any topic belonging within a social circle can change drastically with a few dominant personalities. Another concern is peer pressure involving substance abuse. Adolescents may drink alcohol or do drugs because their friends are doing it and they want to be part of the crowd.

While society and groups impact a person's behavior significantly, institutions also influence human behavior. Institutions have formal and informal rules, and an individual must choose whether they comply with the rules. There are five major types of social institutions that can influence human behavior: family, religion, government, education, and economics.

Family
- Regulates sexual behavior (monogamy)
- Creates and provides for new society members
- Socializes new society members

Religion
- Provides explanations for the unexplainable
- Supports societal norms and values
- Provides a means of coping with life situations

Government
- Institutionalizes norms (by creating laws)
- Enforces laws
- Protects members of society
- Provides a means of resolving conflict

Education
- Prepares society members to contribute to the society in specified roles
- Teaches skills necessary to function within the society

Economics
- Produces and distributes goods needed by society members
- Provides services necessary to the society

Roles of Men, Women, Children, and Families in Historical and Contemporary Cultures

Traditional family structure includes a man, a woman, and one or more children who are either biological or adopted. This is also referred to as a *nuclear family*. In most of human history, the extended family, which includes grandparents, aunts, uncles, and cousins, would live in the same area and work together. The idea of an extended family living and working together broke with the rise of individualism and financial stability in the United States and Europe after World War II. In the modern-day West, the nuclear family is the most common family structure. In addition, the traditional family in the West has grown to include cohabitation families, single-parent families, and same-sex families.

In the Middle East, Africa, Asia, and India, it is still common to have multigenerational households and extended family networks living in close proximity. It is also common to pass down a trade or family business, like a restaurant or masonry business. The role of women is more domestic in these areas. In contrast, women in the United States and Europe more commonly participate in the workforce. In many societies, the wealthier classes educated woman in music and arts but did not encourage much education in mathematics and science. For the most part, the Middle East, Africa, Asia, and India have remained more constant in their family structure and gender roles, while Europe and the United States have seen the most changes in family structure. Examples include divorce and remarriage, evolution of the nuclear family, and change in traditional gender roles.

Until the modern age, girls of the higher classes were often taught housekeeping skills, music, drawing, needlework, and languages. These were often discouraged after marriage, apart from housekeeping, which became a woman's main duties along with childrearing. Boys in the wealthiest class were often educated at elite schools, and though some managed their estates or were members of government, most were expected to use and enjoy their wealth and status without laboring at a job.

Boys of the middle class would seek a profession such as a lawyer, teacher, or minister, often with some college training. Some would be apprenticed to a trade or learn the family business. Girls in the middle class were trained to manage a household, including preparing meals and balancing the family budget, while the higher-class girls focused more on how to entertain guests and manage servants.

Many of the lowest class and orphans, both boys and girls, were used in factory and coalmining work, where quick hands and nimble bodies were useful. For the lower classes, education was not common until the late 1800s. Previously, the wealthier classes suppressed literacy and education for the lower classes, finding it to be a good way of controlling the social and financial status quo. However, girls who received any form of education usually learned domestic skills, simple math, and needlework. Boys of the lower classes would follow the men of their family into whatever work they did, such as coalmining, farming, or factory work.

Nobility and landowners, until World War I, sought to preserve their lineage and wealth through a single male line. The wealth of this class and many of the male heirs were lost in World Wars I and II. Often primogeniture, or the inheritance of an intact estate with all the land, wealth, and titles, was legally passed to the firstborn son. A daughter would only inherit if no male heir was available.

Socialization, Cultural Values, and Norms

Socialization is the term used to refer to the lifelong social experience that develops the potential and cultural values/norms of a person or group of persons. Cultural values/norms therefore vary according to the context—historical time and space—of a person or group of persons. Socialization is varied according to context and the variables of nurture that exist within that context. This is especially evident when one keeps in mind the effects of complete social isolation as in the tragic cases of the abusive childhood deprivation of social experience. Social experience is crucial in forming behaviors and personality/identity, the main components of cultural values/norms. Although socialization is a complex, lifelong process, the early childhood years are the most crucial in personality and cultural development. Nevertheless, the process of socialization can, without a doubt, extend into adulthood as people and groups are exposed to more people, groups, ideas, and contexts. The cultural values/norms acquired through socialization influence the ways in which relationships are built, reinforced, and abandoned in a particular context or set of contexts. Relationships, much like identities, are therefore subjective constructs that are reinforced and/or undermined by the socialization process. The way labor relations are manifested in the hyper-capitalist United States of America is different from the way labor relations are manifested in socialist France, for instance. Location—and time—matter when relationships are discussed from a sociological perspective.

Theoretical Foundations of Psychology

The theoretical foundations of modern-day psychology are usually traced back to the social-scientific analyses of Sigmund Freud. Freud linked human development to biology. Trained as a physician, he believed that human instincts were biologically fixed. He believed certain personality types derived from two basic needs that drove humans from birth: *eros* (life instinct) and *thanatos* (death instinct). Freud believed that life instincts stemmed from biological drives for sex and emotional nurture, and death instincts stemmed from an aggressive, unconscious, animalistic drive in humans. Freud's theories laid the foundations of modern psychology, which tried to understand the biological nature of our behaviors. Freud believed that we internalize social norms and that developmental experiences have a lasting impact on our psyche. Freud's work opened the gateway to future psychological studies on cognitive development (Jean Piaget), moral development (Lawrence Kohlberg), and gender development (Carol Gilligan).

Human Identity, Development, and Learning

Learning is a process in which individuals gain skills or knowledge through experiences, studying, or instruction. Throughout people's lives, human beings are continuously learning and, therefore, the way in which they behave may be affected by new information that is learned. As people learn new things, their behaviors affect how they view their environment, culture, and society. This is also known as a behavioral theory.

Using new technology can affect how people interact with one another. For instance, a new technology allowing people to shop for groceries online and then merely pick up the goods or have them delivered will limit in-store impulse purchases, decrease or eliminate customer service communication, and potentially affect the quality of goods sold if individuals do not personally hand select their own products. Learning processes will constantly change and therefore human behaviors will constantly evolve.

Along with learning, people will continuously adjust their personal identity. Personal identity is a person's own perception of themself throughout their lifespan. Someone's personal identity can relate to where they grew up, race, religion, social class, and many other life experiences. Keep in mind, with new experiences, people learn and may change their viewpoints on topics. Although people may identify with one subgroup or culture now, it does not mean they will agree with that subgroup or culture in the future, or that they have in the past. Personal identity will continue to change an individual's behavior throughout life.

As a person's identity adjusts throughout life, they also develop new skills. Development and learning go hand-in-hand in affecting a person's behavior. Development stems from learning. A person's development progresses through life, and people's behaviors will change many times throughout their lives. New experiences or events, learning something new, identifying with a different group, or natural development in itself will all affect an individual's behaviors.

Psychological Principles and Processes

Early psychologists like Sigmund Freud believed that human motivation and personality stemmed from biological factors and unconscious tensions. For Freud, human motivation— the reasoning behind our behaviors—was almost always rooted in basic instincts, particularly sex. Freud also believed our personalities and perceptions—categorized into the id, ego, and superego—were also derived from basic needs and social experiences. Later psychologists believed Freud's theories were overly simplified and patriarchal, noting that motivation, personality, and perception stemmed from a greater variety of variables than sex and basic needs. Psychologists like Jean Piaget and Lawrence Kohlberg enhanced scholarship on such psychological principles as sensation (experiencing the world through senses) and cognition (experiencing the world through abstract ideas), noting different stages in sensorimotor and moral development. These psychologists departed from Freudian theory by making note of the complexity of biological maturation and social development. Still limited by their sociological models, these psychologists demonstrated that sensation and cognition often moved beyond pain and pleasure to include abstract visions of the senses and perception. Nevertheless, all these psychologists—from Freud to Kohlberg—enhanced scholarship in the social sciences by illustrating the ways in which biological processes and social experiences can come together to create unique behaviors, notions of self, and relationships with others.

Practice Questions

1. Which of the following is the primary problem with map projections?
    a. They are not detailed
    b. They do not include physical features
    c. They distort areas near the poles
    d. They only focus on the Northern Hemisphere

2. Which type of map illustrates the world's climatological regions?
    a. Topographic Map
    b. Conformal Projection
    c. Isoline Map
    d. Thematic Map

3. In which manner is absolute location expressed?
    a. The cardinal directions (north, south, east, and west)
    b. Through latitudinal and longitudinal coordinates
    c. Location nearest to a more well-known location
    d. Hemispherical position on the globe

4. Latitudinal lines are used to measure distance in which direction?
    a. East to west
    b. North to south
    c. Between two sets of coordinates
    d. In an inexact manner

5. Literacy rates are more likely to be higher in which area?
    a. Developing nations
    b. Northern Hemispherical Nations
    c. Developed Nations
    d. Near centers of trade

6. All are true of an area with an extremely high population density EXCEPT which of the following?
    a. Competition for resources is intense
    b. Greater strain on public services exists
    c. Most are found in rural areas
    d. Most are found in urban areas

7. All of the following are negative demographic indicators EXCEPT which of the following?
    a. High Infant Mortality Rates
    b. Low Literacy Rates
    c. High Population Density
    d. Low Life Expectancy

8. Which of the following characteristics best defines a formal region?
    a. Homogeneity
    b. Diversity
    c. Multilingualism
    d. Social Mobility

9. Which statement is NOT true about a person's behavior?
    a. Behaviors change over time.
    b. Behaviors are influenced by a person's environment.
    c. A person will always have the same personal identity.
    d. Cultural changes influence a person's behavior.

10. Which group is more likely to succumb to or be influenced by peer pressure?
    a. Adolescents
    b. Senior Women
    c. Middle-aged men
    d. Small children

11. Which of these is NOT a factor in which education can influence behavior?
    a. A school's rules and regulations
    b. Bullying establishing a system of social ranking
    c. School regulated social situations
    d. Grading

12. Which of these is NOT a true statement about culture?
    a. Culture derives from the beliefs, values, and behaviors of people in a community.
    b. All people are born into a certain culture.
    c. Cultures are stagnant and cannot be changed.
    d. Culture can be embedded within families, schools, businesses, social classes, and religions.

13. Differences in race, gender, sexual orientation, economic status, and language can be denoted as what?
    a. Behaviorism
    b. Peer pressure
    c. Adaptation
    d. Diversity

14. Which of the following are indicators of social class?
    a. Wealth
    b. Education level
    c. Standard of living
    d. All of the above

15. Which is NOT true of nonrenewable resources?
    a. They tend to be used more frequently than renewables.
    b. They are thought to be responsible for climate change.
    c. They are relied upon heavily in developing economies.
    d. They have slowed industrial growth.

16. Which of the following could be considered a pull factor for a particular area?
    a. High rates of unemployment
    b. Low GDP
    c. Educational opportunity
    d. High population density

17. In recent years, agricultural production has been affected by which of the following?
    a. The prevalence of biotechnology and GMOs
    b. Weaker crop yields due to poor soil
    c. Plagues of pests, which have limited food production
    d. Revolutions in irrigation, which utilize salinated water

18. The process of globalization can best be described as what?
    a. The integration of the world's economic systems into a singular entity
    b. The emergence of powerful nations seeking world dominance
    c. The absence of nation-states who seek to control certain areas
    d. Efforts to establish a singular world government for the world's citizens

Answer Explanations

1. C: Map projections, such as the Mercator Projection, are useful for finding positions on the globe, but they attempt to represent a spherical object on a flat surface. As a result, they distort areas nearest the poles, which misrepresent the size of Antarctica, Greenland, and other high latitudinal locations. Map projects can include great detail; some illustrate the physical features in an area, and most include both the northern and southern hemispheres.

2. D: Thematic maps create certain themes in which they attempt to illustrate a certain phenomenon or pattern. The obvious theme of a climate map is the climates in the represented areas. Thematic maps are very extensive and can include thousands of different themes, which makes them quite useful for students of geography. Topographic maps (Choice *A*) are utilized to show physical features, conformal projections (Choice *B*) attempt to illustrate the globe in an undistorted fashion, and isoline maps (Choice *C*) illustrate differences in variables between two points on a map.

3. B: Latitudinal and longitudinal coordinates delineate absolute location. In contrast to relative location, which describes a location as compared to another, better-known place, absolute location provides an exact place on the globe through the latitude and longitude system. Choice A, cardinal directions (north, south, east, west) are used in absolute location, but coordinates must be added in order to have an absolute location. Using other, better known locations to find a location, Choice *C*, is referred to as relative location, and absolute location is far more precise than simply finding hemispherical position on the globe.

4. B: Lines of latitude measure distance north and south. The Equator is zero degrees and the Tropic of Cancer is 23 ½ degrees north of the Equator. The distance between those two lines measures degrees north to south, as with any other two lines of latitude. Longitudinal lines, or meridians, measure distance east and west, even though they run north and south down the Globe. Latitude is not inexact, in that there are set distances between the lines. Furthermore, coordinates can only exist with the use of longitude and latitude.

5. C: Developed Nations have better infrastructural systems, which can include government, transportation, financial, and educational institutions. Consequently, its citizens tend to have higher rates of literacy, due to the sheer availability of educational resources and government sanctioned educational systems. In contrast, developing nations, Choice *A*, struggle to provide educational resources to their citizens. Nations in the Northern Hemisphere, Choice *B*, have no greater availability to educational resources than those in the Southern Hemisphere, and centers of trade, Choice *D*, don't necessarily equate to higher levels of education, as many may exist in poorer nations with fewer resources.

6. C: Population density, which is the total number of people divided by the total land area, generally tends to be much higher in urban areas than rural ones. This is true due to high-rise apartment complexes, sewage and freshwater infrastructure, and complex transportation systems, allowing for easy movement of food from nearby farms. Consequently, competition among citizens for resources is certainly higher in high-density areas, as are greater strains on infrastructure within urban centers.

7. C: Although it can place a strain on some resources, population density is not a negative demographic indicator. For example, New York City, one of the most densely populated places on Earth, enjoys one of the highest standards of living in the world. Other world cities such as Tokyo, Los Angeles, and Sydney also have tremendously high population densities and high standards of living. High infant mortality rates, low literacy rates, and low life expectancies are all poor demographic indicators that suggest a low quality of life for the citizens living in those areas.

8. A: Homogeneity, or the condition of similarity, is the unifying factor in most formal regions. Regions have one or more unifying characteristics such as language, religion, history, or economic similarities, which make the area a cohesive formal region. A good example is the Southern United States. In contrast, diversity and multilingualism, Choices *B* and *C*, are factors that may cause a region to lose homogeneity and be more difficult to classify as a region. Also, social mobility, Choice *D*, is a distractor that refers to one's ability to improve their economic standing in society and is not related to formal regions.

9. C: A person will always have the same personal identity. Even though a person may identify with one subgroup or culture now, does not mean that they will agree with it in the future or that they have in the past. Personal identity will continue to change an individual's behavior throughout life.

10. A: Adolescents are most likely to be influenced by pressure from their peers in making life decisions.

11. B: While bullying may affect a person's life and often happens in schools, it does not establish ranking of any sort, and is not educational or part of the educational system. Choice *A* is correct because the rules established by the school help shape a sense of morals in students, or the lack thereof. Choice *C* is correct because the social situations foster sharing, patience, teamwork, and respect. Choice *D* is correct because grades establish a feeling of desire to meet expectations, as well as a fear of failing.

12. C: Each statement about culture is correct except for Choice *C*. Cultures often will adapt to the settings in which they are found. Some cultures derive from such settings and have continued on adapting to what works best to keep that culture.

13. D: Diversity. Diversity refers to how everything and everyone is uniquely different. Choice *A* (behaviorism) is the study of how behavior influences the way human beings interact with their environment. Choice *B* (peer pressure) is when a group uses the majority vote to try to persuade the minority into changing their minds. Finally, Choice *C* (adaptation) is also incorrect because adaptation refers to how a human being adjusts to their surroundings to create a desired outcome. Therefore, Choice *D* (diversity) is correct.

14. D: All of the above. Each of these answers is an indicator of social class. Wealth and standard of living are often related as the amount of money you have helps determine your standard of living. Often times if the standard of living in an area is high, the education environment fosters a higher education level, which can cause a higher level of social class. The opposite is true if the standard of living is low.

15. D: Most nonrenewable resources are easier to harness and utilize than renewable sources. That may sound counterintuitive, but the reality is that it is harder to develop solar, wind, and geothermal infrastructure than it is to build a coal-fired power plant for the production of electricity. Consequently, developing nations tend to rely on these reliable sources in order to fuel their equally developing economy.

16. C: Pull factors are reasons people immigrate to a particular area. Obviously, educational opportunities attract thousands of people on a global level and on a local level. For example, generally areas with strong schools have higher property values, due to the relative demand for housing in those districts. The same is true for nations with better educational opportunities. Unemployment, low GDP, and incredibly high population densities may serve to deter people from moving to a certain place and can be considered push factors.

17. A: The use of biotechnology and GMOs has increased the total amount of food on Earth. Additionally, it has helped to sustain the earth's growing population; however, many activists assert that scientists are creating crops that, in the long run, will be destructive to human health, even though very little evidence exists to prove such an allegation. Agricultural production has not been affected by poorer soil, plagues of pests, or the use of saline for irrigation purposes.

18. A: Globalization has put students and workers in direct conflict with one another despite their relative level of physical separation. For example, students who excel in mathematics and engineering may be recruited by multinational firms who want the best talent for their business despite where they are educated. Furthermore, products produced in other nations are also in competition with global manufacturers to ensure quality craftsmanship at an affordable price. Globalization does not refer to world domination, an absence of nation-states, or a singular world government.

Government and Citizenship

Democratic Principles and Government in the United States

U.S. Constitution and Other Important Historical Documents

Constitutional Underpinnings

The role of government is to maintain a society and provide public services through its formal institutions, protect the citizens of the state, and regulate the economic system. To determine how a government should perform these functions and to protect the rights and liberties of the citizens, states enact a *constitution*, a written document that typically establishes the form of government and delegation of powers within the government, delineates limits on government, and defines protected rights, liberties, and privileges.

Constitution

The U.S. Constitution was drafted in 1787 at the Constitutional Convention in Philadelphia. The goal was to create a government with checks and balances, and by dividing it into three branches, no single branch had ultimate governmental control. They designated the two legislative bodies—the House and Senate—as the Congress. This document is recognized as the world's first formal plan for a modern democracy and the oldest working constitution in existence.

Many people made significant contributions toward expanding the rights and freedoms of Americans by fighting in the Revolutionary War, signing the Declaration of Independence, and serving as delegates to the Constitutional Convention. The men who shaped the democracy of the United States are often referred to as America's *Founding Fathers*. This prestigious group includes:

- George Washington
- Alexander Hamilton
- James Madison
- John Adams
- Thomas Jefferson
- James Monroe
- Benjamin Franklin

Washington, Adams, Jefferson, Madison, and Monroe became U.S. Presidents, and Washington, Hamilton, and Madison were instrumental in leading the charge for discussion at the Constitutional Convention.

Checks and Balances

The branches of governments have a system of checks and balances between them. This is to ensure that no branch oversteps its authority. They include:

- Checks on the Legislative Branch:
  - The president can veto bills passed by Congress.
  - The president can call special sessions of Congress.
  - The judicial branch can rule legislation unconstitutional.
- Checks on the Executive Branch:
  - Congress has the power to override presidential vetoes by a two-thirds majority vote.

- Congress can impeach or remove a president, and the chief justice of the Supreme Court presides over impeachment proceedings.
- Congress can refuse to approve presidential appointments or ratify treaties.
- Checks on the Judicial Branch:
  - The president appoints justices to the Supreme Court, as well as district court and court of appeals judges.
  - The president can pardon federal prisoners.
  - The executive branch can refuse to enforce court decisions.
  - Congress can create federal courts below the Supreme Court.
  - Congress can determine the number of Supreme Court justices.
  - Congress can set the salaries of federal judges.
  - Congress can refuse to approve presidential appointments of judges.
  - Congress can impeach and convict federal judges.

The three branches of government operate separately, but they must rely on each other to create, enforce, and interpret the laws of the United States.

Checks and Balances

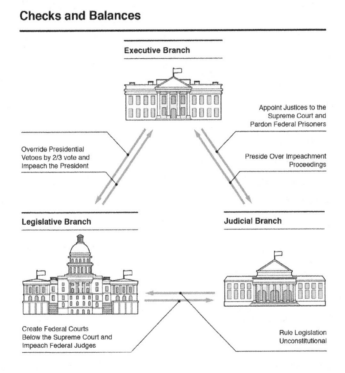

Federalism
To strengthen the central government, while still appeasing the individual states who preferred to remain sovereign over their territories, the framers of the Constitution based the new government upon the principles of *Federalism*—a compound government system that divides powers between a central government and various regional governments. The Constitution clearly defined the roles of both the state governments and the new federal government, specifying the limited power of the federal government and reserving all other powers not restricted by the Constitution to the states in the Tenth Amendment to the Constitution, commonly referred to as the Reservation Clause.

Separation of Powers
The Constitution establishes the specific powers granted to the federal and state governments.

- Delegated powers: the specific powers granted to the federal government by the Constitution
- Implied powers: the unstated powers that can be reasonably inferred from the Constitution
- Inherent powers: the reasonable powers required by the government to manage the nation's affairs and maintain sovereignty
- Reserved powers: the unspecified powers belonging to the state that are not expressly granted to the federal government or denied to the state by the Constitution
- Concurrent powers: the powers shared between the federal and state governments

The Constitution would delegate the following expanded powers to the federal government:

- Coin money
- Declare war
- Establish lower federal courts
- Sign foreign treaties
- Expand the territories of the United States, and admit new states into the union
- Regulate immigration
- Regulate interstate commerce

The following powers were reserved for the states:

- Establish local governments
- Hold elections
- Implement welfare and benefit programs
- Create public school systems
- Establish licensing standards and requirements
- Regulate state corporations
- Regulate commerce within the state

The *concurrent* powers granted to both the federal and state governments in the Constitution include:

- The power to levy taxes
- The power to borrow money
- The power to charter incorporations

Declaration of Independence
The Second Continental Congress met on May 10, 1775 and appointed George Washington as chief of the Continental Army. Although skirmishes began to occur, the Continental Congress made one more attempt to reconcile with the British by sending them the Olive Branch Petition. The petition was refused, and this rejection, combined with a pamphlet written by Thomas Paine in early 1776 called *Common Sense*, pushed the colonists to seek independence in earnest. A committee was chosen to draft a Declaration of Independence, which was written by Thomas Jefferson and approved on July 4, 1776. Another committee was appointed to create an organized government, which was adopted by Congress in November 1777 as the Articles of Confederation. However, this was not approved by all the states until March 1781; therefore, throughout much of the Revolutionary War, there was no official form of government.

<u>Bill of Rights</u>
Collectively referred to as the Bill of Rights, the first ten amendments to the Constitution were added to protect the individual rights of U.S. citizens and to keep the federal government from wielding too much control. These are rights such as *freedom of speech*, *freedom of religion*, *freedom of the press*, and *right to a fair trial*. The Constitution has been amended twenty-seven times in order to accommodate changes and updates. Some of these amendments were made to be more inclusive to the wide range of American citizens. For example, the 14th Amendment, adopted in 1868, abolished slavery and stated that all citizens must be treated equally under Constitutional law and allowed the same protection within each state.

Structure and Functions of the Government Created by U.S. Constitution

The federal government, which is in charge of laws that affect the entire nation, is split into three main branches: executive, judicial, and legislative. It is important to realize that the three segments of the federal government are intended to stand as equal counterparts to the others, and that none of them are "in charge." The executive branch centers on the president, the vice president, and the cabinet. The president and vice president are elected every four years. Also known as the commander-in-chief, the president is the official head of state and serves as the nation's head diplomat and military leader. The vice president acts as the president of the Senate in the legislative branch, while the president appoints members of the cabinet to lead agencies, including the Treasury and Department of Defense. However, the president can only sign and veto laws and cannot initiate them himself.

Instead, the legislative branch, specifically Congress, proposes and debates laws. Congress is bicameral because it is divided into two separate legislative houses. Each state's representation in the House of Representatives is determined proportionally by population, with the total number of voting seats limited to 435. The Senate, in contrast, has only two members per state and a total of one hundred senators. Members of both houses are intended to represent the interests of the constituents in their home states and to bring their concerns to a national level. Ideas for laws, called bills, are proposed in either chamber and then are voted upon according to the body's rules; should the bill pass the first round of voting, the other legislative chamber must approve it before it can be sent to the president. Congress also has a variety of other powers, such as the rights to declare war, collect taxes, and impeach the president.

The judicial branch, though it cannot pass laws itself, serves to interpret the laws. At the federal level, this is done through several tiers of judicial bodies. At the top, the Supreme Court consists of judges appointed by the president; these judges serve for life, unless they resign from their position or are removed by Congress for improper behavior. The Supreme Court's decisions in trials and other judgments rest on the justices' interpretations of the Constitution and enacted laws. As the Constitution remains fundamental to the American legal system, the Supreme Court's rulings on how laws follow or fail to uphold the Constitution have powerful implications on future rulings. Beneath the Supreme Court, there are a number of other federal judicial bodies—courts of appeals, district courts, and courts of special jurisdiction.

Processes by which the U.S. Constitution can be Changed

Ratifying the Constitution
The framers of the Constitution signed the Constitution on September 17, 1787, but the Articles of Confederation required nine of the thirteen states to ratify the document. Conventions were held in all thirteen states and sparked heated debates between those who supported and those who opposed the

new system of government. The Federalists supported the expansion of the federal government, and the anti-Federalists feared that a stronger central government would weaken the states. The anti-Federalists also sought additional protection for civil liberties. The debates between these two parties continued for two years and inspired a series of essays known as the *Federalist Papers* and *Anti-Federalist Papers* authored anonymously by leaders of their respective party.

Notable Federalists and authors of the *Federalist Papers* include:

- Alexander Hamilton: founder of the Federalist Party and advocate for a centralized financial system

- George Washington: commander-in-chief of the Continental Army and future first president of the United States

- James Madison: one of the primary drafters of the Constitution and the future fourth president of the United States

- John Jay: president of the Continental Congress and future first chief justice of the United States

- John Adams: future second president of the United States

Notable anti-Federalists and authors of the *Anti-Federalist Papers* include:

- Thomas Jefferson: primary author of the Declaration of Independence and future third president of the United States

- Patrick Henry: governor of Virginia (1776-1779, 1784-1786)

- Samuel Adams: governor of Massachusetts (1794-1797), lieutenant governor of Massachusetts (1789-1794), and president of the Massachusetts Senate (1782-1785, 1787-1788)

- George Mason: one of only three delegates who did not sign the Constitution at the Constitutional Convention and author of Objections to This Constitution of Government (1787) and the Virginia Declaration of Rights of 1776, which served as the basis for the Bill of Rights

The first state to ratify the Constitution was Delaware in a unanimous vote on December 7, 1787. Several other states followed, and eventually, after ten months, New Hampshire became the ninth state to ratify the Constitution in June 1788. However, some states still remained divided between Federalist and anti-Federalist sentiments and had yet to approve the document, including the two most populous states, Virginia and New York. To reconcile their differing views, the Federalists agreed to include a bill of rights if anti-Federalists supported the new Constitution. Federalist sentiment prevailed, and the remaining states approved the document. On May 29, 1790, the last holdout, Rhode Island, ratified the Constitution by two votes. As promised, the Bill of Rights—the first 10 amendments to the Constitution—was added in 1791, providing expanded civil liberty protection and due process of law.

Enacting Laws in the United States

To enact a new law:

- The bill is introduced to Congress.
- The bill is sent to the appropriate committee for review and revision.

- The approved bill is sent to the Speaker of the House and the majority party leader of the Senate, who places the bill on the calendar for review.
- The houses debate the merits of the bill and recommend amendments.

    o In the House of Representatives, those who wish to debate about a bill are allowed only a few minutes to speak, and amendments to the bill are limited.

    o In the Senate, debates and amendments are unlimited, and those who wish to postpone a vote may do so by filibuster, refusing to stop speaking.

- The approved bill is revised in both houses to ensure identical wording in both bills.
- The revised bill is returned to both houses for final approval.
- The bill is sent to the president, who may

    o Sign the bill into law

    o Veto the bill

    o Take no action, resulting in the bill becoming law if Congress remains in session for ten days or dying if Congress adjourns before ten days have passed

Changes in Role of the U.S. Government Over Time

New Deal Legislation and Wartime Politics

In 1932, in response to the looming global Great Depression of the 1930s, U.S. voters elected President Franklin Delano Roosevelt (FDR) to office because his presidential campaign promised to pull the United States out of economic despair. Unlike his predecessor—President Herbert Hoover—FDR eventually accepted the fact that the federal government would have to play a role in reviving the tattered U.S. economy. On March 4, 1933, FDR pledged a "New Deal" to the American people, one that would regain the trust of down-and-out American workers. This promise of a New Deal was followed by a deluge of socialist-democratic legislation. The New Deal attempted to revive the American economy through public works projects carried out by organizations such as the U.S. Civilian Conservation Corps. These public works projects and government-backed organizations provided jobs to unemployed men and women across the country.

By the end of the 1930s, the FDR administration had spent nearly $10 billion on the construction of hundreds of thousands of public buildings, roads, bridges, and airports. The New Deal also created new government agencies that could help struggling businesses and farms; it dispersed billions of dollars to welfare and relief programs for the poor. The New Deal, however, was just the beginning of socialist-democratic policies being infused into the economic fiber of the United States. Although the New Deal economy only improved slowly prior to the advent of World War II, the changes brought about by FDR's administration transformed the entire essence of the U.S. government's beliefs regarding the role of government in business and the economy. Some describe FDR's policies as the beginning of a New Deal Order that continued well into the Obama administration of the early 2000s. Others pejoratively call his policies the beginning of the U.S. "welfare state." Regardless of the terminology used to describe the New Deal programs, one cannot deny that the New Deal inevitably revolutionized the relationship between the federal government and the economy. The New Deal extended the reach of federal government, paving the way to expanded executive powers.

The New Deal, however, did not solely pull the United States out of the Great Depression—the U.S. involvement in World War II hastened economic recovery through wartime policies and production. During this time, the United States expanded its military-industrial complex, paving the way to the economic excesses of the Cold War and the Space Race with the Soviet Union. This expansion, however, often came at the cost of civil rights, as thousands of Japanese Americans, perceived as a threat to national security, were interned throughout the war via FDR's Executive Order 9066. Executive Order 9066 perhaps sheds light on the "darker side" of the expansion of executive powers during the Second World War. Regardless of ethical analysis or judgment, Executive Order 9066 illustrates the ways in which the FDR administration expanded the reach of federal government, both prior to and during World War II.

Civil Rights

Citizens living in a democracy have several rights and responsibilities to uphold. The first duty is that they uphold the established laws of the government. In a democracy, a system of nationwide laws is necessary to ensure that there is some degree of order. Therefore, citizens must try to obey the laws and also help enforce them because a law that is inadequately enforced, such as early civil rights laws in the South, is almost useless. Optimally, a democratic society's laws will be accepted and followed by the community as a whole.

However, conflict can occur when an unjust law is passed. For instance, much of the civil rights movement centered around Jim Crow laws in the South that supported segregation between black and whites. Yet these practices were encoded in state laws, which created a dilemma for African Americans who wanted equality but also wanted to respect the law. Fortunately, a democracy offers a degree of protection from such laws by creating a system in which government leaders and policies are constantly open to change in accordance with the will of citizens. Citizens can influence the laws that are passed by voting for and electing members of the legislative and executive branches to represent them at the local, state, and national levels.

This, however, requires citizens to be especially vigilant in protecting their liberties because they cannot depend solely on the existing government to meet their needs. To assert their role in a democracy, citizens should be active voters and speak out on issues that concern them. Even with these safeguards, it is possible for systems to be implemented that inhibit active participation. For instance, many southern states had laws that prevented blacks from voting. Under such circumstances, civil rights leaders felt that they had no choice but to resist the laws in order to defend their personal rights. Once voting became possible, civil rights groups strove to ensure that their votes counted by changing state and national policy.

Changing Relationships Among the Three Branches of the Federal Government

War Powers Act

During his first administration, Franklin D. Roosevelt's New Deal political agenda met with a tremendous amount of hostility from the Supreme Court. The Supreme Court overturned many New Deal programs in just a few years because many justices believed Roosevelt's initiative was too radically socialist in nature. Despite these invalidations, Roosevelt won the 1936 election with a landslide victory. Roosevelt fought back against the Supreme Court by attempting to expand the number of appointed justices to a total of fifteen. On February 5, 1937—after initiating his efforts in an address to Congress and in a Fireside Chat—Roosevelt set forward the Judicial Procedures Reform Bill of 1937, which, among other things, attempted to add the six extra Supreme Court justices. The plan was eventually shot down by the checks and balances system of the U.S. government. Congress believed the bill was unconstitutional and placed too much power in the hands of the executive branch and that it would make the government into "one of men rather than one of law." This power increased to the point that Congress eventually passed the War Powers Act of 1973 that officially tried to limit the president's power to declare an armed conflict. This act emerged in the years following the Korean and Vietnam armed conflicts that waged on for many years without an official declaration of war.

Judicial Review
The case of *Marbury vs. Madison* established the policy of judicial review, which declared that the Supreme Court could rule whether or not an act of Congress was constitutional. The case of *McCullough vs. Maryland* affirmed that Congress had the power to pass laws that were "necessary and proper" in order to carry out its other duties. The case also upheld the supremacy of federal laws over state laws when they came into conflict.

Constitutional Amendments

Thirteenth Amendment
The Thirteenth Amendment abolished slavery and involuntary servitude, except as punishment for a crime. The issue of slavery was no longer in the states' hands. Although the Emancipation Proclamation freed slaves in the Confederacy, the status of former slaves remained uncertain as the war neared its conclusion. Many Northerners did not hold strong views on slavery, but most wanted to punish the South and resolve the primary cause of the bloody Civil War. The Northern states all immediately ratified the amendment, and in December 1865, enough reconstructed Southern states ratified the amendment for it to be adopted into law.

Fourteenth Amendment
The Fourteenth Amendment prohibited states from depriving life, liberty, or property without due process and from violating equal protection based on race, color, or previous condition of servitude. Now, all persons born or naturalized in the United States were considered legal citizens. Although revolutionary for the theoretical rights of all American citizens, newly freed or otherwise, the Fourteenth Amendment did not provide actual federally enforced equal protection until the Civil Rights Act of 1964.

Jim Crow Laws
Southern states circumvented the Fourteenth Amendment and imposed what were referred to as Jim Crow laws, which established racial segregation of public facilities. These "separate but equal" facilities included the military, workplaces, public schools, restaurants, restrooms, transportation, and recreational facilities. Despite the label of "separate but equal," most facilities reserved for African Americans were considerably inferior.

In 1896, the Supreme Court handed down a decision in the case of *Plessy vs. Ferguson*, in which Homer Plessy, a Louisiana man of mixed race, attempted to board a railway car reserved for "whites only" and was charged for violating the separate car law. Plessy subsequently filed suit against the state, claiming they violated his Fourteenth Amendment rights. The Supreme Court decided in favor of the state, ruling that the law was not unconstitutional. The Supreme Court upheld separate but equal laws until the 1954 case of *Brown vs. the Board of Education of Topeka* where the Supreme Court ruled that racial segregation of public schools violated the Fourteenth Amendment.

Fifteenth Amendment
The Fifteenth Amendment prohibits the government from denying a citizen the right to vote for reasons of race, color, or previous condition of servitude. Adopted in 1870, the last of the Reconstruction

Amendments, the Fifteenth Amendment sought to protect newly freed slaves' right to vote. As discussed below, most states interpreted the amendment to only apply to male suffrage. In addition, Southern states passed a series of laws to systematically disenfranchise African Americans, like poll taxes, literacy tests, and residency rules. The use of violence and intimidation for political purpose was also common. Meaningful change did not occur until the Civil Rights Movement, nearly one hundred years later. In 1964, the Twenty-Fourth Amendment prohibited the states and federal government from charging a poll tax or fee to vote. Later, the Voting Rights Act of 1965 empowered the federal government to enforce the Fifteenth Amendment on the states for the first time.

Seventeenth Amendment

The Seventeenth Amendment, which was passed in 1913, allows for the direct election of U.S. senators by the American people. This amendment is considered a victory for American liberal democracy and the multicentury efforts for democratization in U.S. society. By allowing the direct election of U.S. senators, the U.S. government continued its transition from a classical republic to a democratic-republic that allowed for limited spheres of popular democratic practices.

Nineteenth Amendment

The Fourteenth Amendment specified equal treatment for all citizens; however, it did not establish women's right to vote in elections, known as women's suffrage. Although landowning women were allowed to vote in New Jersey in the late eighteenth century, the right was removed in 1807. The fight for women's suffrage continued in the middle of the nineteenth century. Famous women's rights activists include Susan B. Anthony, Lucy Stone, and Elizabeth Cady Stanton, who authored the *Declaration of Rights and Sentiments*, which demanded access to the civil liberties granted to all men. Women gained the right to vote in 1869 in Wyoming and 1870 in Utah.

The women's suffrage movement gained momentum in the early twentieth century after their increased participation in the economy during World War I when much of the workforce went overseas to fight. The National Women's Party picketed outside the White House and led a series of protests in Washington, resulting in the imprisonment of the party's leader, Alice Paul. In 1918, Woodrow Wilson declared his support for women's suffrage despite earlier opposition, and in 1920, Congress passed the Nineteenth Amendment, which made it illegal for states to withhold voting rights based on gender.

Twenty-Fourth Amendment

The Twenty-Fourth Amendment prohibited Congress and state governments from instituting poll taxes or any other types of taxes that limit voting rights. Prior to its ratification on January 23, 1964, several states—Virginia, Alabama, Texas, Arkansas, and Mississippi—maintained poll taxes that prohibited low-income voters, specifically black voters, from registering for elections. The passage of the Twenty-Fourth Amendment is considered a tremendous historical victory for the civil rights movement.

Twenty-Sixth Amendment

Signed into law by President Richard Nixon on March 10, 1971, the Twenty-Sixth Amendment to the U.S. Constitution ruled in favor of a uniform national voting age for all local, state, and federal elections. Previously, the 1970 *Oregon v. Mitchell* Supreme Court decision decided that eighteen- to twenty-year-olds in the United States could only vote for the presidential elections, but not for state officials. This decision led to widespread protest, culminating in the Twenty-Sixth Amendment, which made eighteen the uniform national voting age for all elections.

Landmark Supreme Court Decisions

Regents of the University of California v. Bakke was a 1978 court case that witnessed Allan Bakke, a white applicant, sue the Medical School at the University of California at Davis when he was twice denied access to medical school even though his standardized test scores were significantly higher than some minority applicants who were admitted with lower MCAT scores. Bakke claimed that the admissions quotas for students of color violated the Fourteenth Amendment's Equal Protection Clause and Title IV Civil Rights Act of 1964. Although the California Supreme Court agreed that the quota system was discriminatory in nature, the Supreme Court, in a 5–4 decision, ruled that the quota system was constitutionally sound and did not violate the Equal Protection Clause of the U.S. Constitution. Thus, race-based admissions continued in university systems across the United States.

Roe v. Wade was a 1973 court case that determined, in a 7–2 decision, written by Justice Harry Blackman, that a Texas statute that criminalized abortion was unconstitutional for its violation of Jane Roe's right to privacy. According to the Supreme Court decision, abortions occurring within the first trimester of pregnancy (and abortions related to maternal health carried out in the second and third trimesters) rested within a woman's "zone of privacy." The Supreme Court legitimized this "zone of privacy" by citing the First, Fourth, Ninth, and Fourteenth Amendments. This landmark court case legitimized a woman's right to carry out an abortion in the first trimester.

Miranda v. Arizona was a landmark 1966 Supreme Court case that, in a 5–4 decision written by Chief Justice Earl Warren, ruled that police forces and other law enforcement agencies must inform criminal suspects of their constitutional rights, specifically of their right to an attorney and against self-incrimination. Ernesto Miranda, a criminal suspect who was eventually convicted of rape and murder, was detained, interrogated, and convicted without ever being read his rights. Miranda, who had a history of mental illness and low achievement levels in school, never had a counsel present during his interrogation, but he was still sentenced to twenty to thirty years in prison. After a failed appeal to the Arizona Supreme Court, Miranda and his attorney appealed to the U.S. Supreme Court. The court's decision to back Miranda's appeal helped protect individual rights by limiting police powers. Today, every suspected criminal must be read their Miranda Rights.

Prior to the 8–1 Supreme Court decision to *Engel v. Vitale* (1962), New York State law mandated that each school day begin with the Pledge of Allegiance and a nondenominational prayer to God. Although the law stated that students could abstain if they found the nondenominational prayer objectionable, Steven Engel, a Jewish parent, sued on behalf of his child, arguing that the New York State statute violated the First Amendment rights of his child. The 8–1 decision in favor of Engel's case was based on the belief that the purpose of the First Amendment was to prevent government meddling in religious affairs (and vice versa).

Brown v. Board of Education is a landmark unanimous civil rights decision in the Supreme Court in 1954 that made it unconstitutional to segregate public schooling based on race. This decision overturned *Plessy v. Ferguson* (1896), paving the way to the United States of America's first wave of lawful desegregation efforts. Citing the Equal Protection Clause of the Fourteenth Amendment, the Supreme Court, under the leadership of Chief Justice Earl Warren, unanimously decided that Oliver Brown, the parent of a child denied access to a white school in Topeka, Kansas, was justified in his battle against segregation in public schools. The case marked an important victory for the civil rights movement and paved the way to a revolution in race relations in the United States.

Schenck v. U.S. (1919) was a Supreme Court decision that witnessed the creation of a "clear and present danger" test in determining the limitations of free speech in the United States. The decision, which denied Schenck's suit, stated that a citizen's free speech could be limited if that speech presented a "clear and present danger" to the safety and security of the nation and its citizenry. Schenck, a socialist protester, was jailed for posing a clear threat to the United States. The decision reinforced the Espionage Act that placed limits on the First Amendment.

Plessy v. Ferguson (1896) set the stage for Jim Crow and legal segregation by claiming that "separate but equal" public facilities were constitutional. *Plessy v. Ferguson* was later overturned by *Brown v. Board of Education* (1954). Nevertheless, for nearly sixty years, it helped to legally separate U.S. citizens by the color of their skin.

Dred Scott v. Sanford was an infamous 1857 Supreme Court ruling that further decreased the rights of African Americans living in the United States by claiming that they were not citizens and therefore could not sue in federal courts. Additionally, the Supreme Court decision reinforced the belief that slavery could not be outlawed in western territories prior to statehood.

Cherokee Nation v. Georgia was a Supreme Court case in 1831 that solidified the unequal nature of U.S.-Indian relations by declaring that Indian nations, although marginalized and persecuted, were neither independent nor foreign in nature. They, therefore, did not possess constitutional protection, and the Supreme Court could not hear the Cherokee Nation's case against Georgia because they did not have the jurisdiction to resolve the case.

McCulloch v. Maryland (1819) declared that, by unanimous decision, the state of Maryland did not possess the right/power to tax the Bank of the United States. The Supreme Court decision made the Second Bank of the United States a constitutional institution and established the doctrine of "implied powers" that stated the state governments could not interfere with legal actions decided by the federal government.

Marbury v. Madison (1803) increased the power of the Supreme Court by making constitutional the principle of "judicial review" that allows the Supreme Court to strike down any act of Congress that runs counter to the laws of the Constitution.

Relationship Between the States and the National Government of the United States

Federalism is a set of principles that divides power between a central government and regional governments. Sovereign states often combine into a federation, and to do so, they cede some degree of sovereignty to establish a functional central government to handle broad national policies. The United States Constitution structures the central government according to principles of Federalism. Canada is another example of a form of government with a Federalist structure.

Texas State Government and Local Governments

The Texas state government is divided into three major branches: the legislative branch, the executive branch, and the judicial branch.

The legislative branch proposes and ratifies laws for the state. Like the U.S. federal legislative branch, the Texas state legislature is bicameral, which means it's divided into two houses. These are the House of Representatives and the Senate. Senators serve four-year terms; representatives serve two-year terms. In total, there are 31 members of the Texas Senate and 150 members of the Texas House of

Representatives. Each senator and representative is responsible for a district that has roughly the same number of people as other districts. Both senators and representatives must be legal residents of their district for at least one year prior to campaigning for office. Representatives must be Texas citizens for 2 years, and they must be at least 21 years old. Senators must be Texas citizens for at least 5 years, and they must be at least 26 years old.

The legislative branch of Texas can create new laws and bring them to a vote at special periods called sessions. While the House and Senate share many legislative duties, only the House can propose and vote on laws that increase taxes or raise money for the state government. During these scheduled sessions, which can last up to 140 days, the legislature addresses bills and laws. At times, the governor can call special sessions, which last up to 30 days. It's also important to note that the legislature possesses the authority to impeach government officials. The most notorious impeachment in state history occurred in 1917, when Governor James Ferguson was removed for failing to properly enforce banking laws, among other violations.

There's a complex process to create new laws in the Texas state legislature. This process begins when legislators propose a bill. During sessions, clerks read the bill word for word to members of the House and/or Senate. Next, the Speaker of the House or Lieutenant Governor assigns a committee to each bill. Members of each committee—including the lead committee member, known as a chairperson—study the bill, rewrite sections, accept the bill, or reject the bill. The entire house votes and debates a bill once it receives approval by a committee. If the bill is rejected, it "dies." In some cases, a conference committee is created, consisting of members from both houses of state Congress, so that the bill can be rehashed to satisfy more legislators. The governor then has the choice to sign the bill into law, ignore the bill until it becomes law in ten days, or veto the bill. If vetoed, a 2/3 vote by Congress could override the veto so that the bill becomes a law.

The most powerful and important official of the Texas executive branch is the governor. Governors serve four-year terms, with no limit on the amount of terms that a governor can serve. Candidates must be thirty years old to campaign for governor. As the head of the state executive branch, the governor often attempts to sway the motions of the legislature. Although a governor cannot create laws, s/he can urge the legislature to put new bills into motion. Governors can also veto bills. In addition, governors possess the right to use a line-item veto, which allows governors to delete portions of budget bills that they dislike. The governor also collaborates with the legislature by calling special sessions, and s/he can collaborate with the judicial branch by granting pardons for crimes or reprieves from the death penalty. Texas governors also work with the state military and National Guard in times of crisis. In extreme cases, governors can declare martial law or states of emergency.

Although there are thousands of elected executive officials that work with the governor, the most important secondary executive is the lieutenant governor. Lieutenant governors are essentially second in command; they work with the legislature and serve as active governor when the governor is out of state for business or travel. Hundreds of agencies fall under the umbrella of the executive branch in Texas. The largest is the Department of Criminal Justice, which focuses on crime prevention and public safety.

The Supreme Court heads the Texas judicial branch. All judges in the Supreme Court serve four to six year terms and must be U.S. citizens. Within the Texas Supreme Court, there is one Chief Justice and eight other justices. The justices examine cases for both criminal and civil law violations. The lower municipal, county, and district courses each hold trials for their own respective cases. Additionally, appellate courts oversee appeals. High courts in the Texas state judiciary system possess the right to label a law as unconstitutional through judicial review. Citizens also participate in the Texas judicial system as members of petit juries (civil and criminal trials) and grand juries (felony cases).

Citizenship and Political Processes in the United States

Political Parties, Interest Groups, and the Media in the U.S. Political System

Political Parties, Interest Groups, and Mass Media

Political Parties

A *political party* is an organized group of voters who share the same political values and support or oppose the same policies. Members of a political party vote for the candidates from their party who they believe share their values and will approve or reject the policies they support or oppose. Political parties often determine the positions party members take on issues of policy, such as the economy, taxation, and social services.

Slavery divided the nation and created unrest among the political parties, as members took opposing views and splintered into separate sects of the party or started new parties with members who shared their views. The Whig Party, so divided by the differing views of the members, collapsed.

Former Whigs joined or formed the following parties:

- Constitutional Union Party: Devoted itself to a single-issue platform of preserving the Union and recognizing the Constitution as the supreme rule of law. The party did not take a firm issue on slavery, but vigorously opposed secession.

- Democratic Party: Divided into northern and southern factions over slavery, but the Democrats sought to compromise and remain unified.

- Know-Nothing Party: Advocated for an anti-immigration single-party platform, especially immigrants from Catholic countries.

- Republican Party: Formed in response to the Kansas-Nebraska Act, which threatened to extend slavery into new territories, called for the abolition of slavery and argued for a more modernized economy.

Modern Political Parties

The defeat of the South in the Civil War resulted in the Republicans holding power until the 1930s, when Franklin D. Roosevelt, a Democrat, was elected president. Roosevelt instituted the New Deal, which included many social policies that built an expansive social welfare program to provide financial support to citizens during the Great Depression. The Republican Party opposed this interference by the government, and the two parties became more strongly divided. The political landscape again shifted during the Civil Rights Movement, as Southern Democrats fled to the Republican Party over their opposition to enforcing federal civil rights onto states. This strengthened the modern coalition between economic conservatives and social conservatives.

Today, the Democrats and Republicans are still the two major parties, though many third parties have emerged. The Republicans and Democrats hold opposing views on the degree of state intervention into private business, taxation, states' rights, and government assistance. The ideals of these parties include:

Republican (or the Grand Old Party [GOP])
- Founded by abolitionists
- Support capitalism, free enterprise, and a policy of noninterference by the government
- Support strong national defense
- Support deregulation and restrictions of labor unions
- Advocate for states' rights
- Oppose abortion
- Support traditional values, often based on Judeo-Christian foundations, including considerable opposition to same-sex marriage

Democrat
- Founded by anti-Federalists and rooted in classical Liberalism
- Promote civil rights, equal opportunity and protection under the law, and social justice
- Support government-instituted social programs and safety nets
- Support environmental issues
- Support government intervention and regulation, and advocate for labor unions
- Support universal health care

Some prominent third parties include:

- Reform Party: support political reform of the two-party system
- Green Party: support environmental causes
- Libertarian Party: support a radical policy of nonintervention and small, localized government

Interest Groups
An *interest group* is an organization with members who share similar social concerns or political interests. Members of political interest groups work together to influence policy decisions that benefit a particular segment of society or cause. Interest groups might include:

- Activist groups, like the NAACP, American Civil Liberties Union (ACLU), or People for the Ethical Treatment of Animals (PETA)
- Corporations, like pharmaceutical companies or banks
- Small-business advocates
- Religious groups, like the Concerned Women PAC and the Muslim Public Affairs Council
- Unions, such as the Association of Teacher Educators and International Brotherhood of Electrical Workers

Lobbyists
To promote their causes and influence policy in their favor, many interest groups employ *lobbyists*, paid advocates who work to influence lawmakers. Lobbying is a controversial practice, but it is sanctioned and protected as free speech. Lobbying from interest groups has a powerful impact on many policy decisions made in the United States. Examples of lobbyist groups include American Israel Public Affairs Committee (AIPAC) and Pharmaceutical Research and Manufacturers of America.

Mass Media
Mass media refers to the various methods by which the majority of the general public receives news and information. Mass media includes television, newspapers, radio, magazines, online news outlets, and social media networks. The general public relies on mass media for political knowledge and cultural

socialization, as well as the majority of their knowledge of current events, social issues, and political news.

Evolution of Mass Media

- Until the end of the nineteenth century, print media such as newspapers and magazines was the only form of mass communication.

- In the 1890s, after the invention of the radio, broadcast media become a popular form of communication, particularly among illiterate people.

- In the 1940s, television superseded both print and broadcast media as the most popular form of mass media.

- In 1947, President Harry Truman gave the first political speech on television.

- In 1952, Dwight Eisenhower was the first political candidate to air campaign ads on television.

- Today, the Internet is the most widespread mass media technology, and citizens have instant access to news and information, as well as interactive platforms on which they can communicate directly with political leaders or share their views through social media, blogs, and independent news sites.

Influence of Mass Media on Politics

Mass media has a powerful effect on public opinion and politics. Mass media:

- Shapes public interests
- Enables candidates to reach voters wherever they are
- Determines what is and is not considered important in society based on how it prioritizes events and issues
- Provides the context in which to report events
- Is paid for by advertisers who may pressure news outlets to suppress or report information in their own interests

Filling Elective and Appointive Public Offices

As members of a Constitutional Republic with certain aspects of a *democracy*, U.S. citizens are empowered to elect most government leaders, but the process varies between branch and level of government. Presidential elections at the national level use the *Electoral College* system. Rather than electing the president directly, citizens cast their ballots to select *electors* that represent each state in the college.

Legislative branches at the federal and state level are also determined by elections. In some areas, judges are elected, but in other states judges are appointed by elected officials. The U.S. has a *two-party system*, meaning that most government control is under two major parties: the Republican Party and the Democratic Party. It should be noted that the two-party system was not designed by the Constitution but gradually emerged over time.

Electoral Process

During the *electoral process*, the citizens of a state decide who will represent them at the local, state, and federal level. Different political officials that citizens elect through popular vote include but are not limited to:

- City mayor
- City council members
- State representative
- State governor
- State senator
- House member
- U.S. Senator
- President

The Constitution grants the states the power to hold their own elections, and the voting process often varies from city to city and state to state.

While a popular vote decides nearly all local and state elections, the president of the United States is elected by the *Electoral College*, rather than by popular vote. Presidential elections occur every four years on the first Tuesday after the first Monday in November.

The electoral process for the president of the United States includes:

Primary Elections and Caucuses

In a presidential election, *nominees* from the two major parties, as well as some third parties, run against each other. To determine who will win the nomination from each party, the states hold *primary elections* or *caucuses*.

During the primary elections, the states vote for who they want to win their party's nomination. In some states, primary elections are closed, meaning voters may only vote for candidates from their registered party, but other states hold *open primaries* in which voters may vote in either party's primary.

Some states hold *caucuses* in which the members of a political party meet in small groups, and the decisions of those groups determine the party's candidate.

Each state holds a number of delegates proportional to its population, and the candidate with the most delegate votes receives the domination. Some states give all of their delegates (*winner-take-all*) to the primary or caucus winner, while some others split the votes more proportionally.

Conventions

The two major parties hold national conventions to determine who will be the nominee to run for president from each party. The *delegates* each candidate won in the primary elections or caucuses are the voters who represent their states at the national conventions. The candidate who wins the most delegate votes is given the nomination. Political parties establish their own internal requirements and procedures for how a nominee is nominated.

Conventions are typically spread across several days, and leaders of the party give speeches, culminating with the candidate accepting the nomination at the end.

<u>Campaigning</u>

Once the nominees are selected from each party, they continue campaigning into the national election. Prior to the mid-1800s, candidates did not actively campaign for themselves, considering it dishonorable to the office, but campaigning is now rampant. Modern campaigning includes, but is not limited to:

- Raising money
- Meeting with citizens and public officials around the country
- Giving speeches
- Issuing policy proposals
- Running internal polls to determine strategy
- Organizing strategic voter outreach in important districts
- Participating in debates organized by a third-party private debate commission
- Advertising on television, through mail, or on the Internet

<u>General Election</u>

On the first Tuesday after the first Monday in November of an election year, every four years, the people cast their votes by secret ballot for president in a *general election*. Voters may vote for any candidate, regardless of their party affiliation. The outcome of the popular vote does not decide the election; instead, the winner is determined by the Electoral College.

<u>Electoral College</u>

When the people cast their votes for president in the general election, they are casting their votes for the *electors* from the *Electoral College* who will elect the president. In order to win the presidential election, a nominee must win 270 of the 538 electoral votes. The number of electors is equal to the total number of senators and representatives from each state plus three electoral votes for Washington D.C. which does not have any voting members in the legislative branch.

The electors typically vote based on the popular vote from their states. Although the Constitution does not require electors to vote for the popular vote winner of their state, no elector voting against the popular vote of their state has ever changed the outcome of an election. Due to the Electoral College, a nominee may win the popular vote and still lose the election.

For example, let's imagine that there only two states, Wyoming and Nebraska, in a presidential election. Wyoming has three electoral votes and awards them all to the winner of the election by majority vote. Nebraska has five electoral votes and also awards them all to the winner of the election by majority vote. If 500,000 people in Wyoming vote and the Republican candidate wins by a vote of 300,000 to 200,000, the Republican candidate will win the three electoral votes for the state. If the same number of people vote in Nebraska, but the Republican candidate loses the state by a vote of 249,000 to 251,000, the Democratic candidate wins the five electoral votes from that state. This means the Republican candidate will have received 549,000 popular votes but only three electoral votes, while the Democratic candidate will have received 451,000 popular votes but will have won five electoral votes. Thus, the

Republican won the popular vote by a considerable margin, but the Democratic candidate will have been awarded more electoral votes, which are the only ones that matter.

	Wyoming	Nebraska	Total # of Votes
Republican Votes	300,000	249,000	**549,000**
Democratic Votes	200,000	251,000	**451,000**
Republican Electoral Votes	3	0	**3**
Democratic Electoral Votes	0	5	**5**

If no one wins the majority of electoral votes in the presidential election, the House of Representatives decides the presidency, as required by the Twelfth Amendment. They may only vote for the top three candidates, and each state delegation votes as a single bloc. Twenty-six votes, a simple majority, are required to elect the president. The House has only elected the president twice, in 1801 and 1825.

Here how many electoral votes each state and the District of Columbia have:

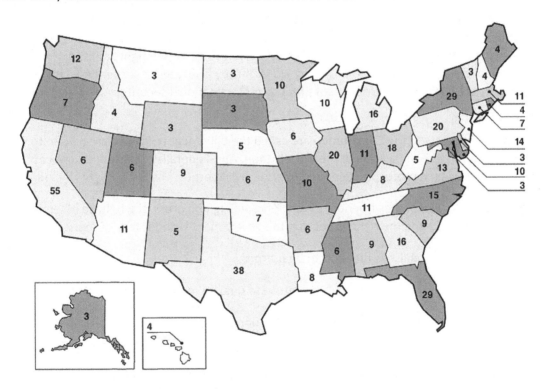

Processes for Making Policy in the United States

The legislative branch of the United States of America is the policy-making branch of the federal government. The legislative branch is made up of two houses: Congress and the House of Representatives. Together, these two branches make laws and amend the Constitution through a federal process of checks and balances. Policies can be enacted through petitions and lobbying efforts by common citizens. Protest is another highly visible way to call for legislative changes. Boycotts and strikes can grab the attention of lawmakers, forcing their hands to enact certain bills or amendments. Conventionally, common citizens change policy by electing officials at the local, state, and federal level via the U.S. voting process. Citizens can also enact change by taking office or joining local lobbying groups or nonprofits. Technology has recently changed the ways in which citizens try to enact change. The Internet and social media have paved the way to a new era of lobbying and protest. Millions of U.S.

citizens now take to their smartphones, tablets, and computers to call for policy changes. This method of enacting policy change has actually been quite successful in the United States and abroad. The Arab Spring in the Middle East, for instance, was largely built upon the instant connection and revolutionary networking available via social media and the Internet.

Rights Guaranteed by the U.S. Constitution

Civil Liberties and Civil Rights

The protection of *civil liberties* is one of the most important political values upon which American society is based. Though the terms *civil liberties* and *civil rights* are commonly used interchangeably, they describe two very distinct types of protections. Civil liberties refer to the legal protections afforded to U.S. citizens against government action, while civil rights refer to equal treatment under the law, especially in relation to minority groups, like women, African Americans, and Hispanics.

Civil Liberties

A civil liberty is a protection from legal action by the government. Civil liberties are granted by the Constitution in the first ten amendments, collectively known as the Bill of Rights, which were added to the Constitution in 1791. Civil liberties are conditional and do not afford protection from government action in every scenario. They can be restricted when they infringe on the rights of others; for example, with defamation, child pornography, or "fighting words." They also may be suspended with just cause, such as in the case of limiting the freedom of press to protect national security.

The Bill of Rights

The first ten amendments of the Constitution are called the Bill of Rights. They were passed to win over anti-Federalists during the ratification of the Constitution. Anti-Federalists wanted assurances that the federal government would protect certain fundamental civil liberties. The Bill of Rights includes:

- Amendment I: Establishes freedom of religion, speech, and press; the right to assemble in peaceful protest; and the right to petition the government without fear of reprisal

- Amendment II: Establishes the right to bear arms

- Amendment III: Establishes the right to refuse to quarter, or house, soldiers in time of war

- Amendment IV: Establishes protection against unreasonable search and seizure and requires a warrant based on probable cause supported by specific information

- Amendment V: Protects against self-incrimination in criminal trials, except in cases of military court martial; protects against being tried more than once for the same crime, known as double jeopardy; and protects against seizure of private property for public use without compensation

- Amendment VI: Establishes extensive set of rights to protect defendants in a criminal trial—the right to a speedy and timely trial before a judge and impartial jury of peers, the right to be informed of criminal accusations, the right to present and compel witnesses in defense of the accused, the right to confront witnesses against the accused, and the right to assistance of counsel

- Amendment VII: Protects the right to a trial by jury in civil cases exceeding a dollar amount of $20

- Amendment VIII: Protects against cruel and unusual punishment and excessive fines

- Amendment IX: Establishes the existence of additional fundamental rights unnamed in the Constitution; protects those rights that are not enumerated

- Amendment X: Reserves all powers that are not specified to the federal government or prohibited to the states or the people, establishing the principles of separation of powers and Federalism

Civil Rights

Civil rights concern who is protected, while *civil liberties* concern what is protected. Civil rights refer to protection against unfair treatment based on characteristics such as gender, race, ethnicity, religion, sexual orientation, and disability. The struggle for civil rights has a long history in the United States. Following the Civil War, the ratification of three amendments—Thirteenth, Fourteenth, and Fifteenth, collectively known as the Reconstruction Amendments—expanded the constitutional protection of equal civil rights.

Democratic Process in the United States

Political Beliefs and Behaviors

Political beliefs are the beliefs held by the citizens of a nation about the government, leaders, policies, and the related political issues of their state. Political beliefs differ among individual citizens, but in America, a strong basis of democracy shapes the political beliefs, behaviors, and attitudes.

Democratic Values

The foundation of democratic values upon which the United States is based include:

- The people are sovereign, and they elect a representative government to exercise that sovereignty.
- The citizens of the nation are equal under the law.
- The peaceful transition of power is valued regardless of election results.
- The private property of individuals cannot be taken by force by the government without due process or fair compensation.
- The civil liberties of the citizens of the state cannot be abridged or violated by the government without due process.
- The government should be accountable to the citizenry.

Political Socialization

American citizens undergo a process of *political socialization* from early childhood to adulthood during which they develop their individual sense of political identity and civic pride. Children learn about politics in the home from an early age, whether from the views, opinions, and facts of family and friends, or through the media to which they are exposed.

In school, they learn about the nation's political history, basic politics, and democratic values, as well as the ideals of patriotism and the processes of government. As they grow older, they join interest groups, labor unions, religious groups, and political organizations that further influence their political beliefs. This socialization shapes not only the political beliefs and values of individual citizens and groups but the political ideals of the nation and public opinion.

Public Opinion

Public opinion is the shared political ideals, opinions, and attitudes of the people of a state regarding the politics, current events, and social issues that influence policy and shape the political atmosphere of a state. Public opinion is the result of political beliefs, socialization, and current events. Political scientists measure public opinion through:

- Distribution of opinion across demographics such as age, race, gender, and religion
- Strength of the opinion
- Stability of the opinion over time

Public opinion refers to the majority opinion in a democratic state. Citizens express public opinion through the interest groups they join, the media they consume and interact with, and the leaders they elect. To measure public opinion, scientists use polls to gather data. Accurate polling requires:

- Random sampling of representative populations
- Unbiased questions
- Clear instructions for how to answer questions
- Controlled procedures such as the use of telephone, mail, Internet, or in-person interviews with an unbiased pollster
- Accurate reporting of the results, including information about methods, inconsistencies, respondents, and possible sources and degree of error

George Washington

George Washington, the first president of the United States of America, envisioned the creation of a classical republic rather than a democracy. Nevertheless, his leadership helped embed democratic values within the governmental fibers of the United States. Specifically, Washington set the precedent for limited terms as president, warning of the dangers of unchecked executive power. Although he also warned about the dangers of democracy, he is still heralded by Americans as a forefather of democracy because he believed in creating a nation that was governed by the people and for the people.

John Marshall

John Marshall served a lengthy tenure as chief justice during the presidencies of John Adams, Thomas Jefferson, James Madison, James Monroe, John Quincy Adams, and Andrew Jackson. He oversaw many crucial U.S. Supreme Court cases such as *McCulloch v. Maryland* (1819) and *Marbury v. Madison* (1803). Marshall is typically lauded for his push to expand the voting electorate to include more white men. As a delegate to the Virginia Constitutional Convention of 1829–1830, Marshall declared that any white man who served in the War of 1812 or promised military service should have the right to vote. His ideas were crucial for paving the way to an expanded white voting bloc during the Age of Jacksonian Democracy.

Frederick Douglass

Frederick Douglass was a former-slave-turned-statesman who vehemently fought for the rights of African Americans in both antebellum America and the era of Reconstruction. Douglass radically campaigned for the civil rights of African Americans, explicitly noting the obvious inequalities in society through his writings and oratory. Douglass, like other reformers at the time, also fought for women's suffrage as well as abolition.

Elizabeth Cady Stanton

Elizabeth Cady Stanton is famous for her *Declaration of Sentiments*, a women's suffrage document presented at the Seneca Falls Convention in 1848. Stanton was not only a leader in women's suffrage and the early women's rights movement, but she was also a dedicated abolitionist. As a social activist, she fought to extend civil and voting rights to African Americans and women fighting against the limitations of racism and patriarchy. Although she died before women's suffrage was fully realized, she paved the way to later democratic victories such as the Nineteenth Amendment.

Franklin D. Roosevelt

Franklin Delano Roosevelt was the president of the United States toward the tail end of the Great Depression and throughout World War II. During his multiterm presidency, FDR expanded the role of the federal government, instituting many famous public works and social welfare projects through his New Deal policies. FDR's policies and public works helped pave the way to an entire "New Deal Order" in American history that gradually socialized many of the United States' federal programs. His blend of democratic-socialism has traditionally been celebrated as a victory for democracy and social welfare.

Dr. Martin Luther King Jr.

Dr. Martin Luther King Jr. helped begin the peak of the civil rights movement in the United States in the 1950s and 1960s, paving the way to the infamous Civil Rights Act of 1964. This legislation helped protect African Americans from unequal voting laws and institutional discrimination. Dr. King is applauded for his willingness to peacefully protest injustice in the name of American democracy.

Major Reform Movements in the U.S. History

Abolitionist Movement

The abolitionist movement—which was driven by an antislavery sentiment—gained steam in the early to mid-1800s as the United States became increasingly sectionalized in character. The abolitionist movement was not a monolithic, static phenomenon, but rather changed over time as different groups created different visions for solving the United States' slave issue. The American Colonization Society (founded 1816), for instance, helped create the African colony of Liberia as a refuge for freed and enslaved blacks living in the United States. Even within this movement, reformers produced different visions. Some simply wanted to send black residents back to Africa for the benefit of creating a less diverse and conflicted society; others saw Liberia as a way to help blacks regain their cultures overseas. Other movements included the American Anti-Slavery Society, the Philadelphia Female Anti-Slavery Society, the Anti-Slavery Convention of American Women, and the Female Vigilant Society. Led and motivated by women, these organizations brought the abolitionist and women's rights movements closer together, planting the seeds of a coalition that would once again join together in American history during the heart of the civil rights movement of the 1950s and 1960s. Abolition was eventually achieved through President Lincoln's Emancipation Proclamation, thanks in part to the efforts of these reformers.

Public Education Reform Movement

The public education reform movement also gained steam during the early to mid-1800s, as reformers like Horace Mann of Massachusetts pushed for universal and compensatory free public education for all children in the United States of America. Mann and other public school reformers believed that free and compensatory public education would strengthen national unity and civic engagement and better prepare adolescents to enter the U.S. economy as laborers, inventors, and businessmen as adults. Mann and his followers wanted to create a more literate citizenry. By the end of the nineteenth century, Mann's dreams were becoming a reality, as public primary school was made compensatory and free for all citizens. Gradually, the movement expanded to fight for free and compensatory secondary education.

Temperance Movement

The temperance movement emerged out of the spiritual fervor of the Second Great Awakening and the urban decline associated with the Industrial Revolution and early Progressive Era. As early as 1874, concerned women had established the Women's Christian Temperance Union (WCTU). Concerned about rising rates of alcoholism in fathers and male laborers, these women fought for the prohibition of alcohol alongside urban religious leaders and organizations. The temperance movement culminated in the passage of the Eighteenth Amendment in 1917—the so-called Prohibition Amendment—that prohibited the sale and consumption of alcohol. Prohibition was one of the most profound victories for progressive citizens and legislators; however, the amendment was eventually repealed due to rising organized crime rates and immediate backlash from citizens.

Prison Reform Movement

Throughout the eighteenth century, religious leaders and legislators came together to establish the prison reform movement, which moved the United States of America away from public forms of execution and embarrassment and toward the construction of institutions dedicated to criminal reform and individual penitence. During this time, Quakers and other religious leaders helped create the first penitentiaries, or prisons. The most famous of these penitentiaries was Eastern State Penitentiary in Philadelphia, Pennsylvania. Nevertheless, despite their efforts to create a more human form of behavioral correction, these institutions were often characterized by inhumane facilities and cruel forms of punishment (at least by today's standards). This movement inaugurated the creation of the prison-industrial complex in the United States, creating later reform movements such as Angela Davis's prison abolition movement.

Women's Rights

Due to the Women's Liberation Movement and the creation of the National Organization for Women (NOW) in 1966, the 1960s and 1970s were an important time for women. Women gained the right to vote in 1920, but still were not on equal terms with men in many areas. Suffragist leader Alice Paul had introduced the Equal Rights Amendment (ERA) in 1923 to help bridge this gap. Congress finally passed the ERA in 1972 and sent it to the states for ratification. However, not all states ratified the amendment, and to date only a total of thirty-five have ratified it, which is three less than the thirty-eight required to pass. In the controversial 1973 court case *Roe vs. Wade*, the Supreme Court gave women the right to legally obtain abortions within the first three months of pregnancy.

Civil Rights Movement

Brown vs. the Board of Education prohibited segregation in 1954, but the Civil Rights Movement, led by the National Association for the Advancement of Colored People (NAACP) and such famous activists as Martin Luther King Jr. and Malcolm X, did not secure the enforcement of the Fourteenth Amendment until the passage of the Civil Rights Act of 1964, which outlawed discrimination based on gender, race, ethnicity, and religion. African American and Native American women, however, did not gain the right to vote until the Voting Rights Act of 1965, which enforced the voting rights articulated in the Fourteenth Amendment and Fifteenth Amendment. Section 5 of the Voting Rights Act prevented states with a history of discrimination from altering their voting laws without getting approval from the attorney general or a federal district court.

Civic Responsibilities

Political Participation
Citizens express their political beliefs and public opinion through participation in politics. The conventional ways citizens can participate in politics in a democratic state include:

- Obeying laws
- Voting in elections
- Running for public office
- Staying interested and informed of current events
- Learning U.S. history
- Attending public hearings to be informed and to express their opinions on issues, especially on the local level
- Forming interest groups to promote their common goals
- Forming political action committees (PACs) that raise money to influence policy decisions
- Petitioning government to create awareness of issues
- Campaigning for a candidate
- Contributing to campaigns
- Using mass media to express political ideas, opinions, and grievances

Voting
In a democratic state, the most common way to participate in politics is by voting for candidates in an election. Voting allows the citizens of a state to influence policy by selecting the candidates who share their views and make policy decisions that best suit their interests, or candidates who they believe are most capable of leading the country. In the United States, all citizens—regardless of gender, race, or religion—are allowed to vote unless they have lost their right to vote through due process, such as felons.

Since the Progressive movement and the increased social activism of the 1890s to the 1920s that sought to eliminate corruption in government, direct participation in politics through voting has increased. Citizens can participate by voting in the following types of elections:

- Direct primaries: Citizens can nominate candidates for public office.

- National, state, and municipal elections: Citizens elect their representatives in government.

- Recall elections: Citizens can petition the government to vote an official out of office before their term ends.

- Referendums: Citizens can vote directly on proposed laws or amendments to the state constitution.

- Voter initiatives: Citizens can petition their local or state government to propose laws that will be approved or rejected by voters.

Types of Political Systems

Major Political Ideas in History

Major Political Concepts

Politics is the process of governance, typically exercised through the enactment and enforcement of laws, over a community, most commonly a state. Political theory involves the study of politics, especially concerning the efficacy and legitimacy of those responsible for governance. The major concepts in political theory include *power* and *authority*. The concepts of power and authority are closely related but possess certain significant distinctions.

Power is the ability of a ruling body or political entity to influence the actions, behavior, and attitude of a person or group of people; in short, power implies a degree of control over a human community. In order to possess *authority*, the ruling body or political entity must be recognized as having the right and justification to exercise power. This is commonly referred to as *legitimacy*. In representative governments, authority is garnered from the citizens through democratic processes, but in more autocratic regimes, influential elites grant that authority. In some cases, a ruling body or political entity may possess authority recognized by its citizens or influential elites but lack the power to influence those citizens and political entities or effect change within the system of governance. When power and authority are not properly aligned, governments are extremely weak, often deadlocked, and at risk of collapse or revolution.

Government is the result of the decisions made by a society during the political process and is a physical manifestation of the political entity or ruling body. The government determines and enforces the power of the state. A government includes the formal institutions of a society with the power and authority to enact, enforce, and interpret laws. The many different forms of government are determined based on this delegation of power between those institutions. Government encompasses the functions of *law*, *order*, and *justice* and is responsible for maintaining the society.

Sovereignty refers to a political entity's right and power to self-govern, including enacting and enforcing its own taxes and laws without interference from external forces. A political entity may possess varying degrees of sovereignty, as some sovereign states may still be subject to influence by outside political entities. For example, the members of the European Union cede some sovereignty in order to enjoy membership. A state's sovereignty is legitimate when outside political entities recognize the right of the state to self-govern. Both sovereignty and legitimacy are requirements to form a state.

The terms *nation* and *state* are often used interchangeably, but in political theory, they are two very distinct concepts. *Nation* refers to a people's cultural identity, while *state* refers to a territory's political organization and government.

Unlike states, there are no definitive requirements to be a nation; the nation just needs to include a group that is bound together by some shared defining characteristics such as the following:

- Language
- Culture and traditions
- Beliefs and religion
- Homeland
- Ethnicity
- History
- Mythology

The term *state* is commonly used to reference a nation-state, especially in regard to their government. There are four requirements for a political entity to be recognized as a state:

- Territory: a clearly defined geographic area with distinct borders

- Population: citizens and noncitizens living within the borders of the territory with some degree of permanence

- Legitimacy: legal authority to rule that is recognized by the citizens of the state and by other states

- Sovereignty: a political entity's right and power to self-govern without interference from external forces

Nation-state is the term used to describe a political entity with both a clearly defined nation and state. In a nation-state, the majority population of the state is a nation that identifies the territory as their homeland and shares a common history and culture. It is also possible to have several nations in the same nation-state. For example, there are Canadians in Canada and nations of Aboriginal peoples. The presence of multiple nations raises issues related to sovereignty.

Example of a nation: Sikhs in India

Example of a state: Vatican City

Example of a nation-state: Germany

Liberty and Freedom
Governments provide different *liberty* and *freedom*, depending on the form of government that, in turn, is influenced by the states' shared history and culture. Philosophers started articulating defined rights and liberties and arguing for their adoption and protection by the government during the Enlightenment. Liberalism advocates for increasing liberty and freedom in society and economics, while authoritarian regimes offer considerably less protection. The terms liberty and freedom both reference the same thing in society. Examples of liberty and freedom relate to speech, religion, press, economic pursuits, etc. The degrees and breadth of protections are context dependent, and they might be fluid and influenced by the political process. Many states delineate liberty and freedoms in their constitution. Rights and privileges are different because they involve something that is legal to do or possible according to the government sanctioning the action; thus, rights and privileges are typically more easily revoked from both specific individuals and larger communities.

Rights and Privileges

A *right* is a freedom, protection, or entitlement afforded to a person. In political theory, a right or *privilege* specifically refers to that which is granted to the citizens of a political territory according to the legal system or the social conventions of the society. Rights and privileges typically cannot be removed without due process under the law, although this depends on the form of government. Like the distinction between liberty and freedom, the difference between rights and privileges is indistinguishable. They are often the concrete representations of liberty and freedom in a society; as rights and privileges grow in number and strength, the society enjoys more liberty and freedom. Rights are the privileges provided by the government; however, the term right is commonly used to refer to a privilege of higher status that receives more scrutiny and protection from the state, usually requiring more due process to revoke or alter.

Example of a right: the right to vote

Example of a privilege: the privilege to receive a driver's license

Law, Order, and Justice

Governments must establish *law*, *order*, and *justice* through the government's political institutions. Protecting citizens' rights under the systems of laws, as well as effectively punishing the violators, is one of government's foundational responsibilities. Establishing law, order, and justice is an exercise in sovereignty—states that do not impose law and order under a reasonable standard of justice risk public unrest and challenges to the regime's legitimacy.

Law is the system of rules, policies, and regulations that govern behavior that is enacted by a political entity and enforced by the formal institutions created by the political entity. *Order* refers to each citizen, institution, and political entity acting as the law. Political entities secure order through the execution of laws through its enforcing institutions, like the police and justice system.

The term *justice* often refers to the fairness in the political entity's treatment of its citizens. When discussing its relation to law and order, justice refers to the necessary, agreed-upon consequences for failure to act according to the law. In political theory, justice is the social contract between the political entity and its citizens in which all parties involved have agreed upon what is considered "fair" in a society and what the consequences of acting contrary to the law should be.

Citizenship and Nationality

Citizenship is the political term referring to the legal status of an individual recognized by the state or government as a protected member. *Citizens* are subject to the laws of their state and granted the rights and liberties afforded by that state, including the right to vote and be elected to office.

Citizenship does not necessarily denote *nationality*, which refers to the relationship between an individual and a nation, rather than a legal status. Nationality is a component of citizenship, but nationality does not afford an individual any of the rights associated with citizenship of a state without official sanction from the state.

Philosophies of Individuals in World History

<u>Major Political Theorists</u>
Aristotle, 384 BC to 322 BC
A student of Plato, Aristotle was a Greek philosopher best known for his theories of rationality and ethics. In *Politics*, Aristotle asserted that "man is a political animal" and that man must actively

participate in politics to further the political well-being of the city-state. He believed that man could only attain the happy life that nature intended through noble acts that bettered the community in which they lived. To this end, he envisioned an ideal society in which the most virtuous and knowledgeable men ruled and the citizens lived virtuous lives in the service of their city-state. Aristotle is one of the leading contributors to Western philosophy and, later, Liberalism. The Roman Republic applied much of his theories on ethics and civics to their government.

Niccolo Machiavelli, 1469-1527

Machiavelli was an Italian diplomat, politician, and historian during the Italian Renaissance. He is most known for his infamous political treatise, *The Prince,* which inspired the political philosophy known as Machiavellianism. In *The Prince,* Machiavelli instructed rulers that it is "better to be feared than to be loved" and asserted that a ruler must be willing to commit any acts necessary to maintain power and establish the stability of their society. He advocated violence, deceit, and immoral acts and advised rulers to seek out and eliminate any potential political rivals within the community. Machiavellianism prioritizes maintaining and consolidating power over all else.

Thomas Hobbes, 1588-1679

Thomas Hobbes was an English philosopher most notable as being the founder of social contract theory. In his 1651 book, *Leviathan,* Hobbes stated that without a strong central authority, the people would live in constant fear; they would go without industry, knowledge, or commodities if there was no system for enforcing good behavior As such, he asserted that the people enacted social contracts with ruling bodies, in which the people agreed to submit to the laws and limitations imposed by the ruling body in exchange for the protection and quality of life afforded to them. Hobbes was responsible for founding many of the fundamentals of liberal thought, stating that all men are naturally equal and that a ruling body may only gain legitimacy through the consent of the people.

John Locke, 1632-1704

John Locke was an English philosopher influenced by Thomas Hobbes' social contract theory. Though he agreed with the theory on some points, he argued against Hobbes' assertion that man requires protection from a ruling body in order to maintain a civilized society, Instead, Locke believed that men are rational and tolerant beings by nature. Locke is considered the "Father of Liberalism." His works on political theory include the famous *Two Treatises on Government*, which contributed significantly to modern ideals of liberal theory, including espousing the need to protect the right to life, liberty, health, and possessions. Locke's philosophy on rights and self-government influenced the writers of the Declaration of Independence.

Jean-Jacques Rousseau, 1712-1778

Jean-Jacques Rousseau was a philosopher, writer, and composer during the Enlightenment in France whose political writings, *Discourse on Equality* and *The Social Contract,* influenced aspects of the French Revolutionary War and many modern political theories. Rousseau thought man was free in the more primitive stage, and this freedom could only be maintained in a state if the people remained sovereign through representative government. He advocated for religious equality and argued that the people are sovereign, rather than a divinely empowered monarch, and that the people should have the right to rule themselves. His work was banned in France, but his ideals influenced the people and inspired many of the political reforms that led to the Revolutionary War.

Immanuel Kant, 1724-1804

A German philosopher, Kant is best known for the set of ideas known as Kantianism, which states that individuals possess dignity and deserve respect. Although more famous for his philosophy, Kant discussed political theory in his essay, *Perpetual Peace: A Philosophical Sketch,* where he argued that world peace may be achieved through universal democracy and international cooperation. In this work, he explained that, in order to end all wars and create lasting peace, all states must form constitutional republics in which elected officials adhere to the rule of the constitutional law to govern the state.

John Stuart Mills, 1806-1873

John Stuart Mills, an English philosopher and political economist, was considered the "most influential English-speaking philosopher of the nineteenth century" and was best known for being the first member of Parliament to advocate women's suffrage. His book *On Liberty* promoted utilitarianism, which advocates that people should always make decisions based on what would be the most net positive. In his work, Mills sought to limit the power exercised upon the individual by any ruling body and stated that moral actions are those that promote utility and increase individuals' and society's well-being. He called for limited constraints upon individual behavior that only restrict those actions that cause harm to others.

Karl Marx, 1818-1883

Karl Marx, a philosopher, social scientist, historian, and revolutionary, is considered one of the most influential Socialist thinkers of the nineteenth century. His ideas became known as Marxism, and Marx heavily influenced powerful Socialist and Communist leaders, such as Vladimir Lenin, with his 1848 pamphlet *The Communist Manifesto.* In this pamphlet, he explained that, in a capitalist society, perpetual "class struggle" exists in which a ruling class (bourgeois) controls the means of production and exploits the working class (proletariat), who are forced to sell labor for wages. He advocated for the working class to rebel against the ruling class and establish a classless society with collective ownership of the means of production. He envisioned world history as a series of stages in which capitalism eventually collapses into Communism.

Vladimir Lenin, 1870-1924

As a leading figure in the Russian Revolution and eventual founding of the Soviet Union, Lenin was one of the most controversial and influential political figures in the international Communist movement. Strongly influenced by Karl Marx, Lenin established the one-party system of government, which advocates pure Communism: a classless, egalitarian society in which the people abide by one rule—from "each according to his ability, to each according to his needs," a slogan coined by Marx. Lenin led the Bolsheviks into power after the Russian Revolution, and his Communist Party dominated the centralized one-party system. Lenin redistributed land among the peasants and nationalized most private industries, and he suppressed all political opposition with aggression, most notably during the Red Terror. Lenin advocated for Communist revolution across the world. Joseph Stalin, who further consolidated power of the increasingly authoritarian centralized government, succeeded Lenin as head of the Soviet Union.

How Governments have Affected Cultural Values and Provided for Social Control

Throughout history, governments have reflected the cultural values of nation-states because they are typically run by political leaders who in some way represent the people they govern, or have risen up from the populace they serve. In rare cases, such as colonial governments, politics do not always reflect the cultural values of the populace. Nevertheless, in most modern instances, the government remains a reflection of the sociohistorical values of a particular group or set of groups.

In some historical cases, governments can suppress the cultural values of the populace through aggressive means of social control. Authoritarian or oligarchical governments, for instance, usually serve a particular class or group of people over the masses. Some dictatorial regimes in Central and South America, for example, have maintained social control through fear and violence. Nazi Germany is another example of an authoritarian regime that controlled its citizens through violence and propaganda. Liberal democracy attempts to dismantle global authoritarianism by reflecting the voices and values of the populace. In some cases, however, even democratic institutions can verge on social control and coercion; some democratic countries tamper with voting practices to maintain hegemony over certain marginalized groups.

Similarities and Differences Between the U.S. Constitutional Republic and Other Contemporary Forms of Government

<u>Forms of Government and Types of Regimes</u>

Government is the physical manifestation of the political entity or ruling body of a state. It includes the formal institutions that operate to manage and maintain a society. The form of government does not determine the state's *economic system*, though these concepts are often closely tied. Many forms of government are based on a society's economic system. However, while the form of government refers to the methods by which a society is managed, the term *economy* refers to the management of resources in a society. Many forms of government exist, often as hybrids of two or more forms of government or economic systems. Forms of government can be distinguished based on protection of civil liberties, protection of rights, distribution of power, power of government, and principles of Federalism.

Regime is the term used to describe the political conditions under which the citizens live under the ruling body. A regime is defined by the amount of power the government exerts over the people and the number of people who comprise the ruling body. It is closely related to the form of government because the form of government largely creates the political conditions. Regimes are governmental bodies that control both the form and the limit of term of their office. For example, authoritarianism is an example of a form of government and type of regime. A regime is considered to be ongoing until the culture, priorities, and values of the government are altered, ranging from the peaceful transitions of power between democratic political parties to the violent overthrow of the current regime.

The forms of government operated by regimes of government include:

Aristocracy

An *aristocracy* is a form of government composed of a small group of wealthy rulers, either holding hereditary titles of nobility or membership in a higher class. Variations of aristocratic governments include:

- *Oligarchy*: form of government where political power is consolidated in the hands of a small group of people
- *Plutocracy*: type of oligarchy where a wealthy elite class dominates the state and society

Though no aristocratic governments exist today, it was the dominant form of government during ancient times, including the:

- Vassals and lords during the Middle Ages, especially in relation to feudalism
- City-state of Sparta in ancient Greece

Communism

Communism is a radical political ideology that seeks to establish common ownership over production and abolish social status and money. Communists believe that the world is split between two social classes—capitalists and the working class (often referred to as the proletariat). Communist politics assert that conflict arises from the inequality between the ruling class and the working class; thus, Communism favors a classless society. Political philosophers Karl Marx and Friedrich Engels argued that Communism is society's destiny since capitalism would ultimately collapse. The collapse of the Soviet Union weakened Communism across the world.

Republican Form of Government

America's Founding Fathers wanted to break away from the monarchy style of rule they had fled from in England. There, equality and freedoms were suppressed or non-existent. They decided to form a democratic style of government and preserving liberties was the core ideal. They realized that this style of government must have checks and balances in order to run smoothly and ensure the rights and freedoms of its citizens. Therefore, they devised a system of three separate branches—legislative, judicial, and executive. Although each has different responsibilities, the three branches work together to ensure that no one section of the government exerts too much power, and the rights of U.S. citizens are not overlooked or disregarded. Realizing the U.S. was such a huge landmass with many citizens spread out over a large area, they decided on a type of democracy referred to as a *democratic republic*— governed by the people in the form of elected representatives.

Democracy

Democracy is a form of government in which the people act as the ruling body by electing representatives to voice their views. Forms of democratic governments include:

- Direct democracy: democratic government in which the people make direct decisions on specific policies by majority vote of all eligible voters, like in ancient Athens

- Representative democracy: democratic government in which the people elect representatives to vote in a legislative body. This form of soft government providing for the election of representatives is also known as representative republic or indirect democracy. Representative democracy is currently the most popular form of government in the world.

The presidential and parliamentary systems are the most common forms of representative democracy. In the presidential system, the executive operates in its own distinct branch. Although the executive and legislative branches might enjoy powers checking each other, as in the American presidential system, the two functions are clearly separated. In addition, the people directly elect the president, and the president is typically both the head of state and head of government. Examples of presidential systems include Brazil, Nigeria, and the United States.

In the parliamentary system, the prime minister serves as the head of the government. The legislative branch, typically a parliament, elects the prime minister; thus, unlike in the presidential system, the parliament can replace the prime minister with a vote of no confidence. This practically means that the parliament has considerable influence over the office of prime minister. Parliamentary systems often include a president as the head of state, but the office is mostly ceremonial, functioning like a figurehead. Examples of parliamentary systems include Germany, Australia, and Pakistan.

The presidential system is a form of government better designed to distribute power between separate branches of government. This theoretically provides more stability. The president serves for a limited term of years, while prime ministers serve until replaced after receiving a vote of no confidence. In the parliamentary system, the interdependence and interconnectedness between the parliament and prime minister facilitates efficient and timely governance, capable of adjusting to developing and fluid situations. In contrast, the presidential system is more prone to political gridlock because there is no direct connection between the legislative and executive branches. The legislature in a presidential system cannot replace the executive, like in the parliamentary system. The separation of powers in a presidential system can lead to disagreement between the executive and legislature, causing gridlock and other delays in governance.

Major Forms of Government in History

Monarchy

Monarchy is a form of government in which the state is ruled by a *monarch*, typically a hereditary ruler. Monarchs have often justified their power due to some divine right to rule, like the ancient Chinese Mandate of Heaven. Types of monarchies include:

- Absolute monarchy: a monarchy in which the monarch has complete power over the people and the state

- Constitutional monarchy: a type of monarchy in which the citizens of the state are protected by a constitution, and a separate branch, typically a parliament, makes legislative decisions. The monarch and legislature would share power, like in England during the Enlightenment.

- Crowned republic: a type of monarchy in which the monarch holds only a ceremonial position and the people hold sovereignty over the state. It is defined by the monarch's lack of executive power.

Examples of monarchies:

- Kingdom of Saudi Arabia is an absolute monarchy.
- Australia is a crowned republic.

Authoritarian

An authoritarian state is one in which a single party rules indefinitely. The ruling body operates with unrivaled control and complete power to make policy decisions, including the restriction of denying civil liberties such as freedom of speech, press, religion, and protest. Forms of authoritarian governments include *autocracy*, *dictatorship*, and *totalitarian*—states or societies ruled by a single person with complete power over society.

Examples of states with authoritarian governments:

- Soviet Union
- Nazi Germany
- Modern-day North Korea

Classical Republicanism

Classical republicanism developed from Renaissance Era reflections on the governmental practices of the Roman Empire in classical antiquity. According to classical republic theory, the Roman Empire created a government based on the principles of popular sovereignty, natural rights, and devotion to citizens for the common good. These principles were some of the major driving forces for the American

Revolution and the founding of the United States of America. Both the Articles of Confederation and the U.S. Constitution employ classical republican principles, pointing to the popular sovereignty of each state and the civic virtue of its leaders and citizens. The United States of America is still, in many ways, a republican nation, though it has democratized rapidly since its inception.

Liberal Democracy
Liberal democracy has its roots in Greek civilization and American history. Ancient Greece is often referred to as the cradle of Western civilization because its governmental institutions continue to influence modern-day nation-states. The Athenian form of democratic leadership has influenced the democratization process in the United States of America. Initially founded as a republic, the United States has adopted the Greek tradition of democracy, though it has limited democracy through its republic electorate system. Liberal democracy today is, therefore, manifested in the limited democratic systems of the United States. The United States is a beacon of electorate-based democracy, and since World War I, has become a leader in global democratization processes. Nevertheless, the United States' limited liberal democracy does not necessarily promulgate popular democratic systems, because many leaders in the United States continue to believe that pure popular democracy is "chaos." Still, citizenship in a liberal democracy bestows upon U.S. citizens voting responsibilities and individual human rights. Citizens in this type of democratic system are eligible to run for office.

Totalitarianism
Democracy runs counter to totalitarian forms of government; democracy and totalitarianism rest on different poles on the political spectrum. Totalitarian governments believe that no single sector of society can exist outside the direct/total control of the state. Both fascist and communist governments can fall under the broader umbrella of totalitarianism. All totalitarian governments—fascist or communist in nature—believe they are acting in the best interest of the citizenship by enforcing complete conformity to state ideals.

Democratic-Republican Government

Originally, during the American Revolution and the Age of the Early Republic, leaders of the United States of America envisioned the creation of a virtuous civic republic modeled after the governmental practices of the Roman Empire. Civic representation was a key component to this early republican system. Equality and popular sovereignty were embedded into the fiber of the Early Republic. These values, over time, gradually incorporated principles of Athenian democracy, paving the way to a mixed democratic-republican system. Gradually, the voting base of the United States expanded from only including white landowners to also including working-class whites, blacks, Native Americans, and finally women. This democratizing process was fueled by both popular uprisings and religious sentiments. American populism slowly chipped away at the parameters of the classical republican model, incorporating more popular practices. Nevertheless, the United States remains a democratic-republic rather than a popular democracy despite its historical populist undercurrents: The United States continues to employ a limited, electorate-based voting system that reigns in the feared excesses of pure popular democracy.

Practice Questions

1. Which political concept describes a ruling body's ability to influence the actions, behaviors, or attitudes of a person or community?
    a. Authority
    b. Sovereignty
    c. Power
    d. Legitimacy

2. Which feature differentiates a state from a nation?
    a. Shared history
    b. Common language
    c. Population
    d. Sovereignty

3. Which political theorist considered violence necessary in order for a ruler to maintain political power and stability?
    a. John Locke
    b. Jean-Jacques Rousseau
    c. Karl Marx
    d. Niccolo Machiavelli

4. Which political theorist is considered the father of the social contract theory?
    a. John Stuart Mills
    b. Thomas Hobbes
    c. Aristotle
    d. Immanuel Kant

5. Which political orientation emphasizes maintaining traditions and stability over progress and change?
    a. Socialism
    b. Liberalism
    c. Conservatism
    d. Libertarianism

6. Which political orientation supports cooperation between states as a means to improve the quality of life for all states, nations, and people?
    a. Fascism
    b. Conservatism
    c. Anarchism
    d. Internationalism

7. Which political orientation emphasizes a strong central government and promotes violence as a means of suppressing dissent?
    a. Communism
    b. Socialism
    c. Nationalism
    d. Fascism

8. After the ratification of the Constitution, which power held by the states under the Articles of Confederation was ceded to the federal government?
   a. Power to levy taxes
   b. Power to establish courts
   c. Power to coin money
   d. Power to regulate trade

9. Under Federalism, which is considered a concurrent power held by both the states and the federal government?
   a. Hold elections
   b. Regulate immigration
   c. Expand the territories of a state
   d. Pass and enforce laws

10. Which check does the legislative branch possess over the judicial branch?
    a. Appoint judges
    b. Call special sessions of Congress
    c. Rule legislation unconstitutional
    d. Determine the number of Supreme Court judges

11. Which part of the legislative process differs in the House and the Senate?
    a. Who may introduce the bill
    b. How debates about a bill are conducted
    c. Who may veto the bill
    d. What wording the bill contains

12. Which of the following is NOT included in the Bill of Rights?
    a. Freedom to assemble
    b. Freedom against unlawful search
    c. Freedom to vote
    d. Reservation of non-enumerated powers to the states or the people

13. Which political party was founded to advocate for the abolition of slavery?
    a. Constitutional Union
    b. Southern Democrat
    c. Republican
    d. Libertarian

14. What is NOT a common characteristic of an interest group?
    a. Seeks to influence public policy
    b. Employs lobbyists
    c. Regulates trade
    d. Benefits a specific segment of society

15. Which of the following is NOT a power of the mass media?
    a. Ability to shape public opinion
    b. Ability to regulate communications
    c. Ability to influence the importance of events in society
    d. Ability to determine the context in which to report events

16. Which form of government divides power between a regional and central government?
    a. Democracy
    b. Constitutional monarchy
    c. Federalism
    d. Feudalism

17. Which form of government most limits the civil liberties of the people?
    a. Authoritarianism
    b. Communism
    c. Socialism
    d. Federal monarchy

18. Which type of electoral system is considered the most proportionate?
    a. Majority
    b. Electoral College
    c. Plurality
    d. Single transferable vote

Answer Explanations

1. C: Power is the ability of a ruling body or political entity to influence the actions, behavior, and attitude of a person or group of people. Authority, Choice *A*, is the right and justification of the government to exercise power as recognized by the citizens or influential elites. Similarly, legitimacy, Choice *D*, is another way of expressing the concept of authority. Sovereignty, Choice *B*, refers to the ability of a state to determine and control their territory without foreign interference.

2. D: Sovereignty is the feature that differentiates a state from a nation. Nations have no sovereignty, as they are unable to enact and enforce laws independently of their state. A state must possess sovereignty over the population of a territory in order to be legitimized as a state. Both a nation and a state must have a population, Choice *C*. Although sometimes present, shared history and common language are not requirements for a state, making Choices *A* and *B* incorrect.

3. D: In his book, *The Prince*, Niccolo Machiavelli advocated that a ruler should be prepared to do whatever is necessary to remain in power, including using violence and political deception as a means to coerce the people of a state or eliminate political rivals. John Locke, Choice *A*, contributed and advocated liberal principles, most prominently the right to life, liberty, and health. Jean-Jacques Rousseau, Choice *B*, heavily influenced the French Revolution and American Revolution by advocating individual equality, self-rule, and religious freedom. Karl Marx, Choice *C*, wrote that the struggle between the bourgeois (ruling class) and the proletariat (working class) would result in a classless society in which all citizens commonly owned the means of production.

4. B: Thomas Hobbes is considered the father of social contract theory. In his book *Leviathan,* Hobbes advocated for a strong central government and posited that the citizens of a state make a social contract with the government to allow it to rule them in exchange for protection and security. John Stuart Mills, Choice *A*, is most commonly associated with the political philosophy of utilitarianism. Aristotle, Choice *C*, believed that man could only achieve happiness by bettering their community through noble acts, while Immanuel Kant, Choice *D*, promoted democracy and asserted that states could only achieve lasting global peace through international cooperation.

5. C: Conservatism emphasizes maintaining traditions and believes political and social stability is more important than progress and reform. In general, Socialism, Choice *A*, seeks to establish a democratically elected government that owns the means of production, regulates the exchange of commodities, and distributes the wealth equally among citizens. Liberalism, Choice *B*, is based on individualism and equality, supporting the freedoms of speech, press, and religion, while Libertarian ideals, Choice *D*, emphasize individual liberties and freedom from government interference.

6. D: Internationalism promotes global cooperation and supports strong unity between the states in order to achieve world peace and improve quality of life for all global citizens. Fascism, Choice *A*, values the strength of a state over all foreign powers and emphasizes the state over individual liberties, and Fascists typically establish an authoritarian government and consider violence necessary to suppress dissent and revitalize a struggling nation. Conservatism, Choice *B*, is focused on maintaining the traditions and political institutions within a single country. Anarchism, Choice *C*, favors a completely free society ruled by a government composed of only voluntary institutions.

7. D: Fascism considers a strong central government, martial law, and violent coercion as necessary means to maintain political stability and strengthen the state. Neither the politics of Communism, a society in which the people own the means of production, nor Socialism, a society in which the government owns the means of production, promote violence but instead advocate a classless society that eliminates the class struggle. Thus, Choices *A* and *B* are incorrect. Nationalism, Choice *C*, emphasizes preserving a nation's culture, often to the exclusion of other cultures, but violence is not officially promoted as a means for suppressing dissent, as is the case with Fascism.

8. C: Under the Constitution, the power to coin money is designated exclusively to the federal government, but both the states and the federal government maintain the power to collect taxes from the citizens under their jurisdictions and establish courts lower than the Supreme Court, though states may only establish regional courts within their states. The states reserve the right to regulate trade within their states (intrastate), while the federal government maintains the power to regulate trade between states (interstate).

9. D: Both the states and the federal government may propose, enact, and enforce laws. States pass legislation that concerns the states in their state legislative houses, while the federal government passes federal laws in Congress. Only states may hold elections and determine voting procedures, even for federal offices such as the president of the United States, and only the federal government may expand any state territory, change state lines, admit new states into the nation, or regulate immigration and pass laws regarding naturalization of citizens.

10. D: The Constitution granted Congress the power to decide how many justices should be on the court, and Congress first decided on six judges in the Judiciary Act of 1789. The Constitution granted the power to appoint judges and to call special sessions of Congress to the president. Only the Supreme Court may interpret the laws enacted by Congress and rule a law unconstitutional and subsequently overturn the law.

11. B: The process by which the House and Senate may debate a bill differs. In the House, how long a speaker may debate a bill is limited, while in the Senate, speakers may debate the bill indefinitely and delay voting on the bill by filibuster—a practice in which a speaker refuses to stop speaking until a majority vote stops the filibuster or the time for the vote passes. In both the House and the Senate, anyone may introduce a bill. Only the president of the United States may veto the bill, so neither the House nor Senate holds that power. Before the bill may be presented to the president to be signed, the wording of the bill must be identical in both houses. Another procedural difference is that the number of amendments is limited in the House but not the Senate; however, this does not appear as an answer choice.

12. C: The first ten amendments to the Constitution are collectively referred to as the Bill of Rights. The Founding Fathers did not support universal suffrage, and as such, the Bill of Rights did not encompass the freedom to vote. The Fifteenth Amendment provided that the right to vote shall not be denied on the basis of race, color, or previous condition of servitude, and women did not receive the right to vote until passage of the Nineteenth Amendment. The other three answer choices are included in the Bill of Rights—the freedom to assembly is established in the First Amendment; the freedom against unlawful search is established in the Fourth Amendment; and the reservation of non-enumerated powers to the states or the people is established in the Tenth Amendment.

13. C: The Republican Party emerged as the abolitionist party during the antebellum period and succeeded in abolishing slavery after the North's victory in the Civil War. The Constitutional Union Party supported slavery but opposed Southern secession, while the Southern Democrats supported slavery and secession. The Whig Party splintered in the 1850s as a result of tension over slavery, leading to the creation of the Republican Party and Constitutional Union Party.

14. C: While interest groups attempt to influence the legislation and organizations that regulate trade, they do not possess the authority to enact or enforce laws necessary to regulate trade. However, they may influence policy through the use of petitions, civil suits against the government, and by the practice of lobbying, in which paid lobbyists put pressure on lawmaking bodies. Interest groups form due to a common connection between the members of a group attempting to bring about change that benefits a specific segment of society, such as teachers or pharmaceutical corporations.

15. B: The mass media does not have the ability to regulate communications. The mass media has the ability to shape public opinion, making Choice A incorrect. Mass media selects which events to report on and thereby influences the perceived importance of events in society and determines the context in which to report events, making Choices C and D incorrect. Only the federal government may regulate communications through agencies such as the Federal Communications Commission (FCC).

16. C: Federalism divides power between regional and federal governments, and it is the form of government upon which the United States is structured, according to the Tenth Amendment. While a constitutional monarchy, Choice B, is typically divided between a monarch, the head of state, and a legislative body, usually a parliament, power is not reserved to the regional government. A democratic government, Choice A, is a government ruled by the people and does not specify division of powers. Feudalism, Choice D, is an economic system popular in medieval Europe where the monarchy granted the nobility land in exchange for military service, and the nobility allowed serfs to live on their land in exchange for labor or percentage of crops.

17. A: An authoritarian government is ruled by a single party that holds complete control over the powerful central government. Authoritarian governments limit political freedom and civil liberties to diminish any opposition. Communism, Choice B, is one in which the class struggle between the ruling and working classes is eliminated because the means of production belongs to the people. Similarly, Socialism, Choice C, is classless, but in this type of government, the government owns the means of production and is often democratic. Unlike a regular monarchy, a federal monarchy, Choice D, is a federal government in which political power is divided between the monarch (head of state) and regional governments, resulting in checks and balances of power.

18. D: Proportional electoral systems reflect the divisions in an electorate proportionately in the elected body. In single transferable vote systems, voters rank individual candidates by their preference, and the top candidates' votes are transferred to the second-place candidate, and so on, once a candidate receives the minimum votes to win a seat in the election; thus, the single transferable vote system is the most proportionate electoral system. The Electoral College is the method of electing the president of the United States. Although the Electoral College apportions a number of electors to each state according to the number of congressional seats in the state, it is not a proportional electoral system. To win a majority vote, a candidate must receive 50 percent plus 1 of the vote, so the minority's preferences are not proportionally reflected in the body. Similarly, a plurality only requires the highest percent of votes among any number of candidates, which often results in most voters voting *against* the winning candidate.

Economics and Science, Technology, and Society

Economic Concepts and Types of Economic Systems

Scarcity and Opportunity Costs

Economics is the study of human behavior in response to the production, consumption, and distribution of assets or wealth. Economics can help individuals or societies make decisions or plans for themselves or communities, dependent upon their needs, wants, and resources. Economics is divided into two subgroups: microeconomics and macroeconomics.

Microeconomics is the study of individual or small group behaviors and patterns in relationship to such things as earning and spending money. It focuses on particular markets within the economy, and looks at single factors that could potentially affect individuals or small groups. For example, the use of coupons in a grocery store can affect an individual's product choice, quantity purchased, and overall savings that a person may later roll into a different purchase. Microeconomics is the study of scarcity, choice, opportunity costs, economics systems, factors of production, supply and demand, market efficiency, the role of government, distribution of income, and product markets.

Macroeconomics examines a much larger scale of the economy. It focuses on how a society or nation's goods, services, spending habits, and other factors affect the people of that entity. It focuses on aggregate factors such as demand and output. For example, if a national company moves its production overseas to save on costs, how will production, labor, and capital be affected? Macroeconomics analyzes all aggregate indicators and the microeconomic factors that influence the economy. Government and corporations use macroeconomic models to help formulate economic policies and strategies.

Microeconomics
Scarcity
People have different needs and wants, and the question arises, are the resources available to supply those needs and wants? Limited resources and high demand create scarcity. When a product is scarce, there is a short supply of it. For example, when the newest version of a cellphone is released, people line up to buy the phone or put their name on a wait list if the phone is not immediately available. The product, the new cellphone, may become a scarce commodity. In turn, because of the scarcity, companies may raise the cost of the commodity, knowing that if it is immediately available, people may pay more for the instant gratification—and vice versa. If a competing company lowers the cost of the phone but has contingencies, such as extended contracts or hidden fees, the buyer will still have the opportunity to purchase the scarce product. Limited resources and extremely high demand create scarcity and, in turn, cause companies to acquire opportunity costs.

Choice and Opportunity Costs
On a large scale, governments and communities have to assess different opportunity costs when it comes to using taxpayers' money. Should the government or community build a new school, repair roads, or allocate funds to local hospitals are all examples of choices taxpayers may have to review at some point in time. How do they decide which choice is the best, since each one has a trade off? By comparing the opportunity cost of each choice, they may decide what they are willing to live without for the sake of gaining something else.

Economic Systems
Economic systems determine what is being produced, who is producing it, who receives the product, and the money generated by the sale of the product. There are two basic types of economic systems: market economies (including free and competitive markets), and planned or command economies.

- Market Economies are characterized by:

    o Privately owned businesses, groups, or individuals providing goods or services based on demand.

    o The types of goods and services provided (supply) are based on that demand.

    o Two types: competitive market and free market.

Competitive Market	Free Market
Due to the large number of both buyers and sellers, there is no way any one seller or buyer can control the market or price.	Voluntary private trades between buyers and sellers determine markets and prices without government intervention or monopolies.

- Planned or Command Economies:

    o In planned or command economies, the government or central authority determines market prices of goods and services.

    o The government or central authority determines what is being produced as well as the quantity of production.

    o Some advantages to command economies include a large number of shared goods such as public services (transportation, schools, or hospitals).

    o Disadvantages of command economies include wastefulness of resources.

Factors of Production
There are four factors of production:

1. Land: both renewable and nonrenewable resources
2. Labor: effort put forth by people to produce goods and services
3. Capital: the tools used to create goods and services
4. Entrepreneurship: persons who combine land, labor, and capital to create new goods and services

The four factors of production are used to create goods and services to make economic profit. All four factors strongly impact one another.

Market Efficiency and the Role of Government (Taxes, Subsidies, and Price Controls)
Market efficiency is directly affected by supply and demand. The government can help the market stay efficient by either stepping in when the market is inefficient and/or providing the means necessary for markets to run properly. For example, society needs two types of infrastructure: physical (bridges, roads, etc.) and institutional (courts, laws, etc.). The government may impose taxes, subsidies, and price

controls to increase revenue, lower prices of goods and services, ensure product availability for the government, and maintain fair prices for goods and services.

The Purpose of Taxes, Subsidies, and Price Controls

Taxes	Subsidies	Price Controls
-Generate government revenue -Discourage purchase or use of "bad" products such as alcohol or cigarettes	-Lower the price of goods and services -Reassure the supply of goods and services -Allow opportunities to compete with overseas vendors	-Act as emergency measures when government intervention is necessary -Set a minimum or maximum price for goods and services

Distribution of Income

Distribution of income refers to how wages are distributed across a society or segments of a society. If everyone made the same amount of money, the distribution of income would be equal. That is not the case in most societies. The wealth of people and companies varies. Income inequality gaps are present in America and many other nations. Taxes provide an option to redistribute income or wealth because they provide revenue to build new infrastructure and provide cash benefits to some of the poorest members in society.

Product Markets

Product markets are marketplaces where goods and services are bought and sold. Product markets provide sellers a place to offer goods and services to consumers, and for consumers to purchase those goods and services. The annual value of goods and services exchanged throughout the year is measured by the Gross Domestic Product (GDP), a monetary measure of goods and services made either quarterly or annually. Department stores, gas stations, grocery stores, and other retail stores are all examples of product markets. However, product markets do not include any raw, scarce, or trade materials.

Theory of the Firm

The behavior of firms is composed of several theories varying between short- and long-term goals. There are four basic firm behaviors: perfect competition, profit maximization, short run, and long run. Each firm follows a pattern, depending on its desired outcome. Theory of the Firm posits that firms, after conducting market research, make decisions that will maximize their profits since they are for-profit entities.

- Perfect competition:
    - In perfect competition, several businesses are selling the same product at the same time.
    - There are so many businesses and consumers that none will directly impact the market.
    - Each business and consumer is aware of the competing businesses and markets.
- Profit maximization:
    - Firms decide the quantity of a product that needs to be produced in order to receive maximum profit gains. Profit is the total amount of revenue made after subtracting costs.

- Short run:
  - A short amount of time where fixed prices cannot be adjusted
  - The quantity of the product depends on the varying amount of labor. Less labor means less product.
- Long run:
  - An amount of time where fixed prices can be adjusted
  - Firms try to maximize production while minimizing labor costs.

Overall, microeconomics operates on a small scale, focusing on how individuals or small groups use and assign resources.

Macroeconomics

Macroeconomics analyzes the economy as a whole. It studies unemployment, interest rates, price levels, and national income, which are all factors that can affect the nation as a whole, and not just individual households. Macroeconomics studies all large factors to determine how, or if, they will affect future trend patterns of production, consumption, and economic growth.

Measures of Economic Performance

It is important to measure economic performance to determine if an economy is growing, stagnant, or deteriorating. To measure the growth and sustainability of an economy, several indicators can be used. Economic indicators provide data that economists can use to determine if there are faulty processes or if some form of intervention is needed.

One of the main indicators to measure economic performance is the growth of the country's Gross Domestic Product (GDP). GDP growth provides important information that can be used to determine fiscal or financial policies. The GDP does not measure income distribution, quality of life, or losses due to natural disasters. For example, if a community lost everything to a hurricane, it would take a long time to rebuild the community and stabilize its economy. That is why there is a need to take into account more balanced performance measures when factoring overall economic performance.

Other indicators used to measure economic performance are unemployment or employment rates, inflation, savings, investments, surpluses and deficits, debt, labor, trade terms, the HDI (Human Development Index), and the HPI (Human Poverty Index).

Unemployment

Unemployment occurs when an individual does not have a job, is actively trying to find employment, and is not getting paid. Official unemployment rates do not factor in the number of people who have stopped looking for work, unlike true unemployment rates that do, causing them to be higher.

There are three types of unemployment: cyclical, frictional, and structural.

Cyclical
The product of a business cycle. This usually occurs during a recession.
Frictional
The difficulty of matching qualified workers for specific jobs. An example would be a person changing careers.
Structural
When a person no longer qualifies for a specific job, or failing out of a retraining course for a job.

Given the nature of a market economy and the fluctuations of the labor market, a 100 percent employment rate is impossible to reach.

Inflation
Inflation is when the cost of goods and services rises over time. Supply, demand, and money reserves all affect inflation. Generally, inflation is measured by the Consumer Price Index (CPI), a tool that tracks price changes of goods and services over time. The CPI measures goods and services such as gasoline, cars, clothing, and food. When the cost of goods and services increase, the quantity of the product may decrease due to lower demand. This decreases the purchasing power of the consumer. Basically, as more money is printed, it holds less and less value in purchasing power. For example, when inflation occurs, consumers in the United States are spending and saving less because the U.S. dollar is worth less, and therefore the consumer cannot buy or save as much money. However, if inflation occurs steadily over time, the people can better plan and prepare for future necessities.

Inflation can vary from year to year, usually never fluctuating more than 2 percent. Central banks try to prevent drastic increases or decreases of inflation to prohibit prices from rising or falling far from the minimum. Inflation can also vary based on different monetary currencies. Although rare, any country's economy may experience hyperinflation (when inflation rates increase to over 50 percent), while other economies may experience deflation (when the cost of goods and services decrease over time). Deflation occurs when the inflation rate drops below zero percent.

Business Cycle
A business cycle is when the Gross Domestic Product (GDP) moves downward and upward over a long-term growth trend. These cycles help determine where the economy currently stands, as well as where the economy could be heading. Business cycles usually occur almost every six years, and have four phases: expansion, peak, contraction, and trough. Here are some characteristics of each phase:

- Expansion:
  - Increased employment rates and economic growth
  - Production and sales increase
  - On a graph, expansion is where the lines climb.
- Peak:
  - Employment rates are at or above full employment and the economy is at maximum productivity.
  - On a graph, the peak is the top of the hill, where expansion has reached its maximum.
- Contraction:
  - When growth starts slowing
  - Unemployment is on the rise.
  - On a graph, contraction is where the graph begins to slide back down or contract.
- Trough:
  - The cycle has hit bottom and is waiting for the next cycle to start again.
  - On a graph, the trough is the bottom of the contraction prior to when it starts to climb back up.

When the economy is expanding or "booming," the business cycle is going from a trough to a peak. When the economy is headed down and toward a recession, the business cycle is going from a peak to a trough.

Four phases of a business cycle:

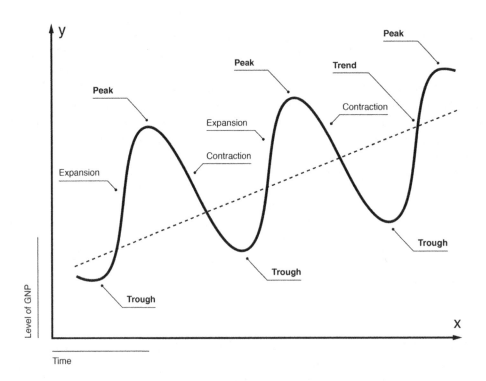

Fiscal Policy
A fiscal policy is when the government is involved in adjusting spending and tax rates to assist the way in which an economy financially functions. Fiscal policies can either increase or decrease tax rates and spending. These policies represent a tricky balancing act, because if the government increases taxes too much, consumer spending and monetary value will decrease. Conversely, if the government lowers taxes, consumers will have more money in their pockets to buy more goods and services, which increases demand and the need for companies to supply those goods and services. Due to the higher demand, suppliers can add jobs to fulfill that demand. While the increase of supply, demand, and jobs are positive for the overall economy, they may result in a devaluation of the dollar and less purchasing power.

Money and Banking
Money is the universal form of currency used throughout goods and services exchanges that holds its value over time. Money provides a convenient way for sellers and consumers to understand the value of their goods and services. As opposed to bartering (when sellers and consumers exchange goods or services as equal trades), money is quick and easy for both buyers and sellers.

There are three main forms of money: commodity, fiat, and bank. Here are characteristics of each form:

- Commodity money: Money as a valuable good, such as precious metals
- Fiat money: The value of the good set by supply and demand rather than the actual value it represents, such as paper money
- Bank money: Money that is credited by a bank to those who deposit it into bank accounts, such as checking and savings accounts or credit

While price levels within the economy set the demand for money, most countries have central banks that supply the actual money. Essentially, banks buy and sell money. Borrowers can take loans and pay back the bank, with interest, providing the bank with extra capital.

A central bank has control over the printing and distribution of money. Central banks serve three main purposes: manage monetary growth to help steer the direction of the economy, be a backup to commercial banks that are suffering, and provide options and alternatives to government taxation.

The Federal Reserve is the central bank of the United States. The Federal Reserve controls banking systems and determines the value of money in the United States. Basically, the Federal Reserve is the bank for banks.

All Western economies have to keep a minimum amount of protected cash called *required reserve*. Once banks meet those minimums, they can then lend or loan the excess to consumers. The required reserves are used within a fractional reserve banking system (fractional because a small portion is kept separate and safe). Not only do banks reserve, manage, and loan money, but they also help form monetary policies.

Monetary Policy
The central bank and other government committees control the amount of money that is made and distributed. The money supply determines monetary policy. Three main features sustain monetary policy:

1. Assuring the minimum amount held within banks (bank reserves). When banks are required to hold more money in reserve funds, banks are less willing to lend money to help control inflation.

2. Adjusting interest rates. For example, if the value of money is low, companies and consumers buy more (products, employees, stocks) because prices are cheap. Just like an investment, it is risky, but can pay off in the long term.

3. The purchase and sales of bonds (otherwise known as open market operations). When buying bonds to increase money and selling bonds to reduce the supply, the central bank helps control the money supply.

In the United States, the Federal Reserve maintains monetary policy. There are two main types of monetary policy: expansionary monetary policy and contractionary monetary policy.

- Expansionary monetary policy:
    o Increases the money supply
    o Lowers unemployment
    o Increases consumer spending
    o Increases private sector borrowing
    o Possibly decreases interest rates to very low levels, even near zero
    o Decreases reserve requirements and federal funds
- Contractionary monetary policy:
    o Decreases the money supply
    o Helps control inflation
    o Possibly increases unemployment due to slowdowns in economic growth
    o Decreases consumer spending
    o Decreases loans and/or borrowing

The Federal Reserve uses monetary policy to try to achieve maximum employment and secure inflation rates. Because the Federal Reserve is the "bank of banks," it truly strives to be the last-resort option for distressed banks. This is because once these kinds of institutions begin to rely on the Federal Reserve for help, all parts of the banking industry—such as those dealing with loans, bonds, interest rates, and mortgages—are affected.

Economic Growth

Economic growth is measured by the increase in the Gross National Product (GNP) or Gross Domestic Product (GDP). The increase of goods and services over time indicates positive movement in economic growth. Keep in mind that the quantity of goods and services produced is not necessarily an indicator of economic growth. The value of the goods and services produced matters more than the quantity.

There are many causes of economic growth, which can be short- or long-term. In the short term, if aggregate demand (the total demand for goods and services produced at a given time) increases, then the overall Gross Domestic Product (GDP) increases as well. Not only will the GDP increase, interest rates may decrease. With reduced interest rates, spending and investing will increase. Consumer and government spending will also increase because there will be more disposable income. Real estate prices will rise, and there will be lower income taxes. All of these short-term factors can stimulate economic growth.

In the long term, if aggregate supply (the total supply of goods or services in a given time period) increases, then there is potential for an increase in capital as well. With more working capital, more infrastructure and jobs can be created. With more jobs, there is an increased employment rate, and education and training for jobs will improve. New technologies will be developed, and new raw materials may be discovered. All of these long-term factors can also stimulate economic growth.

Outside of the short- and long-term causes for economic growth, other factors include low inflation and stability. Lower inflation rates encourage more investing versus higher inflation rates that cause instability in the market. Stability encourages businesses to continue investing. If the market is unstable, investors may question the volatility of the market.

Potential Costs of Economic Growth:

- Inflation: When economic growth occurs, inflation tends to be high. If supply cannot keep up with demand, then the inflation rate may be unmanageable.
- Economic booms and recessions: The economy goes through cycles of booms and recessions. This causes inflation to increase and decrease over time, which puts the economy into a continuous cycle of rising and falling.
- Account inefficiencies: When the economy grows, consumers and businesses increase their import spending. The increase of import spending affects the current account and causes a shortage.
- Environmental costs: When the economy is growing, there is an abundance of output, which may result in more pollutants and a reduction in quality of life.
- Inequalities: Growth occurs differently among members of society. While the wealthy may be getting richer, those living in poverty may just be getting on their feet. So while economic growth is happening, it may happen at two very different rates.

While these potential costs could affect economic growth, if the growth is consistent and stable, then growth can occur without severe inflation swings. Also, as technology improves, new ways of production can reduce negative environmental factors as well.

Circular-Flow Model of the Economy

The circular-flow model of the economy (depicted below) illustrates the interdependence between households and businesses. In both the resource market (households sell; businesses buy) and product market (businesses sell; households buy), inputs and outputs are exchanged based on the model of the market. Businesses (buy resources; sell products) accrue costs from the resource market, but gain resources from these costs. Households (sell resources; buy products) provide the resource market with labor, land, capital, and entrepreneurial ability, receiving money income (wages, rents, interest, profits) from the resource market. Households interact with the product market by providing consumptive expenditures in return for goods and services. Likewise, businesses provide goods and services to the product market in return for the incoming revenue from the households.

Circular Flow Model

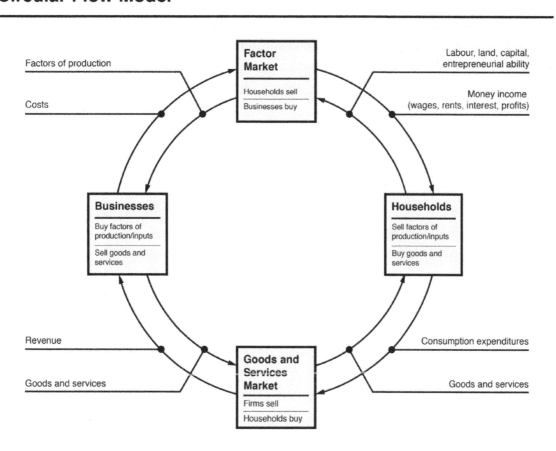

Supply and Demand

Shifts in supply and demand inevitably affect the prices of goods and services while also affecting the relationship of supply and demand to one another. Take the graphs below as evidence of the changes initiated by shifts in supply and demand. An increase in demand moves the demand curve to the right (D1 to D2) on Panel (a). The equilibrium price rises in this case. The actual supply curve (S1) does not

177

shift on the graph in this instance; rather, the intersection between supply and demand experiences a slight movement. A decrease in demand shifts the demand curve to the left rather than the right (D1 to D2 on Panel (b). The equilibrium price falls in this case. The supply curve does not shift; rather, there is movement along the supply curve. An increase in supply will shift the supply curve to the right (S1 to S2) on Panel (c). The equilibrium price will fall with this shift. In this case, the demand curve (D1) does not move; rather, the intersection between supply and demand experiences a slight movement. An increase in supply shifts the supply curve to the left (S1 to S2) on Panel (d). The equilibrium price rises in this instance, and the quantity demanded increases. In this case, the demand curve (D1) does not move; rather, the intersection between supply and demand experiences a slight movement.

Factors for an increase in demand can include a shift in preferences that lead to greater consumption, a lower price for a complementary good/service, a higher price for a substitute good/service, an increase in income, or an increase in population.

Factors for a decrease in demand can include a shift in preferences that lead to a decrease in consumption, an increase in the price of a complementary good/service, a reduction in a substitute good/service, a reduction in income, or a reduction in population.

Factors leading to an increase in supply can include a reduction in the price of input/labor, a decline in returns for alternative uses of the inputs, an improvement in manufacturing or technology, or an increase in the number of firms.

Factors leading to a decrease in supply can include an increase in the price of input/labor, an increase in returns for alternative uses of the inputs, manufacturing or technology problems, or a reduction in the number of firms.

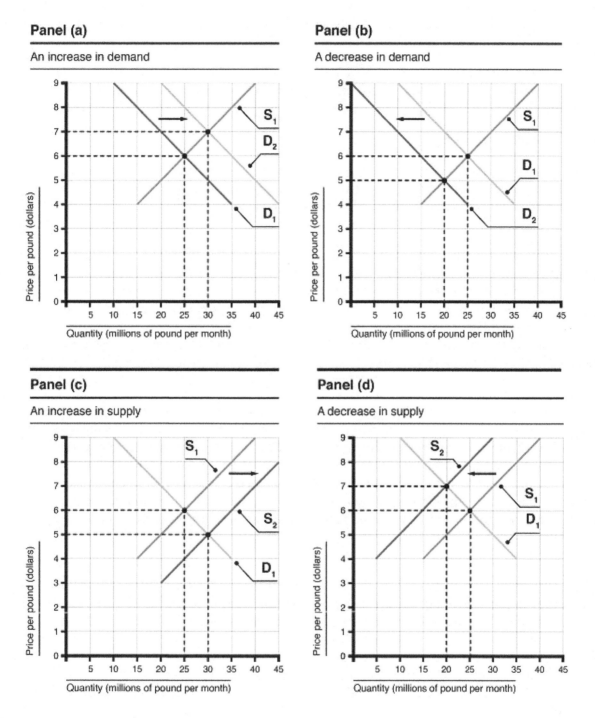

Contemporary Economic Systems

Communism is a political system and ideology characterized by a classless social system and communally controlled property. Communism encourages state control of the production and distribution of goods.

It is an extreme branch of Marxist theory that blends Karl Marx's revolutionary theories with visions of a one-party government.

Socialism is a more moderate offshoot of Marxism. In a socialist nation, the state does not own the means of production, but exercises some influence over them. This political system takes a guiding role in the economy, but usually promotes democracy over dictatorship.

Capitalism is the free enterprise economic system that stemmed from the philosophies of Adam Smith and John Maynard Keynes. Capitalism promotes competition by denying government influence over the economy.

Types of Market Structures

Competition in a capitalist economy like the U.S. economy is determined by market structure. Throughout U.S. and world history, there have been various forms of market structures, such as pure competition, monopolistic competition, oligopoly, and monopoly.

Pure Competition
A pure competition market system is the most competitive; it is dictated by the "pure knowledge" of all its buyers and sellers. In a pure competition market system, there are a large number of firms that create standardized products; the products become so homogenous in nature that consumers become indifferent about their company choices. This pure competition system has low barriers for entering and exiting a particular industry. Thus, firms are more likely to come and go as they please. In this pure competition market system, prices are determined by consumer demand, and no supplier maintains any significant influence over prices. In this system, suppliers are often called price takers.

Monopolistic Competition
Monopolistic competition is much like pure competition in terms of the number of suppliers and barriers. Monopolistic competition structures also have low barriers to entering and exiting the industry, so there are many suppliers. In a monopolistic competition market, suppliers often try to attain price advantages through product differentiation. Suppliers justify higher prices as a result of this differentiation of similar products. Monopolistic competition is only successful when suppliers actually convince consumers of the higher quality of their standard products. Beauty supplies and other retail vanity goods are great examples of products that may achieve higher sales through monopolistic competition.

Oligopoly
Oligopolies are markets that establish a few large firms as the major sellers/distributors. A good example of an oligopoly is the American automobile industry. Each automobile firm tries to maximize profit by producing marginal costs that equal marginal revenues. High barriers to entry limit the number of firms that can enter an oligopoly. These firms, therefore, maintain a great deal of influence over the market prices of their products. In the case of the American automobile oligarchy, auto manufacturers tend to limit entry into the industry by maintaining high costs for manufacturing.

Monopoly
Pure monopoly is very different from pure competition. Pure monopolies seek to create barriers for entry into the industry. In this system, there is only one seller of a particular product or commodity, and the sole seller attempts to restrict firms from exiting and entering the industry at will.

International Trade

International trade is when countries import and export goods and services. Countries often want to deal in terms of their own currency. Therefore, when importing or exporting goods or services, consumers and businesses need to enter the market using the same form of currency. For example, if the United States would like to trade with China, the U.S. may have to trade in China's form of currency, the *Yuan*, versus the dollar, depending on the business.

The exchange rate is what one country's currency will exchange for another. The government and the market (supply and demand) determine the exchange rate. There are two forms of exchange rates: fixed and floating. Fixed exchange rates involve government interventions (like central banks) to help keep the exchange rates stable. Floating or "flexible" exchange rates constantly change because they rely on supply and demand needs. While each type of exchange rate has advantages and disadvantages, the rate truly depends on the current state of each country's economy. Therefore, each exchange rate may differ from country to country.

Advantages and Disadvantages of Fixed Versus Floating Exchange Rates			
Fixed Exchange Rate: government intervention to help keep exchange rates stable		Floating or "Flexible" Exchange Rate: Supply and demand determines the exchange rate	
Advantages	*Disadvantages*	*Advantages*	*Disadvantages*
-Stable prices	-Requires a large	-Central bank	-Currency speculation
-Stable foreign	amount of reserve	involvement is not	-Exchange rate risks
exchange rates	funds	needed.	-Inflation increases
-Exports are more	-Possibly mispricing	-Facilitates free trade	
competitive and in turn	currency values		
more profitable	Inflation increases		

While each country may have differing economic statuses and exchange rates, countries rely on one another for goods and services. Prices of imports and exports are affected by the strength of another country's currency. For example, if the United States dollar is at a higher value than another country's currency, imports will be less expensive because the dollar will have more value than that of the country selling its good or service. On the other hand, if the dollar is at a low value compared to the currency of another country, importers will tend to defer away from buying international items from that country. However, U.S. exporters to that country could benefit from the low value of the dollar.

Structure and Operation in the U.S. Free Enterprise System

Free Enterprise System in the United States

In a free enterprise, or capitalist, economic system, business can be conducted without interference from government. Without government interference, business owners, entrepreneurs, and corporations can decide how they want to run their companies with limited direction from local, state, and federal legislators. The free enterprise market system in the United States of America is heavily tied to the laws of supply and demand rather than government regulations. Supply is the term used to describe the quantities of goods and/or services that sellers are willing and able to sell at varied prices over an established period of time. Demand is the term that refers to how much of the goods/services buyers are willing to purchase from sellers. Along with competition, supply and demand affect pricing in a free enterprise system. Prior to the Industrial Revolution of the eighteenth and nineteenth centuries, many towns and cities in the United States were centered on a single economic activity. Mill towns produced and processed grains. Members of farming communities devoted their whole lives to agriculture and animal husbandry. Mining towns and logging towns focused all their energies on resource extraction and refinement. The economic activities of these towns and cities were limited by the lack of modern communication and transportation.

All this changed with the Industrial Revolution of the eighteenth and nineteenth centuries. Towns and cities began to realize that an overreliance on one economic activity could result in financial catastrophe. The Industrial Revolution brought about changes to human civilization by increasing and diversifying productivity through technological advancement, improving the reach and efficiency of transportation and communication, and standardizing parts and services for mass production. As a result, many business conglomerates, oligopolies, and monopolies emerged, and these companies extended the reach of the economy while also limiting access to entry in the industry. The Industrial Revolution is responsible for embedding the free enterprise market system into the American economy; nevertheless, it also planted the seeds of discontent, paving the way to a socialist and anarchist backlash against big business. Although the government began to regulate business, especially during the trust-busting years of the Progressive Era, free enterprise remained at the heart of the American economic system, leading to a multicentury debate over the role of government in business.

U.S. Economic Growth from the 1870s to the Present

The American economy has changed dramatically since the 1700s, a century where agriculture was the main economic activity. The First Industrial Revolution began in the early 1800s when steam-powered machines were used to increase productivity, especially in the textile industry. The invention of steamboats and railroads made it much cheaper and faster to ship goods across the country in the mid-1800s as well. After the Civil War, the Second Industrial Revolution led to increased productivity and efficiency in the many industries, including metallurgy, chemicals, telecommunications, and energy. This led to significant social changes as immigration and urbanization increased. Workers began to form labor unions in order to demand better wages and working conditions, which led to strikes and conflict with law enforcement officials.

In the early 20th century, Henry Ford introduced the moving assembly line to the automobile manufacturing industry, which made it easier for middle- and working-class families to buy cars. Other industries adopted Ford's methods, which led to lower prices for many consumer goods. The stock market crash in 1929 helped trigger the Great Depression, which resulted in a vicious downward economic spiral. Franklin D. Roosevelt introduced the New Deal to try and boost the economy, but only the outbreak of World War II led to full employment. The United States emerged from World War II as the world's largest economy and pent-up consumer demand fueled prosperity during the post-war era.

The development of computers in the latter part of the 20th century improved communications and led to greater economic efficiency. However, it also marked the beginning of the post-industrial economy in the United States. Traditional manufacturing jobs began to disappear as robots replaced unskilled workers. On the other hand, careers in the information technology sector grew and became a key component of the new high-tech economy. Many unskilled manufacturing jobs also went overseas to countries in Asia and South America as the global economy became more interconnected.

Types of Business Ownership

Within the United States' free enterprise system, there are four major types of business ownership: sole proprietorships, partnerships, limited liability companies, and corporations. Sole proprietorships are unincorporated companies that have one owner who pays all the income taxes on profits made from the business. Partnerships bring together two or more individuals to establish and maintain business at large. In a partnership, both owners share responsibilities and are equally liable for debts. Limited liability companies reduce the risk of investing in a business by making investors responsible only for investments and not debts. Corporations are legal entities that enjoy most of the responsibilities of individuals (i.e., the right to enter into contracts, sue and be sued, loan and borrow money, etc.), but the shareholders of the corporation maintain limited liability despite their right to profit from dividends.

Saving, Investing, and Borrowing

All economic markets strive for an efficient allocation of resources. The supply of loanable money comes from institutional or personal savings. Savings are dollars of postponed spending. In terms of investing, many financial institutions offer interest rates on savings to "compensate" households for postponing their spending in the name of saving money. Higher interest rates typically lead to higher saving rates. The supply of loanable funds increases as savings' interest rates increase. Loans are a form of financial borrowing. People who receive loans are willing to pay an interest price on the funds they borrow. Loans are preferred at lower interest rates; higher interest rates mean more money lost. Much like market prices, market interest rates perform locative functions. Some companies or individuals take loans out to invest in such things as construction or education. Financial institutions, such as banks and credit unions, typically dictate interest rates for both saving and borrowing.

Goals of Economic Growth, Stability, Full Employment, Freedom, Security, Equity, and Efficiency

In the U.S. free enterprise system, the main reason for the government regulation of private business is to control prices. Since investment and economic growth are important for increasing and stabilizing the U.S. gross domestic product (GDP), the government often works with the financial market to create growth or equilibrium. In certain cases, antitrust laws may be enacted, such as the Sherman Antitrust Act, to deter or "bust" monopolistic mergers or predatory practices that restrict competition. Throughout history, government regulation has increased and decreased based on the political context of the time. On both sides of the debate over regulation and deregulation, legislators have full employment, freedom, security, equity, and efficiency in mind. The ways each side of the debate define these terms differ based on political disposition. During the 1980s, under the leadership of President Ronald Reagan, for example, the U.S. government entered an era of considerable deregulation in business. Reagan believed lessening regulation would promote freedom, security, equity, and efficiency in business so that the United States could push forward toward full employment for its citizenry. Proponents of increased regulation point to the growing socioeconomic gap between the rich and the poor that is created by rampant deregulation in free enterprise. These proponents of increased regulation see pure free enterprise as a threat to the freedom, security, equity, and efficiency of the American citizenry.

Consumers, Labor, and Business in the U.S. Free Enterprise System

In a free enterprise system, labor is provided to the resource market—and, in turn, business—from the household. In this system, laborers not only extract/provide goods and services for business, but they also double as consumers in the market economy. Labor and consumption are both tied to business. As laborers, they produce the goods/services that give themselves and others satisfaction or utility in everyday life. As consumers, they buy the goods/services for satisfaction or utility. As laborers and consumers, citizens in the U.S. free enterprise system can affect business efficiency and profits. They can choose to strike as laborers or boycott goods/services as consumers. On the flip side, businesses can affect the lives of consumers/laborers by decreasing or increasing wages, cutting or creating jobs, or controlling the prices of goods and services. The rights and responsibilities of consumers and laborers are to offer—or deny—work and expenditures to business. The rights and responsibilities of businesses are to protect the rights of workers and provide adequate goods/services to consumers. At times throughout history, these rights and responsibilities have been denied or disrupted, leading to labor unrest and/or business collapse.

Personal Financial Literacy and Consumer Economics

There is only so much time and money a household can offer to the economy as laborers and consumers. Consumers do not have the money or time to buy everything they want. Laborers do not have the time or capacity to work all the time. This indicates that time and money are scarce resources. If a consumer spends too much time doing one activity (i.e., working too much or enrolling in evening educational classes), then that means that consumer must sacrifice another activity. There are only twenty-four hours for laborers and consumers to affect the economy. The scarcity of time and money affects personal financial management in consumer economics. Buying one service or good means that a person must sacrifice another service or good. Scarcity means the households, businesses, and governments—as well as society as a whole—cannot always have all the time and money that they need/want. Households—and consumers living within those households—must therefore budget their time and money accordingly, paying close attention to the ways in which their decisions and choices affect the quality of life in their households.

Science, Technology, and Society

Major Scientific and Mathematical Discoveries and Technological Innovations

The following section looks at the ways the three major agricultural revolutions in history—the First Agricultural Revolution, the Second Agricultural Revolution, and the Green Revolution—affected technological innovations throughout history.

First Agricultural Revolution

For several millennia after Cro-Magnon human beings first developed their modern physical appearances some forty thousand years ago, the men and women of the Old Stone Age survived by wandering from place to place in search of animals and plant life. These early nomads roved in bands of no more than forty people, living off the land and hunting game for survival. The Paleolithic hunter-gatherers of this era separated their bands into gendered, skill-based categories: The majority of men developed wood, bone, and stone toolkits to slay prehistoric beasts, while the majority of women fashioned digging sticks and storage containers to unearth, uproot, gather, and store the land's available roots, fruits, grains, grasses, plants, and berries. By inventing these basic tools, Paleolithic hunter-gatherers managed to increase their food supplies. Cro-Magnon humans sharpened stones into knives to kill and butcher wild animals. Wooden spears helped roving nomadic tribes kill game at greater distances. Lion claws and mammoth tusks transformed into hooks and harpoons for fishing. Bone needles helped Cro-Magnons sew the animal-hide gear they needed to hunt for long periods of time in the cold and stampede wild animals off icy cliffs. Together, these Stone Age innovations laid the paradigmatic foundations for later technological shifts such as the Neolithic Revolution, also known as the First Agricultural Revolution.

The First Agricultural Revolution began around ten thousand-plus years ago when early nomadic men and women began scattering seed near regular campsites. As early human beings witnessed crops growing from these seed disposal locations, they recognized that they had some relative power over ecological conditions. This seemingly insignificant (and likely accidental) realization inaugurated a shift from food gathering to food producing methods at early human campsites, and the subsequent ideas and ideals that stemmed from these new tactics sewed the seeds for a broader agricultural revolution that, to this day, represents one of the greatest breakthroughs in human history. The revolutionary Neolithic transformation from hunting-gathering bands to farming-based societies had far-reaching effects on technological innovation, population, and human culture at large. For the first time in history, humans across the globe developed innovative food production methods effective enough for sustaining highly populated, complex city-states and civilizations.

Scientists and historians have not come to a consensus as to why the agricultural revolution occurred around ten thousand years ago. However, most theories tend to highlight the broader impact climate change had on the First Agricultural Revolution in some capacity. Around ten thousand years ago, the end of the last Ice Age in human history set the stage for rising worldwide temperatures and longer growing seasons. Specifically, favorable Neolithic temperatures and drier landscapes made grasses and grains more readily available for immediate nourishment and future cultivation. Warmer climates also eliminated many weather- and starvation-induced deaths, which contributed to a small population boom of sorts. The coinciding climate and population changes of the Neolithic Age created a global context that demanded a more sustainable food source. Farming, in particular, became an attractive alternative to hunting and gathering because it placed more control in the hands of burgeoning human populations. Farming, unlike hunting and gathering, offered human beings a rich supply of grains, roots, fruits, and vegetables that could be planted and harvested on a systematic basis.

In fact, human communities became more systematic as a whole during the First Agricultural Revolution. Independently, Neolithic villages across the globe evolved into sophisticated city-states and civilizations sourced from the same central, revolutionary milieu. The favorable climate changes and population booms of the Neolithic Age coalesced into a collection of unique, independent global "culture hearths." These culture hearths took root in such divergent places as Egypt, Iraq, Pakistan, China, Mexico, Central America, and Peru. Known as hearths of domestication to some scholars, the globe's earliest Neolithic villages eventually evolved into complex, fertile centers of systematic social advancement, allowing many of the unconscious participants of the First Agricultural Revolution to cling closely to the new, institutionalized processes of permanent human settlement.

The microcosmic processes of war, trade, migration, drought, famine, personal contact, and mass communication catalyzed this larger process of cultural diffusion, forcing each civilization into a sort of cultural symbiosis with the other. Each burgeoning city-state relied on other city-states for obtaining new objects, ideas, and customs. The transformation from village to city-state—and the accompanying cultural diffusions that followed—spanned several generations, making it difficult for scholars to pinpoint the origins of many specific agricultural-based practices. The cultural diffusion spawned by the First Agricultural Revolution created a web of interrelated objects, ideas, and practices that multilaterally affected the social institutions and geographic dispositions of many of the world's first civilizations.

Second Agricultural Revolution
Prior to the eighteenth century, most village farms in England and its colonies remained family owned and operated; these small farms, fashioned by pastoral notions of freedom and virtue, emphasized family values and familial subsistence over mass production and financial gain. All this changed, however, as the English Empire turned into a colonial powerhouse in the early to mid-1700s, marking a transition from family farming to early agribusiness. At this time, an expanding English economic catalyzed the broader transformative processes of the Industrial Revolution and the coinciding Second

Agricultural Revolution. The English Crown (and its vassal colonies) reaped the benefits of imperial resources and cheap labor forces, paving the way to simultaneous paradigm shifts in industry and agriculture.

The economic strength and political stability of England in the early to mid-1700s made its burgeoning empire the perfect candidate for the growing global demand for new technologies and greater food production. Industrialization—the process by which mechanized technologies produce both natural and synthetic products for human beings—required a tremendous amount of resources and human labor. By the mid-eighteenth century, England could readily industrialize because it had:

- Enough water power and coal to fuel new technologies
- An extensive slave system, indentured servant system, and tenant farm system that offered free/cheap labor
- Established iron ore mines for new machines and buildings
- Extensive river systems and canals for intranational trade
- Extensive colonial structures for international trade
- A powerful navy to protect trade
- Elaborate harbor systems to welcome trade
- A complex and highly developed banking system to back industrial growth

In all, England had the three major factors necessary for fruitful industrialization: land, labor, and capital. And, to make matters even better, although England suffered its fair share of wars during the eighteenth century, none of these international military crises occurred on English soil. Consequently, eighteenth-century England became the home of some of the most unique inventors, inventions, businessmen, and businesses in world history. Moreover, the broader processes of English industrialization created beneficial, symbiotic relationships with the budding processes of the English agricultural revolution that eventually witnessed a massive increase in the output of machine-made goods and textiles.

The Second Agricultural Revolution shadowed the Industrial Revolution as it spread from England to Continental Europe and North America (and later to South America, Africa, and Asia). Much like the First Agricultural Revolution, the Second Agricultural Revolution spawned an increase in technological innovation and food production. During the Second Agricultural Revolution, wealthy capitalist landowners began buying out family-owned farms and creating tenant farm systems that forced former village farmers into essential waged servitude. Similarly, the worldwide system of slavery continued to grip the globe in the eighteenth century: Slavery and capitalism joined hand in hand on plantations, as wealthy landowners forced African slaves into perpetual submission for the sake of mass production. Slavery existed long before the Second Agricultural Revolution, but persisted during this era, even with technological advancements and calls for abolition. This excess in free/cheap labor, coupled with near-perfect economic conditions, encouraged wealthy landowners and businessmen to experiment with new machinery and new farming methods. The resulting agricultural revolution sewed the seeds of technological and scientific advances.

The coinciding Industrial and Second Agricultural Revolutions impacted society at a time when the Enlightenment had also reached its full fruition. Thus, it makes sense that science, scientific inquiry, scientific research, and scientific advancement—all crux characteristics of the Enlightenment Era—inevitably impacted the paradigmatic shifts of the Industrial and Second Agricultural Revolutions. Prior to the Enlightenment, many agriculturalists in Europe and North America relied heavily upon Christian theology and dogma to influence their decision-making processes: Most pre-Enlightenment farmers spoke of the "Floods of God" rather than the "Minds of Men" when analyzing ways to till, plant, and harvest the soil. In other words, these early farmers placed a greater emphasis on the mysteries of God than on the capabilities of science. While a belief in God did not totally perish with Enlightenment advances, scientific practice began to slowly take precedence over prayer, especially when it came to strategic farming. As a result, the Second Agricultural Revolution witnessed an intense wave of new technology and new agricultural practices that relied heavily on scientific objectivity.

The Second Agricultural Revolution helped create an entirely new class of "scientific farmers." This new class of farmers criticized and abandoned outdated farming tools and techniques in favor of scientific approaches and mechanized practices. Perhaps one of the most recognizable "scientific farmers" in history was Jethro Toll of Berkshire, England. Toll was an agriculturalist who believed scattering seed across the ground by hand was wasteful and inefficient. Recognizing that much of the seed failed to take root once scattered, Toll decided to bank on new industrial advances to create a complex agricultural machine called the seed drill. Invented in 1701, Toll's seed drill capitalized on the advancements of the Industrial Revolution: It employed a grooved, artisan-made rotating cylinder that methodically sowed well-spaced rows of seed into channels dug at specified depths by a cutting-edge, front-end steel plough. A rear-end, mechanized harrow provided closure to the entire process by immediately covering the sewn seeds with soil. The seed drill boosted crop yields by mechanically designating the necessary depths and spaces needed for seeds to germinate at a more efficient rate. The invention also cut farmers' costs by conserving seed for future crops.

The Second Agricultural Revolution also witnessed the rise of various textile industries in England and its Anglo-American colonies. During this time period, the English Empire became a world leader in wool, linen, and cotton manufacturing and exports, thanks to new technological advancements in the textile industries. Colonial merchants unified smaller mills and spinneries under the umbrella of big business and a burgeoning global capitalist system in England and North America. Similarly, businessmen and landowners formed partnerships with the expanding plantation system in agriculture so that these mills and factories could be supplied with an excess of textile materials. These merchants, businessmen, landowners, and plantation farmers boosted their overall profits by mechanizing the formerly arduous spinning and weaving processes. Inventors not only transformed planting and harvesting processes by introducing new technologies, but they also revolutionized merchant machinery in the first-ever textile factories. These large warehouses of industry depended on the efficient production capabilities of new machineries such as John Kay's "flying shuttle," James Hargreave's "spinning jenny," and Eli Whitney's "cotton gin." Each of these new machines assisted early capitalists in their efforts to enhance wool, linen, and cotton production.

Green Revolution

The beginnings of the "Green Revolution" have traditionally been traced to the agricultural theories and practices developed by Norman Borlaug—often referred to as the "Father of the Green Revolution"—in Mexico in the 1940s. In 1944, the Mexican Ministry of Agriculture recruited Borlaug, an American biologist who received his PhD in plant pathology and genetics from the University of Minnesota in 1942, to conduct research on wheat production. In a joint venture with the world-famous Rockefeller Foundation, Borlaug and several other American scientists founded a new scientifically driven movement to increase agricultural production and catalyze economic growth in developing nations all over the world.

Traditional histories of the Green Revolution place Norman Borlaug and the high-yielding variety of seeds he developed at the praxis of a global paradigm shift in agricultural techniques and technologies. As the story goes, it is Borlaug and his team of scientists who inaugurated a paradigmatic revolution that helped stave off world hunger by ensuring disease resistance through techniques such as dwarfing, which, in turn, led to high crop yields and agricultural production.

According to this narrative, Borlaug, who later received a Nobel Peace Prize for his scientific advances in the 1970s, set forth a revolutionary wave of agronomic activity that placed chemical engineering, mechanized farming, and scientifically enhanced, disease-resistant cultivars at the forefront of global agro-capitalist interests and enterprises. The positive results of his efforts, according to this narrative, were:

- A newfound reliance on high-yield varieties (HYV) of seed
- Highly efficient methods of chemical and mechanized farming
- Increased food production
- Reduction in hunger on a global scale
- Economic stimulation, thanks to an increase in crop production and a higher demand for chemicals and mechanized farming equipment
- Increased income
- Sustained population growth

This "Master Narrative," however, places too much emphasis on the positive impact of one man and, consequently, fails to shed light on the broader, highly complicated historical picture.

In many ways, Borlaug was the inheritor of a "Green Revolution" that has its roots in the arid soil of the Dust Bowl and Great Depression of the 1930s. Borlaug, who came of age during an era of widespread American poverty and famine, inherited the technological shifts and scientific efforts of the Dust Bowl and Depression that sought to refertilize the American agricultural landscape with new ideas and economic opportunities. Borlaug's work in the 1940s was a direct cultural correlate of the agricultural failures of America in the 1930s and the transformative efforts to retake the soil of the Republic. During the tumultuous thirties, the United States came to terms with the fact that poor decisions and a lack of agricultural and cultural foresight had ravaged the banks and breadbaskets of America, bringing both Wall Street and the Heartland to their knees. Borlaug, who had a brief stint in the Civilian Conservation Corps in the 1930s, was well aware of federal and global efforts to bring labor and agriculture closer together for the sake of economic stimulation.

The "Green Revolution," in this sense, can be interpreted as a direct cultural response to the Dust Bowl and the Depression rather than a revolution inaugurated by one man. Borlaug is, without a doubt, a crucial character in this broader narrative, but he is by no means the only revolutionary. Borlaug inherited a cultural context ripe for agricultural advances and a marriage between science and the economy.

The Green Revolution responded to an increased need for global food production during the Great Depression, World War II, and the post–World War II baby boom era. The scientific and technological advances of the Green Revolution, without a doubt, helped combat global hunger and poverty. Nevertheless, as is the case with any revolution, the effects of the Green Revolution were not only positive. The economic excesses of the Green Revolution, which were often tied to capitalist interests, also fed global inequality. The Revolution was not spread evenly around the world; it did not always take hold in the so-called Third World countries of Africa and Southeast Asia. The Green Revolution tended to impact the United States and the West more positively than nations residing outside these global alliances. Nevertheless, the Green Revolution also took its toll on the United States and the West.

Some of the negative consequences of the Green Revolution include:

- Ecological damage from over-irrigation
- Ecological damage from a dependency on harmful chemicals and pesticides
- Indiscriminate use of toxic fertilizers
- Pollution from an overreliance on gas-powered agricultural machines
- Overproduction and an increased amount of food waste
- An inflation in the cost of agricultural technology and high-yield seeds
- Economic disparity; greater disparities between the rich and poor
- Uneven development (even in the United States, especially in poorer rural areas such as Appalachia)
- Increased ground water extraction
- Water table depletion
- Overpopulation

In all, the Green Revolution, like any other revolution in history, had both its positive and negative effects. Today, historians and scholars of human geography continue to debate the historical legacy of the Green Revolution and its impact on the globe.

Mathematics, Science, and Technology in River Valley Civilizations

Under the leadership of the infamous Alexander the Great, during the Hellenistic period of the Greek civilization, Ancient Greece entered an era of intercultural exchange with Egypt, Persia, India, the Near East, and the Mediterranean world. During this time, Alexander created military trading posts all over his empire, establishing Greek as the dominant language of communication. Throughout this era, the center of scholarship shifted away from Athens and toward Alexandria. Alexandria became the center of mathematical and scientific discoveries; it became a hub of technological innovation. Hellenistic astronomers, such as Ptolemy, flocked to Alexandria's world-renowned observatory. Scholars such as Eratosthenes skillfully computed the earth's circumference in Alexandria's library. Mathematicians such as Eratosthenes and Aristarchus previewed geometry texts written by Euclid; these texts, housed in Alexandria's library, stirred the intellect of these mathematicians, helping them to make advances in geometry and physics.

Alexandria became the West's greatest beacon of intercultural exchange; hundreds of Indian, Egyptian, and Persian scholars flocked to the center of Hellenistic culture, which unified and synthesized the ideas and technologies that had been amassed over time in the earliest hearths of civilization: the River Valley Civilizations, Classical India, Ancient Egypt and Persia, and Classical Greece. By the time the Roman Empire came to power, Alexandria had already endured centuries of scholarly advancement. The Roman Empire inherited Alexandria as an academic center, and it remained the capital of Roman and Byzantine Egypt for almost a thousand years.

Following the Muslim conquests of the seventh century, Alexandria shifted into the hands of Arab caliphates until 1200. During this period, Alexandria remained a center for intercultural exchange as famous Arab mathematicians, such as al-Khwarizmi of Baghdad, disseminated new ideas, such as "Arab numerals," across the Arab world. These Arab numerals were actually based off his study of Indian math, illustrating the dramatic ways in which the Arab world interacted with other cultures during the era of the Muslim caliphates. Thousands of miles away, China was also entering a "Golden Age" in mathematics as the Chinese developed concepts such as zero and negative numbers throughout the Tang and Song Dynasties. The vast expansion of the Mongol Empire brought many Chinese ideas and technologies to the Middle East and Europe, furthering cultural exchange. Thus, by the time of the Ming Dynasty, China was beginning to create stronger ties with the West through the Silk Road. This exchange paved the way to the Age of Exploration and a new era of scientific exchange and advancement.

Affects of Scientific and Mathematical Discoveries and Technological Innovations

From 1750 onward, the world experienced dramatic cultural, political, social, and economic shifts brought about by the processes of industrialization, modernization, and urbanization. Throughout this vast period, human beings were able to produce steam-powered mechanics, coal-and-gas-powered forms of transportation, and electric-powered urban infrastructure and communications. The discoveries of coal, oil, and electricity revolutionized technology. As mathematicians and scientists mastered subjects such as trigonometry, calculus, nuclear physics, and quantum theory, the world became both a more interesting and dangerous place for global citizens. Nikola Tesla and Thomas Edison helped create and domesticate the power of electricity. Edward Jenner and other medical professionals helped lessen the severity of such diseases as smallpox through vaccination discoveries. Albert Einstein and other physicists helped the United States and other countries obtain nuclear capabilities. Watson and Crick discovered DNA, paving the way to a better understanding of the human genome. President Kennedy and NASA helped fund a voyage to the moon that only could take place because of advances in rocket engineering. Inventors and entrepreneurs such as Bill Gates and Steve Jobs revolutionized the computer industry. All these scientific advances have helped the United States of America evolve from an agricultural new nation to a technological world leader. These changes have affected society in a positive way, but also in a negative manner. Industrialization has led to environmental pollution. Computer technologies have spawned drone attacks. Nuclear energy has led to the threat of nuclear war and the reality of nuclear meltdowns. Genetic advances have created so-called Frankenfoods that can sometimes cause more environmental harm than help.

Developments in Science, Technology, and the Free Enterprise System

Advances in science and technology have waxed and waned with the economy of the United States throughout the nineteenth and twentieth centuries. Since the advent of the Industrial Revolution in the nineteenth century, the U.S. economy has changed dramatically. Shifts in the free enterprise system of the United States have led to a fair share of economic panics and depressions. The most notable of these economic downturns was the Great Depression of the 1930s. Prior to this time, technological advances in consumer culture encouraged an era of excess and inflation. The consumer practices of the Roaring Twenties, therefore, gave way to the economic collapse of the 1930s. Ironically, it was also advances in science and technology that helped resuscitate the U.S. free enterprise system during World War II. The expansion of the military-industrial complex helped lead the United States out of the Great Depression and into the Golden Age of the 1950s. Consumer capitalism and military spending, therefore, can be a double-edged sword: On the one hand, in excess, it can create economic panic; on the other hand, within reason, it can induce economic stimulation.

Standard of Living in the United States

The impact of science and technology reaches well beyond the realm of free enterprise upswings and downturns and into the very heart of morality/ethics as well as into standards of living in the United States. Excesses in consumer science and technology can spawn economic depressions, which, in turn, may lower the overall standard of living. In the case of the Great Depression, the standard of living in the United States dropped to an all-time low. This, in turn, also affected people's morality in both a positive and negative manner. In a positive way, the Great Depression brought people together through economic struggle, encouraging many to cling to the ethics of their faith. In a negative way, the Great Depression also brought many doubts to the moral consciences of the nation; some citizens began to question whether God was on America's side during this time. Technological advances are also often accompanied by power and hegemony. In the case of the expansion of the military-industrial complex in the Cold War era, financial excess led to economic stimulation and a higher standard of living on average. Nevertheless, the global hegemony and moral weight spawned by this expansion also created a tremendous amount of fear, calling into question the ethics of nuclear capabilities.

Practice Test

1. Which of the following is the subgroup of economics that studies large-scale economic issues such as unemployment, interest rates, price levels, and national income?
    a. Microeconomics
    b. Macroeconomics
    c. Scarcity
    d. Supply and demand

2. A homeowner hires a landscape company to mow the grass because they would like to use that time to do something else. The trade-off of paying someone to do a job to make more valuable use of time is an example of what?
    a. Economic systems
    b. Supply and demand
    c. Opportunity cost
    d. Inflation

3. Which kind of market does not involve government interventions or monopolies while trades are made between suppliers and buyers?
    a. Free
    b. Command
    c. Gross
    d. Exchange

4. Which is NOT an indicator of economic growth?
    a. GDP (Gross Domestic Product)
    b. Unemployment
    c. Inflation
    d. Theory of the Firm

5. In a business cycle, a recession occurs between which cycles?
    a. Expansion, peak
    b. Peak, contraction
    c. Contraction, trough
    d. Trough, expansion

6. What is the name of the central bank that controls the value of money in the United States?
    a. Commodity Reserve
    b. Central Reserve
    c. Federal Reserve
    d. Bank Reserve

7. Which option does NOT sustain monetary policies?
    a. Closed market operations
    b. Open market operations
    c. Assuring bank reserves
    d. Adjusting interest rates

8. What determines the exchange rate in a "floating" or "flexible" exchange?
   a. The government
   b. Taxes
   c. The Federal Reserve
   d. The market

9. Which statement is true about inflation and purchasing power?
   a. As inflation decreases, purchasing power increases.
   b. As inflation increases, purchasing power decreases.
   c. As inflation increases, purchasing power increases.
   d. As inflation decreases, purchasing power decreases.

10. Which statement is true about goods and services?
    a. The quantity of goods and services matters more than their value.
    b. The value of goods and services matters more than their quantity.
    c. The quality of goods and services matters more than their production.
    d. The production of goods and services matters more than their quality.

11. Which of the following refers to the value of a good set by supply and demand rather than the actual value it represents?
    a. Commodity money
    b. Fiat money
    c. Bank money
    d. Reserve money

12. Which of the following is not a characteristic of contractionary monetary policy?
    a. Increases the money supply
    b. Possibly increases unemployment due to slowdowns in economic growth
    c. Decreases consumer spending
    d. Decreases loans and/or borrowing

13. Which of the following lists all four phases of the business cycle?
    a. Expansion, crest, peak, trough
    b. Expansion, contraction, peak, trench
    c. Peak, trough, contraction, expansion
    d. Peak, rise, trough, decline

14. Frictional unemployment is best described by which of the following?
    a. When a person is no longer qualified for a job
    b. When a qualified person cannot be matched to a job
    c. When a person is laid off because of the business cycle
    d. When a person is unemployed for longer than six months

15. How is economic growth measured?
    a. By the rise in the inflation of a country
    b. By the amount of reserves that a country holds
    c. By the amount of exports that a country has
    d. By the GDP of a country

16. If a store has a large supply of *Widget X* and they are not selling many of them, what should they do?
    a. Raise the price so that when they do sell one, they will make a large profit.
    b. Lower the price to hopefully increase demand so they can offload supply.
    c. Raise the price so that people will think that it is a limited, high value product and buy it.
    d. Offer the product in a low price bundle with other unrelated products.

17. Who is in control in a command economy?
    a. The consumer
    b. Private businesses
    c. The government
    d. Manufacturers

18. Which of the following correctly lists the factors of production?
    a. Land, labor, material, entrepreneurship
    b. Land, labor, capital, equity
    c. Land, a building, capital, labor
    d. Land, labor, capital, entrepreneurship

Answer Explanations

1. B: Macroeconomics. Macroeconomics studies the economy on a large scale and focuses on issues such as unemployment, interest rates, price levels, and national income. Microeconomics, Choice *A*, studies more individual or small group behaviors such as scarcity or supply and demand. Scarcity, Choice *C*, is not correct because it refers to the availability of goods and services. Supply and demand, Choice *D*, is also incorrect because it refers to the quantity of goods and services that is produced and/or needed.

2. C: Opportunity cost. Opportunity cost can trade time, power, or anything else of value in exchange for something else. Economic systems, Choice *A*, determine what is being produced and by whom. Supply and demand, Choice *B*, refers to the quantity of goods and services that is produced or needed. Finally, inflation, Choice *D*, refers to how the cost of goods and services increases over time.

3. A: Free. A free market does not involve government interventions or monopolies while trading between buyers and suppliers. However, in a command market, the government determines the price of goods and services. Gross and exchange markets refer to situations where brokers and traders make exchanges in the financial realm.

4. D: Theory Of The Firm. Behaviors of firms is not an indicator of economic growth because it refers to the behavior that firms follow to reach their desired outcome. GDP, unemployment, and inflation are all indicators that help determine economic growth.

5. C: Contraction and trough. A recession occurs between the contraction and trough phases of the business cycle. Between expansion and peak phases, employment and productivity are on the rise, causing a "boom." Between the peak and contraction, unemployment rates are starting to fall, but have not yet hit an all-time low. Between trough and expansion phases, the economy is getting back on its feet and starting to increase employment again.

6. C: Federal Reserve. The Federal Reserve is the bank of banks. It is the central bank of the United States and controls the value of money. A commodity is the value of goods such as precious metals. While the Central Reserve and Bank Reserve may sound like good options, the term "bank reserve" refers to the amount of money a bank deposits into a central bank, and the Central Reserve is simply a fictitious name.

7. A: Closed market operations. Monetary policies are sustained by assuring bank reserves, adjusting interest rates, and open market operations. Closed market operations do NOT uphold monetary policies.

8. D: The market. The market, through supply and demand, determines the exchange rate with a "flexible" or "floating" exchange rate. The government, Choice *A*, is not the correct answer because it is involved in "fixed" exchange rates to help keep exchange rates stable. Taxes, Choice *B*, is also incorrect because they create government revenue. The Federal Reserve, Choice *C*, is the bank of banks.

9. B: As inflation increases, purchasing power decreases. As more money is printed, the monetary value of the dollar drops and, in turn, decreases the purchasing power of goods and services. So, as inflation increases, consumers are not spending as much and the value of the dollar is low.

10. B: The value of goods and services matters more than their quantity. For example, in the real estate industry, if a realtor sells ten houses valued at $200,000, their commission would be the same as a realtor who sells one house valued at $2,000,000. Even though one realtor sold more homes, the value of ten houses adds up to the same amount as the single home that the other realtor sold. Therefore, the number of goods and services produced does not determine economic growth—the value of the goods and services does.

11. B: Fiat money. Commodity money, Choice *B*, refers to a good that has value, such as a precious metal. Bank money, Choice *C*, is money that is credited by a bank to those people who have their money deposited there. The term Reserve money, Choice *D*, does not refer to anything.

12. A: In contractionary monetary policy, the money supply is decreased. All of the other choices are characteristics of contractionary monetary policy.

13. C: The four phases of the business cycle are peak, trough, expansion, contraction. The other answer choices include at least one wrong phase.

14. B: Frictional unemployment occurs when a qualified person is unable to find a job. Cyclical unemployment occurs as a product of the business cycle, such as during a time of recession. Structural unemployment occurs when a person is no longer qualified for that particular job.

15. D: The GDP is used to measure an economy's growth. The inflation of a country doesn't tell us anything about their growth. A country may hold a lot of money in reserves but this does not tell us if they are growing or not. The same can be said for having a lot of exports. It does indicate that an economy is necessarily growing.

16. B: As the price of a product is lowered the demand should rise. Raising the price on an already hard to sell item would just make it harder to sell. If you offer it in a bundle of unrelated products then people are unlikely to want to buy those products together.

17. C: In a command economy, the government controls the prices as well as what and how much of a product is produced.

18. D: The factors of production are land, labor, capital, and entrepreneurship. The other choices all include at least one option that is not a factor of production.

Social Studies Foundation, Skills, Research, and Instruction

Social Studies Foundations and Skills

Social Studies Terminology

There is no denying that social studies classrooms are some of the most demanding for students when it comes to literacy and language acquisition. In social studies, students will not only have to comprehend basic verbs, nouns, and adjectives, but they will also have to understand complex social studies terms for particular contexts, places, eras, persons, movements, and groups. Social studies standards across different states typically demand that students obtain a relative amount of terminological specificity. In other words, literacy in a social studies classroom can be hyperspecific, which poses problems with students of all learning types and grade levels. In particular, social studies terminology can pose problems for Section 504 students, special education (SPED) students, and English language learners (ELLs). It is important that social studies teachers introduce students to best practices such as 1) using study cards, cognitive maps, and organizational charts for understanding social studies terms, 2) finding individualized structures and styles for note-taking, 3) employing memory games and mnemonic devices for recalling important information, and 4) using timelines and charts for understanding the importance of context, time, and sequence when it comes to social studies terms. Understanding and using social studies terminology correctly is almost always contingent on properly understanding the notion of time and context in history.

Knowledge Generated by the Social Science Disciplines

Teachers must first assist students with understanding their own identities before they try to expose them to diverse identities and communities within the social sciences. Implementing social and emotional learning (SEL) activities can help students understand themselves as well as their peers. SEL activities, such as personal reflections or class diaries, can help students in the social sciences prepare for interacting within the broader world. SEL activities help students understand the idea of community while also helping them *build* community in the classroom. Student growth and development in the social sciences should begin with identity and gradually branch out to classroom community, family, and personal community. Once students understand themselves better and the ways in which their ideas and emotions operate, then they will be more ready to comprehend the similarities and differences they have with their teachers and peers. As the complex components of the in-class community are more readily understood, students should be ready to deconstruct their relationships to their individual families and communities.

Teachers should prompt students to understand the *why* of their beliefs and emotions as well as the source. This is crucial in a social sciences classroom because students are consistently analyzing identity, culture, society, and social relations. Without this basic foundation, it is difficult for students to respect their own cultures. Moreover, it may be difficult for them to share about their own cultures and collaborate with people who may reside outside of their cultures. The routines and expectations of every social sciences classroom should therefore be mandated by some sort of community agreement or constitution. To design and implement effective learning experiences, the entire community must "buy into" a particular social contract. Teachers should create nonnegotiable aspects of class culture, but they should also call upon students as experts and engineers of their own context. Social science

197

classes with poor management typically fail to implement "student voice and choice" when it comes to routines and expectations, especially for working cooperatively within the community.

How Social Science Disciplines Relate to Each Other

As mentioned earlier, teachers must extend interdisciplinary study to include fields and content areas that exist outside the traditional social sciences (i.e., history, political science, social studies, geography, psychology, government, ethics, economics, environmental studies, and sociology). The future of the social sciences depends heavily on communication with fields that traditionally fall under the STEM (Science, Technology, Engineering, and Math) or STEAM (Science, Technology, Engineering, Art, and Math) categories. Disassociating the social sciences from these other fields is not beneficial for young students. In an increasingly technological world, students must be prepared to incorporate skills, ideas, concepts, and practices from STEM and STEAM courses into their social science classrooms. It is difficult to imagine future historians, political scientists, social studies teachers, geographers, psychologists, government officials, ethicists, economists, environmentalists, and sociologists functioning without science, technology, engineering, art, and mathematics. Future historians, for example, will likely have to be forensic computer scientists who sift through old files and data to better understand history and historical agents. Whenever possible, teachers should explicitly expose students to the ways in which these fields perpetually affect each other within the global economy and popular culture.

Sources of Social Studies Information; Interpreting and Communicating Social Studies Information

Primary and Secondary Sources

Traditionally, historical documents have been separated into two major categories: primary sources and secondary sources. Understanding the features of each is crucial for building foundational historical inquiry skills in the K-6 classroom. Students must learn to deconstruct primary and secondary sources to gain a better understanding of historical context and personal perspective.

Primary sources contain firsthand documentation of a historical event or era. Primary sources are provided by people who have experienced an historical era or event. Primary sources capture a specific moment, context, or era in history. They are valued as eyewitness accounts and personal perspectives. Examples include diaries, memoirs, journals, letters, interviews, photographs, context-specific artwork, government documents, constitutions, newspapers, personal items, libraries, and archives. Another example of a primary source is the Declaration of Independence. This historical document captures the revolutionary sentiment of an era in American history.

Authors of secondary sources write about events, contexts, and eras in history with a relative amount of experiential, geographic, or temporal distance. Normally, secondary source authors aren't firsthand witnesses. In some cases, they may have experienced an event, but they are offering secondhand, retrospective accounts of their experience. All scholars and historians produce secondary sources—they gather primary source information and synthesize it for a new generation of students. Monographs, biographies, magazine articles, scholarly journals, theses, dissertations, textbooks, and encyclopedias are all secondary sources. In some rare instances, secondary sources become so enmeshed in their era of inquiry that they later become primary sources for future scholars and analysts.

Teachers and students alike must spend a great deal of time analyzing the relationships between primary sources, secondary sources, and their historical scopes. Juxtaposing primary sources with secondary sources helps teachers and students attain a deeper understanding of the material they are studying.

Outlines, Reports, Databases, Narratives, Literature, and Visuals

Students should not only be able to analyze maps and other infographics, but they should also be able to create graphs, charts, tables, documents, maps, timelines, and other visual materials to represent geographic, political, historical, economic, and cultural features. Students should be made aware of the different options they have to present data. They should understand that maps visually display geographic features, and they can be used to illustrate key relationships in human geography and natural geography. Maps can indicate themes in history, politics, economics, culture, social relationships, demographic distributions, and climate change. Students can also choose to display data or information in a variety of graphs: Bar graphs compare two or more things with parallel bars; line graphs show change over time with strategic points placed carefully between vertical and horizontal axes; and pie graphs divide wholes into percentages or parts. Likewise, students can choose to use timelines or tables to present data/information. Timelines arrange events or ideas into chronological order, and tables arrange words or numbers into columns or rows. These are just some of the visual tools teachers and students can use to help visually convey their historical questions or ideas.

Maps and Other Graphics

Geographers utilize a variety of different maps in their study of the spatial world. Projections are maps that represent the entire world (which is spherical) on a flat surface. *Conformal projections* preserve angles locally, maintaining the shape of a small area in infinitesimal circles of varying sizes on a two-dimensional map. Conformal projections tend to possess inherent flaws due to their two-dimensional nature. For example, the most well-known projection, the *Mercator projection*, drastically distorts the size of land areas at the poles. In this particular map, Antarctica, one of the smallest continents, appears massive, almost rivaling the size of North America. In contrast to the poles, the areas closer to the central portion of the globe are more accurate. Other projections attempt to lessen the amount of distortion; the *Equal-area projection*, for example, attempts to equally represent the size of landforms on the globe. Nevertheless, equal-area projections like the *Lambert projection* also inherently alter the size of continents, islands, and other landforms, both close to Earth's center and near the poles. Other projections are a hybrid of the two primary models. For example, the *Robinson projection*, also referred to as the *Goode's homolosine projection*, tries to balance form and area in order to create a more visually accurate representation of the spatial world. Despite the efforts to maintain consistency with shapes, projections cannot provide accurate representations of the Earth's surface, due to their flat, two-dimensional nature. In this sense, projections are useful symbols of space, but they do not always provide the most accurate portrayal of spatial reality.

Unlike projections, *topographic maps* display contour lines, which represent the relative elevation of a particular place and are very useful for surveyors, engineers, and/or travelers. Hikers of the Appalachian Trail or Pacific Crest Trail, for instance, may call upon topographic maps to calculate their daily climbs.

Thematic maps are also quite useful to geographers because they use two-dimensional surfaces to convey complex political, physical, social, cultural, economic, or historical themes.

Thematic maps can be broken down into different subgroups: *dot-density maps* and *flow-line maps*. A *dot-density map* is a type of thematic map that illustrates the volume and density in a particular area. Although most dots on these maps represent the number of people in an area, they don't always have to do that. Instead, these maps may represent the number of events, such as lightning strikes, that have taken place in an area. *Flow-line maps* are another type of thematic map, which utilize both thin and thick lines to illustrate the movement of goods, people, or even animals between two places. The thicker the line, the greater the number of moving elements; a thinner line would, of course, represent a smaller number.

Similar to topographic maps, an *isoline map* is also useful for calculating data and differentiating between the characteristics of two places. In an *isoline map*, symbols represent values, and lines can be drawn between two points in order to determine differences. For example, average temperature is commonly measured on isoline maps. Point A, which is high in the mountains, may have a value of 33 degrees, while point B, which is in the middle of the Mojave Desert, may have a value of 105 degrees. Using the different values, it is easy to determine that temperatures in the mountains are 72 degrees cooler than in the desert. Additionally, isoline maps help geographers study the world by creating questions. For example, is it only elevation that is responsible for the differences in temperature? If not, what other factors could cause such a wide disparity in the two values? Utilizing these, and other sorts of maps, is essential in the study of geography.

Social Studies Research

Research Questions

To formulate solid research questions, students must act like a detective by gathering clues in primary and secondary sources. These clues help them understand and explain past events from multiple perspectives. To reconstruct the past, students must cross-reference these sources to determine valuable research questions and the established historiography of a particular historical context or question. Working from this historiography—the lineage of secondary sources covering a particular historical context or question—students must cite previous arguments as a means to create new questions. Research questions should emerge not only from personal interest, but also scholarly discourse.

Supportable Judgments and Conclusions in Social Studies

To reach supportable judgments and conclusions in social studies, teachers and students must be prepared to categorize and synthesize a variety of primary and secondary sources, paying close attention to which sources are legitimate sources of fact or opinion. Students must also be able to justifiably quote information from these sources to establish historical generalizations, or "general statements that identify themes that unite or separate source materials." Often, a generalization identifies key features, relationships, or differences found throughout multiple sources.

Research Methodologies

Acting as amateur social scientists and historians, students should formulate research questions and reconstruct the past by locating sources in libraries, online sites, and physical and digital archives. Once students gather a diversity of sources, they should organize, analyze, synthesize, and interpret these sources by determining the meanings, points of view, frames of reference, biases, main ideas, and validity of each source. Once this is accomplished, students will be able to create new historical research questions. Throughout the process, students should keep an eye out for both qualitative and quantitative data to gain a greater understanding of a particular historical context or question.

Analyzing Social Studies Information

Social studies students must understand how to determine the timeline/chronology of events through a process called sequencing. Sequencing allows student to gain a better understanding of change over time in history. Social studies classrooms often employ test questions that force students to recall the correct chronology, or time order, of important historical events.

Along with sequencing, social studies students should be able to carry out a process known as categorizing. Categorizing is the process by which historical themes, events, agents, persons, movements, or ideas are placed in designated categories that help students understand their historical significance. Categorization is usually most effective when certain words or phrases are organized by themes or concepts. For instance, the categorical concept of "economic depression" could help students better understand such historical events as the Panic of 1819, the Great Depression, and the Great Recession. Categorization allows students to link unrelated events in history.

Identifying associations and cause-and-effect relationships strengthens a student's ability to sequence events in history. All U.S. history is a series of associated events leading to still other events. A cause is what made something happen. An effect is what happens because of something. Understanding cause-and-effect helps students to understand the proverbial *why* of history; it helps them breathe more meaning into history.

Comparing and contrasting is another strategy that will make students more historically informed. In history, we often compare two or more things to understand their similarities and differences better. Part of the historical process is understanding what historical characteristics are unique or utterly common. Students might, for instance, compare and contrast the American Revolution to the Texas Revolution to gain a better understanding of the ways in which such variables as time, geographic location, and contributing persons affect history.

Summarizing is a strategy that is also used often throughout the historical process in a social studies classroom. Students will not only have to summarize the meaning of historical events or eras, but they will also need to know how to summarize the important points of primary and secondary sources. Summaries allow students to convey their knowledge in a short, concise, digestible fashion. Part of summarizing requires that students find the main idea of a particular article, source, or paragraph. Main ideas help students make their summaries even more concise and effective. Summarizing sometimes requires students to make generalizations or draw inferences/conclusions. Often there are "gaps of information" in the sources provided to students. Students will have to use background knowledge and critical-thinking skills to fill in these gaps with generalizations (broad, sweeping statements) or inferences/conclusions (educated guesses, predictions, or assumptions).

Analyzing Social Studies Data

Being "literate" in social studies means that teachers and students must be ready to interpret a variety of forms of data. In social studies, data is usually numerical or statistical information offered in the form of a graph, chart, table, document, map, or timeline.

In social studies, teachers and students will encounter many types of graphs. The two most common graphs used in social studies classes are bar graphs and line graphs. Bar graphs are made of parallel bars of varying lengths. Bar graphs help teachers and students compare two or more things. Line graphs are composed of a series of strategically placed points that are connected by one or more lines. Line graphs, much like timelines, help teachers and students of social studies gain a better understanding of change over time.

Sometimes valuable data can also be embedded in documents, maps, or timelines. Thus, it is important that every student is also exposed to these data-based tools in a social studies classroom. Much like all sources, students should be challenged to determine the validity of the data presented in graphs, charts, tables, documents, maps, and timelines.

Social Studies Instruction and Assessment

Promote Students' Use of Social Science Skills

In social studies, vocabulary terms typically focus on particular people, places, groups, or features that happened or existed in the past (or present). Social studies vocabulary terms can be particularly challenging because there is a certain specificity that goes along with complex identities, groups, and events. To promote student understanding of these complex vocabulary terms, it is important that teachers connect the terms to larger concepts (i.e., "words or phrases that refer to categories of information"). Concepts allow social studies students to organize large amounts of information using historical context and change over time. When analyzing concepts, students should pay close attention to the definition of the concept and examples of the concept. For instance, one concept that can be bequeathed to students is the concept of "war in American history." Under the umbrella of this concept, students can chronologically or thematically organize such disparate vocabulary terms as *French and Indian War, American Revolution, War of 1812, Mexican-American War, Civil War, Spanish-American War, World War I,* and *World War II*. Students may even broaden this concept to include such terms as *Cold War* and *War on Drugs*.

To promote study skills in the classroom, teachers can introduce students to such strategies as using study cards. This is particularly helpful for visual learners who need to see a certain term or concept to make an impression in their minds. Additionally, teachers can introduce students to the "art of note-taking," which will help them succeed in both K–12 and higher-education classrooms. Students should be explicitly taught how to underline, highlight, color-code, and take notes in the margins. Test-taking skills should also be explicitly taught to students—students should know the E.R.A. approach to standardized tests that encourages them to "Examine the Question," "Recall What They Know," and "Apply What They Know." Lastly, students should be exposed to research tools such as libraries, databases, archives, citation styles, and public museums. To be prepared for the twenty-first century, students should also be exposed to digital versions of these tools. It is quite possible that students can even go on "digital tours" of museum collections, thanks to the Internet and computer technologies.

Current Technology as a Tool for Teaching

Computer technology—especially with regard to the Internet, smartphones, tablets, and social media—is progressing at a rate that is often difficult for teachers to "keep up" with what is pertinent, effective, and relevant for their students. With the world becoming increasingly connected (and separated) by technology, it is important for every student in the social sciences to be exposed to contemporary techniques and practices for incorporating technology into the classroom. Students must know how to use the Internet, smartphones, tablets, and social media in their social sciences classroom to adequately prepare for the next era of college learning and professional research. Teachers must acquaint themselves with up-to-date, research-based practices for incorporating technology in the classroom. Specifically, in a social studies classroom, students must be prepared to access sources online and differentiate whether they are primary or secondary sources. More importantly, students must be able to assess whether the sources are legitimate enough to incorporate into research or presentations. Teachers should explicitly teach students how to research on technological devices while also teaching them how to assess the validity of sources and databases. In an increasingly digitized world, it is important to expose students to digital museums and databases. It is also important to use technology—specifically social media and smartphone apps—to "hook" students onto a particular topic or area of inquiry.

Instructional Strategies to Ensure Reading Comprehension

Social science students should not solely be focused on history and the past. Students should be exposed to disciplines such as political science, social studies, geography, psychology, government, ethics, economics, environmental studies, and sociology. These disciplines all emphasize present-day issues and trends in society; students should use these disciplines to determine the essence of their own historical context. Students must be able to not only understand social science concepts, but also apply the problem-solving and decision-making skills of the social sciences to the real world. Even history can help students better understand the present and have enough foresight to protect the future. The social sciences, in this sense, are as much about civic engagement as they are about content acquisition.

Making Connections Between Methods in Social Studies and Other Content Areas

Over the course of the last twenty-five years, the K–12 and higher-education systems in the United States have been gradually adopting interdisciplinary practices that encourage teachers and students to integrate skills, concepts, and ideas across a variety of different disciplines. This has become especially true in the social sciences at the K–12 level, where teachers and students must continually combine theories and practices from such disparate fields as history, political science, social studies, geography, psychology, government, ethics, economics, environmental studies, and sociology. Additionally, twenty-first-century teachers and students will be expected to make connections between the social sciences, sciences, arts, and mathematics. While teachers should strive to enrich their knowledge of content in their particular field of inquiry, they should also strive to make connections between fields. This means they should employ instructional practices in the classroom that explicitly and implicitly expose students to the interconnected nature of all learning. One way this could be accomplished is through collaboration with colleagues who are experts in other fields. Another way is by introducing textbooks, articles, and materials from other fields into content-specific social science classrooms. Lastly, teachers can help students to relate skills, concepts, and ideas across different social science disciplines by incorporating project-based learning (PBL) activities into the classroom that require students to analyze/approach/solve real-world problems through collaboration with peers, professionals, and public agencies with unique, discipline-specific experiences. PBL activities ensure that students not only grasp interdisciplinary content, but also *apply* this content to real-life problems, projects, and scenarios.

Value of Social Studies Education

Teachers and students must also engage parents/caregivers, colleagues/peers, and the community to convey the overall importance of a social studies education. When challenged about the importance of a social studies education, teachers and students can illustrate the ways in which a social studies education can help people become better writers, researchers, and presenters. Moreover, a quality social studies education will also make teachers and students better problem solvers, decision makers, and civic engagers. A knowledge of social studies can help teachers and students understand many problems faced in present-day global society. Politicians, businessmen, and common citizens all could benefit from enriching their historical consciousness so that they can effectively diagnose and implement positive changes for their government, customers, families, or fellow citizens. Social studies can help rebuild communities and prevent international conflicts; it can help teachers and students become better citizens in an often-conflicted global society.

Practice Questions

1. What is the name of the wealthy Venezuelan creole who helped stir revolutions across South America in the nineteenth century?
    a. Simon Bolivar
    b. Nelson Mandela
    c. Dr. Martin Luther King Jr.
    d. Antonio Lopez de Santa Anna

2. What country did Nelson Mandela become president of in 1994?
    a. Liberia
    b. Vietnam
    c. South Africa
    d. Argentina

3. The era following the Civil War is known as what?
    a. Antebellum Era
    b. Reconstruction
    c. Progressive Era
    d. Civil rights movement

4. Who did the state of Texas side with during the Civil War?
    a. North
    b. Union
    c. Mexican Republic
    d. Confederacy

5. What became the scholarly capital of the Hellenistic world during the reign of Alexander the Great?
    a. Jerusalem
    b. Athens
    c. Alexandria
    d. Constantinople

6. Which of the following religions is not a monotheistic Abrahamic religion?
    a. Hinduism
    b. Christianity
    c. Islam
    d. Judaism

7. What is the name given to institutional segregation in South Africa?
    a. Jim Crow
    b. Atlantic Slave Trade
    c. Apartheid
    d. Black Codes

8. Who was a naval officer who pushed the United States of America toward oceanic imperialism in the late nineteenth century?
    a. Alfred Thayer Mahan
    b. Christopher Columbus
    c. Theodore Roosevelt
    d. Matthew Perry

9. The First Agricultural Revolution occurred roughly how many years ago?
    a. 50
    b. 1000
    c. 200
    d. 10,000

10. What is the name of the policies developed by President Franklin Delano Roosevelt during the Great Depression?
    a. The Great Society
    b. The War Against Poverty
    c. Progressivism
    d. The New Deal

11. Which of the following fields falls under the umbrella of the "social sciences"?
    a. Biology
    b. English
    c. Psychology
    d. Geometry

12. Which of the following are markets that establish a few large firms as the major sellers/distributors?
    a. Free enterprise economies
    b. Pure monopolies
    c. Oligopolies
    d. Command economies

13. Which of the following is the best definition for a pure monopoly?
    a. When there is only one seller of a particular product or commodity, and the sole seller attempts to restrict firms from exiting and entering the industry at will
    b. When prices are determined by consumer demand, and no supplier maintains any significant influence over prices
    c. When people are completely free to buy the goods and services they want/need
    d. When a few large firms become the major sellers/distributors of an industry

14. The Third Agricultural Revolution is often referred to as what?
    a. Green Revolution
    b. Texas Revolution
    c. Industrial Revolution
    d. Computer Revolution

15. Which of the following is an example of a New Deal program?
    a. Head Start
    b. NASA
    c. Eisenhower Interstate System
    d. Civilian Conservation Corps

16. What does the following graph represent?

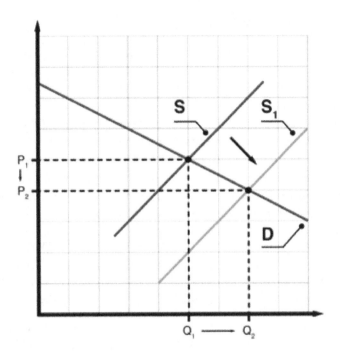

    a. Decrease in supply
    b. Increase in supply
    c. Decrease in demand
    d. Increase in demand

17. Who is considered the "Father of Socialist Theory"?
    a. John Maynard Keynes
    b. Adam Smith
    c. Alfred Thayer Mahan
    d. Karl Marx

18. Communism is more attuned for which of the following?
    a. One-party system
    b. Liberal democracy
    c. Free enterprise economy
    d. Capitalist economy

Answer Explanations

1. A: Bolivar was a creole revolutionary who waged several revolutionary wars in South America. Nelson Mandela (Choice *B*) was the leader of South Africa at the end of apartheid. Dr. Martin Luther King Jr. (Choice *C*) was the southern civil rights leader who helped end segregation in the United States. And Antonio Lopez de Santa Anna (Choice *D*) was the leader of the Mexican army at the Battle of the Alamo.

2. C: Nelson Mandela became the president of South Africa after the fall of apartheid. Liberia (Choice *A*) was the black colony established by Americans to send slaves and free blacks back to Africa. Vietnam (Choice *B*) was the center of a U.S. military dispute over Communism in the 1960s and 1970s. Argentina (Choice *D*) is a South American country that drew support from both the right and the left under the leadership of Juan Peron.

3. B: Reconstruction was the Postbellum Era in which the United States tried to reinstate former Confederate states into the Union and rebuild the South through occupation. The Antebellum Era (Choice *A*) was the time frame that preceded the Civil War. The Progressive Era (Choice *C*) was the era of widespread reform in the late nineteenth and early twentieth century that set the stage for Prohibition. The civil rights movement (Choice *D*) is the era of U.S. history that witnessed desegregation, reaching its culmination in the mid-1960s under the presidency of Lyndon B. Johnson.

4. D: Texas sided with the Confederate States of America during the Civil War, seceding from the Union (Choice *B*). Texas helped the South fight the North (Choice *A*). The Mexican Republic (Choice *D*) is also not the right answer because it played only a limited role during the Civil War, and Texas most certainly did not side with the country it declared independence from decades earlier.

5. C: Alexandria became the capital. Jerusalem (Choice *A*), although the epicenter of Judaism and Christianity, did not host as many scholars as Alexandria during the Hellenistic period. Constantinople (Choice *D*) is incorrect because it was not yet created during the Hellenistic period. And Athens (Choice *B*), the former capital of Greek scholarship, is not the answer because scholarly culture shifted from Athens to Alexandria during this period.

6. A: Hinduism is a polytheistic religion that originated in India and is not Abrahamic in character. Judaism (Choice *D*), Christianity (Choice *B*), and Islam (Choice *C*) are the so-called Abrahamic monotheistic religions.

7. C: Apartheid is the name given to institutional segregation and precolonial and postcolonial South Africa. Jim Crow (Choice *A*) refers to segregation in the southern United States in the early twentieth century. The Atlantic Slave Trade (Choice *B*) refers to the centuries of slavery that sparked trade across the Atlantic Ocean. Black Codes (Choice *D*) refer to the codes instituted to strip freed African Americans of their rights during Reconstruction.

8. A: Mahan wanted the United States to become an imperial power through naval prowess and seaward expansion. Christopher Columbus (Choice *B*) is the European explorer who discovered the New World during the Age of Exploration. Although Theodore Roosevelt (Choice *B*) was a strong proponent of both imperialism and the navy, he was a president and not a naval officer. Matthew Perry (Choice *D*) was a naval officer who opened Japan to the West in 1854.

9. D: The First Agricultural Revolution occurred 10,000 years ago. Choice *A* and Choice *C* respectively point to the Second Agricultural Revolution (200 years) and the Green Revolution (50 years). Choice *B*— 1000 years—is just an erroneous number listed to trick the test takers.

10. D: Following his election during the Great Depression, Franklin Delano Roosevelt pledged a "New Deal" for the American people, inaugurating an era of social welfare and public works programs. The Great Society (Choice *A*) also set forth social welfare and public works programs, but under the presidency of Lyndon B. Johnson (LBJ). The War Against Poverty (Choice *B*) was a subcategory of LBJ's Great Society—it promised to declare war on poverty like any nation would declare war on a foreign threat. Progressivism (Choice *C*) brought about reforms much like the New Deal, but during the early twentieth century, prior to the Great Depression and FDR's administration.

11. C: Psychology is a social science that studies the ways in which the mind and cognition affect social relationships and identities. Biology (Choice *A*) is a hard science that studies life. English (Choice *B*) would be placed under the umbrella of the humanities. Geometry (Choice *D*) would fall under the category of mathematics.

12. C: Oligopolies are markets that establish a few large firms as the major sellers/distributors. Free market economies (Choice *A*) allow for more competition, while command economies (Choice *D*) allow for greater government control. Choice *B* is incorrect because pure monopolies are typically dominated by one firm rather than a few.

13. A: A pure monopoly is when there is only one seller of a particular product or commodity, and the sole seller attempts to restrict firms from exiting and entering the industry at will. Choices *B* and *C* describe a free enterprise economy. Choice *D* describes an oligopoly.

14. A: The Green Revolution is often the name given to the Third Agricultural Revolution, which witnessed the rise of a scientifically driven movement in the early twentieth century to increase agricultural production and catalyze economic growth in developing nations all over the world. The Texas Revolution (Choice *B*) had nothing to do with agriculture and everything to do with politics and independence. The Industrial Revolution (Choice *C*) coincided with the Second Agricultural Revolution. The Computer Revolution (Choice *D*) took place in the 1980s and 1990s with the advent of personal computers, video games, and the Internet.

15. D: The Civilian Conservation Corps was a New Deal program that assisted with the conservation of federal and state parks. Head Start (Choice *A*) was an early childhood education program of the Great Society. NASA (Choice *B*) was a Cold War aeronautics program that launched astronauts to the moon during the Kennedy administration. The Eisenhower Interstate System (Choice *C*) was a highway system built in the United States well after the death of FDR.

16. B: The graph shows an increase in supply because an increase in supply will shift the supply curve to the right (S1 to S2). A decrease in supply (Choice *A*) will shift the supply curve to the left. A decrease in demand (Choice *C*) shifts the demand curve to the left rather than the right. An increase in demand (Choice *D*) will move the demand curve to the right.

17. D: Marxist economic theories helped pave the way to the rise of Socialism (as well as Communism). Alfred Thayer Mahan (Choice *C*) was an imperialist naval captain who did not contribute greatly to economic theory. John Maynard Keynes (Choice *A*) and Adam Smith (Choice *B*) were economists whose theories paved the way to free enterprise economics.

18. A: Communism advocates a one-party system. It does not mix well with the democratic policies of liberal democracy (Choice *B*) and competitive economic systems of free enterprise or capitalist economies (Choices *C* and *D*). Although Communism is not always separate from democracy, its more radical ideals separate it from the moderations of liberal democracy. Moreover, the communal economic frameworks of Communism run counter to the competitive practices of capitalism/free enterprise.

Dear TExES Social Studies 7 - 12 Test Taker,

We would like to start by thanking you for purchasing this study guide for your TExES Social Studies 7 - 12 exam. We hope that we exceeded your expectations.

Our goal in creating this study guide was to cover all of the topics that you will see on the test. We also strove to make our practice questions as similar as possible to what you will encounter on test day. With that being said, if you found something that you feel was not up to your standards, please send us an email and let us know.

We would also like to let you know about other books in our catalog that may interest you.

TExES ELAR 7 - 12

This can be found on Amazon: amazon.com/dp/1628454342

TExES Mathematics 7 - 12

amazon.com/dp/1628454350

We have study guides in a wide variety of fields. If the one you are looking for isn't listed above, then try searching for it on Amazon or send us an email.

Thanks Again and Happy Testing!
Product Development Team
info@studyguideteam.com

Interested in buying more than 10 copies of our product? Contact us about bulk discounts:

bulkorders@studyguideteam.com

FREE Test Taking Tips DVD Offer

To help us better serve you, we have developed a Test Taking Tips DVD that we would like to give you for FREE. **This DVD covers world-class test taking tips that you can use to be even more successful when you are taking your test.**

All that we ask is that you email us your feedback about your study guide. Please let us know what you thought about it – whether that is good, bad or indifferent.

To get your **FREE Test Taking Tips DVD**, email freedvd@studyguideteam.com with "FREE DVD" in the subject line and the following information in the body of the email:

    a. The title of your study guide.

    b. Your product rating on a scale of 1-5, with 5 being the highest rating.

    c. Your feedback about the study guide. What did you think of it?

    d. Your full name and shipping address to send your free DVD.

If you have any questions or concerns, please don't hesitate to contact us at freedvd@studyguideteam.com.

Thanks again!

Made in the USA
Coppell, TX
24 January 2020